THE CHINESE SOVIETS

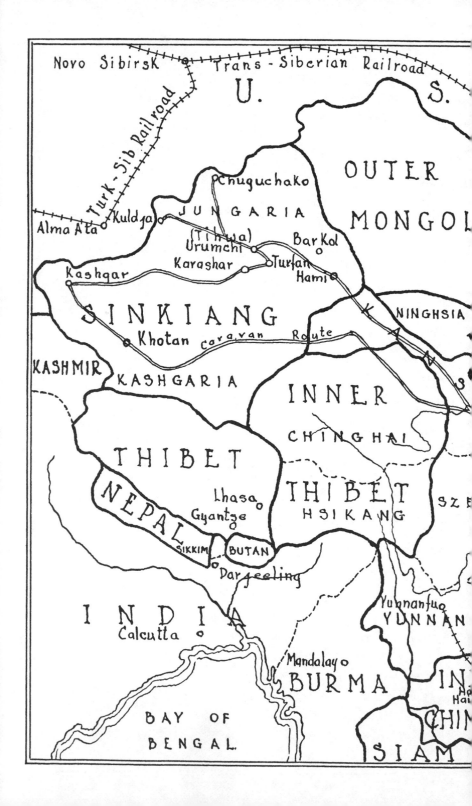

THE CHINESE SOVIETS

By

Victor A. Yakhontoff

Author of "Russia and the Soviet Union in the Far East," etc.

GREENWOOD PRESS, PUBLISHERS
WESTPORT, CONNECTICUT

The Library of Congress has catalogued this publication as follows:

Library of Congress Cataloging in Publication Data

Yakhontoff, Victor A   1881-
    The Chinese soviets.

    1. Chung-kuo kung ch⁶an tang. 2. Communism--
China. 3. China--Politics and government--1912-1949.
4. Chung-kuo kuo min tang. 5. Soviets--China.
I. Title.
DS775.Y3 1972   320.9'51   78-138195
ISBN 0-8371-5290-9

Originally published in 1934
by Coward-McCann, Inc., New York

Reprinted with the permission
of Victor A. Yakhontoff

First Greenwood Reprinting 1972

Library of Congress Catalogue Card Number 78-138195

ISBN 0-8371-5290-9

Printed in the United States of America

TO MY BEST FRIEND

DR. M.

PREFACE

THE subject of this book is its apology for existence, and its scope and purpose are fully discussed in the Introductory Chapter. A few preliminary words should, however, be spoken regarding its origin and the extent and limitation of its sources.

It was while he was still working on his volume entitled *Russia and the Soviet Union in the Far East,* published in 1931, about one month before the commencement of the latest Japanese aggression in Manchuria, that the idea of writing a book on the Chinese Soviets occurred to the author. At that time the Communist movement in China had already reached a stage of development which rendered it, in the writer's opinion, a matter of great potential influence on the rest of the world. This potential influence is greater than ever today. The aggression of the Japanese, though carried on under the pretext of combating Bolshevism and "saving the world for civilization" has actually served to intensify the Communist movement in China.

By 1932, accordingly, the author was already engaged in attempts to arrange a visit to China to study this problem on the spot; but in spite of the keen interest shown in this project by a number of American organizations engaged in the study of Far Eastern questions, it was found impossible to finance the undertaking at that time. In 1933, however, the author was more fortunate, and was able to make a tour around the world. Starting from and returning to the United States, he visited en route all the countries which have important interests in Northeastern Asia, such as Great Britain, the Soviet Union, Japan, and China herself, including "Manchukuo."

On this trip the author limited his work to the accumulation of available material on the Communist and Soviet movements in China. In Moscow, where profound interest in this topic exists and much research is carried on, he found a veritable gold mine of facts and information. In China too—and especially at Nanking and Shanghai—he was fortunate in discovering, with the help of a few native and foreign residents, a great deal of valuable material. But the author was greatly interested, if not exactly astonished, to find how difficult it was to procure anything on this "dangerous" subject in the Chinese shops. The booksellers seemed to have a thorough fear of the Nanking "terror," and certainly preferred not to keep anything of the sort in their establishments.

This reticence concerning things Communistic is, of course, no proof at all that the inhabitants of Eastern Asia are either unfamiliar with, or unreceptive to, the "dangerous" doctrines of Communism. Rather, the attempts at censorship not only in China proper but at points further north, are in themselves strong indications to the contrary.

An experience of the author at the border between Siberia and the "independent state" of Manchukuo may serve to illustrate the extremes to which the censorship fever may be carried. At the Japanese-controlled custom house the over-zealous inspectors attempted to confiscate all the material pertaining to the subject of this work, explaining that no books published in the USSR or anything on Communism could be imported into their country. The announcement that the author had no intention of keeping these books in Manchukuo, but wished them sent "in bond" directly to Peiping, was of no avail; the poor fellows seemed too excited and indignant at coming into contact with such unholy literature to listen to arguments. In the end, however, certain letters of introduction from prominent persons to no less prominent Japanese officials in Man-

chukuo persuaded the superiors of these over-zealous functionaries that the affair was greatly exaggerated, and the subversive
books and pamphlets eventually proceeded on their way with
their owner. But this irritating incident had not been without
its amusing aspect. For the impounded material had contained
not only the various publications of the Foreign Policy Association and the American Council of the Institute of Pacific Relations, and the English Memoranda on Communism in China
prepared for the Lytton Commission by Wellington Koo, but
the Japanese official documents on the same subject as well.

It should be made clear that the author does not pretend to
offer personal impressions of the Soviets in China, for a visit
to the Communist districts of that country proved more than he
could attempt on an already long and hazardous trip. His book,
therefore, is primarily a compilation with a certain amount of
critical comment. But the compilation is—the author believes—
the first of the kind to be attempted in English, and it is a con-
scientious attempt to fill a void. Furthermore, much of the
material included has never before been made available in
English. Hence the author hopes that his book may, despite
its necessary limitations, be of some little use to students of
things Chinese and—since it deals with a matter which will
probably soon be one of general concern—to the reading public
at large.

In conclusion the author wishes to express his sincere appreciation to Mr. T. A. Bisson, of the Foreign Policy Association,
to Dr. Chih Meng, of the China Institute in America, and Miss
Agnes Smedley, the author of that brilliant book *Chinese Desti-
nies,* who were kind enough to read the manuscript. His warm
thanks go to his dear friend, J. Fletcher Smith, for patient
struggles with the author's inadequate English; to his daughter
Olga for reading most of the manuscript, and, of course, to his
wife, M. V. Yakhontoff, for her encouragement.

TABLE OF CONTENTS

THE CHINESE SOVIETS

CHAPTER I

INTRODUCTORY

In the years 1931-32 a tide was turning in China. Something was taking place of vast importance to the former Celestial Empire—something, probably, of more vital significance to the rest of the world than the Occident yet realizes.

During the greater part of 1931 and the earlier part of 1932 a series of four military campaigns was being waged. On the one side were the forces of the "Red Bandits," as their enemies called them, or of the Chinese Communists as they are otherwise known; and on the other the troops of the "Nationalist Revolution," instituted by the famous and radically inclined Dr. Sun Yat-sen, but now subservient to the so-called "Nanking régime," dominated by the reactionary and redoubtable General Chiang Kai-shek. The Nanking Generalissimo was out, so he said, to "annihilate" the Red Bandits. But at the end of the campaign, if we may accept the estimates of the winners, more than two hundred thousand rifles, five thousand machine guns, hundreds of cannon, twelve airplanes, and much other booty including food supplies, were in the hands of the victorious "Communists." A "punitive expedition" on an even larger scale was sent out in the latter part of the second year, but the Reds were again victorious. Another campaign was started in the Autumn of 1933 with similar results. Chinese "Communism" is today in strikingly improved position. With the best army in the strife-torn country at its beck and call, it may very

1

well be in a stronger position tomorrow. If it was once a joke, it is a joke no longer, and it does more than merely deserve the attention of the outside world.

What is Chinese Communism? How did the movement begin? Where does it hold sway, and what are its characteristic features? Is it, or is it not, genuine Communism? Can it be an enduring success? These are some of the questions we must ask ourselves and endeavor to answer.

On one of these questions at least—that of the nature and strength of Chinese Communism—there is a wide divergence of opinion. Different students approach the subject from different angles and reach different judgments. Furthermore, there is little adequate material available on which the public may base its own conclusions. To make clear the extent of this divergence of opinion, and to avoid bias, let us begin by quoting a number of views from a variety of sources.

First of all, let us take the opinion of Dr. Wellington Koo, former Minister of Foreign Affairs and now the Chinese Minister at Paris, well known in the United States as the former Minister of his country at Washington. Dr. Koo is, it must be kept in mind, a high official of the Nanking régime. It must be remembered, too, that the paper in which his opinion is embodied—Document No. 24 on Communism in China—was submitted as part of the *Memoranda* he presented in 1932 to the Lytton Commission of the League of Nations, to which he was Chinese Assessor. The document, in other words, was prepared in the hope of impressing the Powers with the advisability of handling the Japanese invasion of Manchuria with energy, so that the evacuation of the Japanese troops might be brought about, leaving China unhindered in her important task of crushing Communism.

"In spite of the renewed efforts in the course of the last few years for its destruction," wrote Dr. Koo, "Communism remains in China a serious danger because it has threatened the country during one of those crises of social and political evolution which always leave a nation in a state of temporary weakness, and because the internal crisis is complicated, for the last year, by an external crisis of the greatest importance and magnitude. . . . It is not to be doubted, however, that if a prompt remedy cannot be found, the Communist danger may continue to extend to the point of threatening the very foundations of the social organization of China."

Elsewhere in the same *Memoranda*, Dr. Koo stresses the particular nature of this threat. "The Communist danger in China assumes a special form," he declares. "The Communists here are not like those in countries outside of Soviet Russia who simply form a political party, spreading propaganda, seeking to increase their membership, presenting candidates for the elections, succeeding sometimes to have a majority in the municipal council of a city or community, but with a few exceptions, confining their activity within the limits fixed by the legislation of the country, and seeking, if only for the moment, to realize their policy only by constitutional methods. In China, the Communist Party is in open rebellion against the Constitution, against the laws, against the National Government and against the constituted provincial authorities. It has its own army or armies, which oppose the regular forces, and sometimes even baffle them. It has its own government, its own administration organized in conformity with its own principles; it has its own laws, formulated after those of the USSR. In the regions brought within its authority, it puts into practice at least a part of its socialistic theories. It is in these respects that the Chinese Communist Party differs from that of the rest of the world and is altogether unique." [1]

Whatever the object of this expression of opinion may have

[1] *Memoranda* presented to the Lytton Commission, p. 778.

been, it remains the recorded and considered statement of a high official of China, painting the Communist "menace" in no pale colors. Another Chinese of high standing in the Kuo-min-tang, or Nationalist Party, and the Nanking régime, took a no less serious view. Mr. Yang Chien, Assistant Director of the National Research Institute, visited Kiangsi province for the purpose of studying the Communist situation, and in July, 1931, furnished the Kuo-min News Agency with an article, repub-ₗished later in booklet form, in which he uttered warnings to all concerned about the gravity of the situation.[2]

"The time has come," wrote Mr. Yang Chien, "to be frank and open with the people so that the extent of the Red danger will be realized, however damaging this exposé may be to indi-vidual reputations. We are presenting a dark and grim picture, but if we had brought the people to face the situation squarely and courageously, progress would have already been made." In his conclusion, Mr. Yang Chien declared: "Far more important . . . however, is the problem of the conditions that make for Communism . . . objectively necessary for the growth of Communism are the miserable economic conditions that drive famished and exploited humanity to despair. What is happen-ing in Kiangsi may well happen to any province in China, and it is nothing short of a miracle that the famished and back-ward regions of the North-west, which are contiguous to Soviet Russia, have not become infected with the virus of Commu-nism. . . ."

Poor Mr. Yang Chien! When he wrote his pamphlet, and expressed the hope that "the drive will in the near future suc-ceed in shattering the main body of Communist troops," the crushing defeats suffered by Chiang Kai-shek at the hands of the Communists were things of the future.

[2] Yang Chien. *The Communist Situation in China.* Nanking, July, 1931.

The next witness is a prominent student of labor issues, a Chinese high in the councils of the Y.M.C.A. movement. In his book entitled *Facing Labor Issues in China*, published at Shanghai in 1933, Mr. Lowe Chuan-hua writes as follows:

"A factor that must not be overlooked in studying the economic and social conditions in China is the rapid growth of Communism since 1919. Within a little more than a decade the Communists have apparently elevated themselves from a plane of harmless Marxian theorists into that of a powerful political movement and, for good or for ill, they now command amongst the workers and the peasants an influence that is bound to produce far-reaching effects in the future of China. Since the split between the Kuo-min-tang and the Communist Party in April, 1927, continuous attempts have been made by the National as well as the provincial authorities to exterminate the Red menace from the political arena; but despite these efforts the Soviets in the South and Central China remain a vexed question today. The reason behind this failure is not far to seek. Incessant civil strife, the break-up of the agricultural system, unemployment, increase of banditry, natural calamities and the lack of security in the peaceful pursuits of life—these and a host of other causes have made China a most fertile field for Communist propaganda and agitation. Those who have been holding the reins of government during the last few years have not done as much as they have promised to mend the ways of the former war lords and *tuchuns,* or to ameliorate the growing economic burdens of the masses. On the contrary, the situation in China has been very much aggravated by the fact that brutal force, and force alone, has been applied to eliminate the Communists from the political horizon. For not until the causes which have precipitated the rise of Communism are removed by efforts of economic reconstruction, can one hope for any measurable decline in its influence amongst the masses in China." [3]

On the other hand, in the lengthy Document prepared by the Japanese Government and communicated, late in 1932, to the Commission of Enquiry,[4] appointed by the Council of the League of Nations in pursuance of its resolution of December 10, 1931, we read: "The future of the Chinese Communist movement is a matter of serious concern and difficult to deal with. On the surface, the movement may appear like a casual phenomenon, begun in 1920 with the formation of the Chinese Communist Party and through Comintern machinations. But as a matter of fact, its origin lies deep in the peculiar social, economic and political conditions of China; and unless these are removed, the movement will not end but in all likelihood will expand. The Nanking Government in its present state of impotency cannot be expected to accomplish the task of clearing China of Red armies and Soviet areas. Fortunately the latter are yet geographically separated from Russia. In the event they should establish direct geographic contact along the borders of Siberia, Outer Mongolia, or Turkestan, a situation might arise that no Chinese Government could ever cope with alone. The sovietization of entire China is not an absolute impossibility. And what the combination of a Red China with 400,000,000 people and immeasurable natural resources and the Soviet Russia possessing one-sixth of the earth's surface might mean to the world—to say nothing of their neighbor states, such as Japan— is a question that should be borne in mind in following the trend of the Communist movement in China."

In this summary, as in that of the Chinese Assessor, there is more than a trace of exaggeration, since the Japanese Govern-

---

[3] Lowe Chuan-hua. *Facing Labor Issues in China.* Shanghai, 1933, p. 144.

[4] *I.e.,* the so-called "Lytton Commission."

ment was anxious to impress the League of Nations and the Powers, and to induce a more lenient attitude toward its actions in Manchuria. The Tokyo Government, according to its own official statements, was anxious to beat back the tide of Communism, which through China "threatens to engulf the Orient," and this "Red Peril scare" was expected to enlist the sympathy of the Westerners on behalf of Japan, the self-styled "bulwark against Bolshevism in this part of the world." This plea has been brought forward not only as justification for the Japanese invasion of Manchuria and the occupation of China's northeastern provinces, but for other aggressive acts as well. Count Uchida, the former Japanese Minister of Foreign Affairs, declared in the Diet that "the Red movement in the Yangtze Valley and South China was a serious menace to peace in the Orient against which Japan must be on guard," and added that "the suppression of Communism in China is one of Japan's great and noble tasks for which she should have the gratitude of all right-thinking people."

Observing the opposition of Tokyo to the alleged coöperation of the United States with Nanking, which supposedly might have assisted the suppression of the Communists with airplanes and loans, a Chinese writer ironically suggested: "Perhaps someone can explain this strange case of a nation bearing with such difficulty the burden of a war to crush Communism and maintain peace, but objecting vehemently to any allies in her noble aim. But it would be best of all if the Tokyo Government itself would explain. Pending explanation, many will assume that the 'war against Bolshevism' is pretence pure and simple, and Japan's invasion of China, and assertion of hegemony over the Far East under an Asiatic Monroe Doctrine, is simply a form of naked aggression devoid of any redeeming features." [5]

[5] An editorial in *The People's Tribune*, September 1, 1933. Shanghai.

Now let us turn to the views of a few calmer, and presumably more disinterested, observers. In the Memorandum of May 31, 1932, the authoritative American Council of the Institute of Pacific Relations summarized its views on Communism in China as follows:

"Rapid extension of the area and population under Communist control in China in recent months, the threat that this movement may force the evacuation of foreigners from the ports on the southeastern coast and on the middle sections of the Yangtze River, the repeated failure of the Chinese Government troops in their attempts to defeat the Communists, and the gradual admission on the part of Kuo-min-tang leaders that Communism can be dealt with only if the social and economic conditions on which Communism thrives are eliminated—these are indications of the importance of Communism in China today."

The very able summary on the Communist movement in China in the Foreign Policy Association's Report of April 26, 1933, prepared by Mr. T. A. Bisson, concludes, however, by pointing out that "wide divergence of opinion exists among qualified observers regarding the extent to which the Chinese Communist movement constitutes genuine Communism and regarding the movement's future prospects. The majority of Western observers are inclined to minimize its significance, contending that it represents little more than a desperate peasant revolt against unbearable economic conditions." This also appears to be the view of Nathaniel Peffer in his article, "The Chinese Idea of Communism," published in the July, 1932, issue of *Current History;* while in his *China: The Pity of It,* Mr. J. O. P. Bland would remind us that "agrarian revolts have always arisen during epochs of social upheaval in China" and that "it is inconceivable that the present revolt can remold China's social and economic institutions along Communist lines." But a few Western writers take the opposite view. They argue that China is ripe for a change—that its masses are hungry and distressed, its intellectuals disillusioned, its youth humiliated. For the achievement of such a revolutionary change, they feel that the Chinese Communist Party is the most effective agent. Success, they hold, is not ruled out in advance, since, in the words of George Sokolsky, "it is possible to believe that a large section of the army will go over if the Communists win a decisive victory." [*]

Having noted the impressions of various neutral, unaffiliated, and anti-Communist observers, both Chinese and foreign, we must now give ear to the pronouncements of Communist authorities upon the situation. "The Chinese Communist Party and the Soviet régime which is supervised by it," wrote Mr. Wang Ming, a prominent Chinese Communist, in the *Communistichesky Internazional* of July 23, 1933, "will be able, following the example set by the Russian Communist Party of the Bolsheviks, to transform China from a semi-colony of International Imperialism, and the constant object of military interventions by foreigners aiming to dismember and to partition her, into an independent country, strong and able to defend itself, like the Soviet Union of Russia." Mr. Wang Ming further observes that, "the prospects for the future victory of the Soviet Revolution in China are favorable. But this does not mean that the Kuo-min-tang after its defeat in the Fifth Campaign, cannot organize a new one against the Red armies; or that the Kuo-min-tang is already dead, as certain comrades contend. The reason for this statement lies not only in the fact that the Kuo-min-tang is the Agency of International Imperialism, helping it to inaugurate an armed intervention into Soviet China, but also in the fact that the Chinese landlords and the bourgeoisie had suffered a defeat only in one-sixth of the whole territory of the country, and not in the most important

[*] George Sokolsky, *The Tinder Box of Asia.*

part too; they still possess an army one million men strong. They will continue to fight till the last drop of blood to keep the power in their hands. . . . Nor does it mean that along with the development of the Soviet Revolution the Red Army will meet a diminishingly powerful enemy. On the contrary, the more successful the Red Army over the Kuo-min-tang will be, the more real will become the menace of an open armed intervention by the Imperialists against the Soviet régime and the Red Army of China."

It is interesting in this connection, however, to note that *Humanité*, the official organ of the French Communist Party, in describing the "sweeping victory" of the First and the Third Red Armies over the Fifth Anti-Communist Campaign of Chiang Kai-shek, in July, 1932, in the southern part of Kiangsi and Kwangtung provinces, stressed the point that this victory was made possible by the whole-hearted support rendered to the "Reds" by the population at large. The Nanking soldiers, deserting *en masse* and joining the "Red" ranks, made this victory still easier. Even Chiang Kai-shek, himself, declared in July, 1932, that "the main trouble is not in the number of the Communists but in the psychology persisting in our ranks, psychology of fear. Our armies are afraid of the Reds, and prefer to stay near the railroad stations away from the Soviet areas." [7]

The distressing conditions which made so natural this "whole-hearted support rendered to the 'Reds' by the population at large" have been intensified rather than lessened by events subsequent to the Summer of 1932. They have been succinctly summed up by one of the leading Soviet experts on Far Eastern problems in a strong article entitled "Five Years of the Soviet Régime in China," which appeared in No. 11, 1933, of the *Problemi Kitaia*. The author of the article, Mr. Yolk, writes as

[7] In the Chinese newspaper *Da Gun-bao*.

follows: "The great crisis into which China was plunged by the annexation of Manchuria and the beginning of the partitioning of the country by the Imperialist Powers, is thoroughly enlightening the toiling masses of China. It shows them the truth as it is. And this truth is found in an appalling poverty and hunger, resulting from the unlimited robbery by the landlords, the usurers and the tax-collectors; in the arbitrariness of the police and in cruel exploitation by the capitalist-owned factories; in the enslaving of the nation, and the shameless servility of the ruling classes before arrogant foreign Imperialism.

"The gist of the Revolutionary situation in China at this historical moment lies in the fact that the basic requirements of the workers and the farmers cannot be reconciled with the existing régime of bourgeois-landlord reaction and imperialistic pressure; the struggle for decent living is now developing into a nation-wide struggle against Imperialism and the ruling classes. At the head of this struggle are the Soviets. That is why the Soviet movement is becoming the natural centre of the national anti-imperialist and anti-feudal revolution. That is why the soldiers of the Kuo-min-tang are fighting so badly against the Soviet areas, and take advantage of any and every opportunity to desert and join the Reds."

Last but far from least, Mr. Manuilsky, the head of the Comintern, had this to say in his address before the XVIIth Congress of the Communist Party, held in Moscow early in 1934: "The first place after the Communist Party of USSR belongs to the Communist Party of China, the militant activity of which is playing an important rôle in the acceleration of the ripening of the revolutionary crisis. The Communist Party of China has enlisted the support of the toiling masses in the Sovietized areas. Its influence on the proletarians outside of the Sovietized areas is growing daily. This spread of the Communist influence in China is witnessed by the growth of the membership in the Chinese Communist Party, which now has over 400,000 members, as compared with less than 300,000 a year ago. She possesses an Army 350,000 strong in the regular ranks alone, and over 600,000 in the armed volunteer troops. That Army is considered even by its worst enemies as the best army in China. . . ."

Such are the views of many different observers, independent ⸱or official, "Red" and "Anti-Red," Chinese and foreign, on the present position of Communism in China. Almost all, whether with feelings of satisfaction or alarm, agree that it is a potentially strong position. But the fight is by no means over. The problem, in a nutshell, now seems to be whether the "radicals" will be able to construct a permanent Communist or Socialist State, and thereby keep China away from the usual capitalist development, or whether the "rights" or "Conservatives" will succeed in pushing aside the radicals. In that event China would become susceptible to the growth of Capitalism and to industrialization on the old lines. The corollary, of course, would then be the militarization of that enormous country, with all its attendant dangers to the rest of the world.

Dr. Wellington Koo is of the opinion that "Chinese common sense detests Communism," and in enumerating the "profound causes" which account for the Chinese aversion to this doctrine, he writes: "At first, Communism has a certain mystical halo around it. It is a belief, and for some of its followers, a religion. But the Chinese, brought up in the positivist and pragmatic philosophy of Confucius, are not mystical at all. The human element always ultimately triumphs over the speculative element. Mysticism is an innate spiritual disposition. It cannot be carried in a milieu which is unfavorable to it. Even when the Chinese is carried away by a fit of passion, his strong common sense comes back to him after a period of mental unequilibrium, and he again lives in his traditional concepts.

"What is more, the Chinese is very individualistic in his opinions. It is necessary to appeal to his reason in order to make him change them. He is not inclined to follow the ways of the others by simple discipline, but that and the subordination of the faculty of individual criticism to dictation by the Party are precisely the essential characteristics of Communism."

In a paragraph designed to prove that the Chinese family is opposed to Communist individualism (?), Dr. Koo writes: "Communism considers society as being formed of individuals grouped according to their social functions, but not according to their personal sentiments or affections. This idea is alien to the Chinese, who regard family duties as being of great importance. Communism tends to destroy the family by the relaxation of the conjugal bonds, by entrusting the State with the care and education of children and by the abolition of private property. But tradition and the respect for ancestors are important Chinese social characteristics. It is the family which for the Chinese is at the bottom of social structure. . . ." Then after a short paragraph stressing the "attachment" of the Chinese to individual property, Dr. Koo offers the solution, saying: "The Kuo-min-tang expresses the political ideas of the population!"

Having heard and read opinions of other Chinese, and some of them, apparently, not less erudite and representative of their people, opinions which are almost diametrically different from what Dr. Koo wrote in his *Memoranda* for the Lytton Commission, we may perhaps defer our conclusion till after examination of the facts. To this examination the following pages are devoted.

CHAPTER II

THE HISTORICAL BACKGROUND: THE TAIPING REBELLION

GENERAL REMARKS ON CHINA'S PAST

THROUGH many centuries China's strength was dissipated by a lack of real unity. Potent central governments were rare. The Imperial title was little more than a name. Political and economic power was divided among various predatory groups of landlord-warriors and wealthy merchants, who were often also usurers, and who exploited and oppressed the masses. It was this decentralization of the Empire's administrative power and the almost feudal nature of its economic structure, which made it so easy for the Occidental Powers to force, first, the opening of the "treaty ports" as unrestricted centers of their trade, and then virtually to partition China into "spheres of influence" and to lop off from her domain numerous "concessions," "leased territories," and even colonies.

From the earliest days of their mutual intercourse the attitude of the Powers toward the Celestial Empire had been far from friendly. It is true that the Chinese themselves were not disposed to welcome an influx of foreigners, whom they regarded as barbarians and intruders. But they lacked that certain proof of Western superiority—the possession of firearms. Furthermore they neither admired nor cultivated the martial spirit. So they were unable effectively to resist, and their failure was followed by a long and mounting series of foreign abuses, among which the importation of opium was conspicuous. The

14

lot of the Chinese masses, meanwhile, was increasingly miserable. For many decades they had been the most luckless victims of the economic chaos produced by the misgovernment and corruption of those dishonest officials who represented the nominal central power of the degenerate Empire. The provincial landlords and war lords were the virtual masters of the people's lives.

It is small wonder, consequently, that this misery, coupled with the long list of abuses committed by foreigners in later years, prompted intermittent demonstrations of popular discontent. Among these demonstrations the uprising in the South between 1851 and 1864 is most notable. It is known as the "Taiping Rebellion," and is regarded by many students as the first chapter in the story of the modernization of China. This revolt, caused to a considerable extent by resentment against foreign abuses and directed against the Peking authorities (who were charged, among other things, with incompetence in dealing with the foreigners), was for a time successful, and attracted much sympathy even among Europeans, and, especially, Americans. Finally, however, it was put down with foreign help, particularly from British troops led by General Gordon.

But the popular discontent continued. Widespread unrest followed the Sino-Japanese War of 1894-95, which was quieted only for a time by the quasi-reforms of 1898. In 1900 occurred the so-called "Boxer" uprising, involving great numbers of peasants who had suffered from the agrarian policy of the Manchu Dynasty. Other sporadic outbursts of indignation on different grounds followed, necessitating the Constitutional reforms planned—though too late—by the famous Dowager Empress. All these factors worked, in one way or another, toward the Revolution, which broke out in 1911, and at the same time inaugurated the building of the "New" China.

The building of the "New" China, far from being complete, is still going on. In an immense country such as the former Celestial Empire, with its population of well over four hundred million, the task of creating a modern political state, a democratic republic, from a nation accustomed to forty centuries of monarchical régime, was naturally overwhelming. Equally formidable is the problem of educating this mass of people, for it is intensified by the scarcity of modern means of communication, by widespread poverty, by the inefficient political organization of the populace, by dependence upon foreigners, and by the abuses of the war lords, who, themselves a heritage of the past, live by means of all the evils left by the "Old" China to the "New."

Though renowned for the elaborate organization of family and clan, the powerful economic structure of her guilds and her numerous secret societies, China seemed to ignore purely political formations in the Western sense. Indeed, until recent years, the only really well organized political group was the Kuo-min-tang, or People's Party, founded in 1912 by the "Father of the Chinese Revolution," Dr. Sun Yat-sen. The Kuo-min-tang, frequently referred to by foreigners as the Nationalist Party, undoubtedly played an important rôle in the Revolution, and it is still a factor to be considered.

But before turning our attention to the Kuo-min-tang, we must first examine the events and conditions which preceded and prompted its foundation.

The Taiping Rebellion

The Taiping Rebellion was directed against the Manchu Dynasty. It originated in 1850 in those wild and mountainous districts in the Southern Province of Kwangsi, near which, also, the center of Sovietized China is found today. Being a dynastic revolt it had as a goal the far-away city of Peking, then the capital of the Manchu Emperors; and the rebels accordingly moved northward, taking the route through Hunan. At the Yangtze River they turned—as did the Nationalists in their recent campaign against the North—toward Nanking, where they established headquarters. But the northward advance did not cease; and, indeed, their columns had almost reached Tientsin when the Taiping advance was at last checked. Twelve provinces, including some of the richest in China, and an area almost half the size of Europe, had been devastated in the course of the Rebellion. Some twenty million people were reduced to poverty. The Dynasty was all but extinguished. And by 1854 there had been—by all but the Manchu partisans—a general repudiation of civil administration throughout China.[1]

But it had been more—a great deal more—than a mere dynastic revolt. The Taiping Rebellion was, at the same time, a revolutionary movement with a definite social program [2]—a movement of such a character and significance that Mr. G. E. Taylor, writing in the light of recent study, speaks of it as "a revolution against Chinese civilization, a revolution born of the fact that economic change had outrun the growth of social theory." [3] And this economic change, Mr. Taylor believes, was directly related to the increasing density of population. Then, as now, the agricultural population of China—particularly south of the Yangtze, where the peasant holdings were especially meager—lived not only in poverty, but also under the constant stress of economic insecurity. Practically every inch of available ground was already cultivated at an immense expenditure of human labor. Furthermore, the growing population had mean-

[1] H. B. Morse, *International Relations of the Chinese Empire*, V. I., p. 450. London, 1910-1918. And B. Favre, in his *Sociétés Secrètes en Chine*, gives even larger estimates: sixteen provinces devastated and many millions of lives lost.
[2] See Spillman, *The Peasant's War in China* (in Russian), with an introduction by Karl Radek. 1925.
[3] G. E. Taylor, "The Taiping Rebellion," in the *Social and Political Review*, January, 1933, p. 548.

while not only reached an unprecedented total, but was out of all proportion to the acreage under cultivation; for while the increase in cultivated land between 1661 and 1883 was—if the records are accurate—from 550 million to 742 million *mou*, or roughly 35%,[4] the increase of population from 1722 to 1812 alone was 190%, according to one authority,[5] and even about 200% according to another.[6] A further factor which aggravated the situation was the development of foreign trade, which encouraged the commercialization of land tenure. The volume of this trade has been sufficient to build up considerable fortunes for the Chinese merchants in the Open Ports; and this new wealth prompted the development of large estates, especially near the big towns. This process conspired to make the rich richer and the poor poorer, forcing a large number of pauperized farmers into vagabondage, and augmenting a large floating population—which had existed ever since the beginning of the Nineteenth Century, if not earlier—for which the economic and social system was unable to provide, and which was always the raw material for rebellion and revolution. The importation and use of opium, developments in currency, the unequal incidence of the antiquated system of taxation, falling revenues, mounting expenditures and corrupt officialdom, not to mention famine and revolt, were other factors in fomenting discontent or in degrading the position of the peasant almost to serfdom.

It is argued, therefore, that the Taiping Rebellion should be considered first and fundamentally as an agrarian revolution; secondly, as a moral and religious movement which, for all its inspiration from the West, shaped itself in many ways to meet the requirements of Chinese life; and only thirdly as a dynastic

[4] Cheni, *System of Taxation in the Ch'ing Dynasty.*
[5] S. Wells Williams, *The Middle Kingdom.*
[6] E. H. Parker, *China, Her History, Diplomacy, and Commerce.*

revolt against the Manchus, fostered by the secret societies and sanctioned by the apparent "exhaustion of the Mandate from Heaven." Nor was it by any means the first popular uprising in Chinese history. In the early part of the Fourteenth Century, for instance, hardly a year passed without revolt in some part of the Bogdohan's domain. Plague, pestilence, and famine, without adequate relief, produced banditry at best, rebellion at the worst. In the south-eastern provinces of Kwangtung, Kwangsi, and Hunan particularly, a tradition of rebellion existed which goes back to a northward drive at the time of the Ming Dynasty. Subjected by the Manchu Emperors, these provinces now maintained allegiance to the Throne only under compulsion of military force and political tyranny. The racial minorities of this area, the so-called Tao and Miao tribes, were always ready to revolt. For many generations they had been used as slaves and menials; and their multiplied and bitter grievances inflamed them with a spirit of revenge.

Furthermore, in the South, the clan, family and village were economic units of considerable power. The pressure on the land invited collective action, and these and other local economic associations did all they could to resist the intrusion of outsiders who, migrating from their own districts, sought to settle in a new and less crowded neighborhood with more fertile soil. In the towns and villages, likewise, a community of economic interest promoted the formation of influential guilds and associations for keeping peace in trade, and for passive resistance against heavy taxation.

Such associations for economic purposes might work openly. Those of a political character could not. However, the latter managed to survive under oppression, and though forced underground, spread and fostered the revolution.

"The right to revolt against the government has been always considered as an essential element in Chinese political philosophy, and to include not only open rebellion but all those forms of passive resistance, suited to varying circumstances, which even today are employed in resistance to tyranny, injustice, and oppression." The words are those of T. Meadows, a British consul of the time, whose book entitled *The Chinese and their Rebellions* was published in London in 1856.

It is not surprising, therefore, that these secret societies flourished. "By their methods, their extent, the revolts they fostered and the psychology they bred, by their participation in the opening stages of the Taiping Rebellion, and by the light that they threw on the condition of the Chinese society," writes Mr. G. E. Taylor,[7] "the secret societies take an important place in the history of this period." Indeed, their influence can scarcely be underestimated, and this subject will be touched upon later in considerable detail.

The general economic plight and political inequality suffered by the Chinese masses at this time were indeed bad, and their financial situation was no better. Particularly was this true of the South: and a serious decrease in actual revenues of the rural population was noticeable in Kwangtung, Kwangsi, and Hunan —provinces which were constantly the scene of revolts and acute distress aggravated by foreign wars, such as the "Opium War," which ended in 1842.[8] The growing trade in opium, indeed, was draining the country—again, particularly the South— as may be seen from the following table given by A. Skorpileff in an article published in *Problemi Kitaia* (No. I, 1929):

Years	Number of Cases	Cost in American Dollars
1818	3,200	3,567,000
1820	4,770	8,400,000
1825	9,621	7,608,000
1830	8,760	12,900,000
1832	2,670	15,338,000
1837	34,000	20,000,000
1847	50,000	35,000,000

[7] G. E. Taylor, *ibid.*, p. 570.
[8] Another war started by the Franco-British Coalition in 1858.

Of course there was no lack of wealth in the China of that period. But the taxes were heavy. There were constant wars to be financed, rebellions to be suppressed; there were corrupt bureaucrats and greedy landlords to be satisfied. The load naturally fell most heavily on the peasants, since the privileged and commercial classes had been escaping their fair share. In the southern provinces, too, the silver tax on people's land was the highest, and silver was scarce. Prices on silver rose 200% between 1830 and 1848, and in the three following years (1849-51) went up 470% of the 1830 rate.[9] Here was an additional reason why these provinces became the scene of the Rebellion.

It was under such conditions that the Taipings, or Chang-ti, appeared. They were known as the "Advocates of Universal Peace" (the word "Taiping" means "Great Peace"), and their leader, Hung Siu-tsuen—also spelt Hung Shou-Chuan—preached that land should be owned by those who cultivate it and given to those who have none; that the outcasts must be recognized and set on an equal footing with all others; that no racial or other discrimination should be tolerated; that the existing Dynasty must go, since in the minds of the people there was a deep-rooted association between economic distress and dynastic decline; and that the brotherhood of man shall prevail. These tenets, actually derived from popular slogans of the masses themselves, breathed into the hardy mountaineers the hopes and ideals wherewith they started a movement which "developed from a mere agrarian revolution into a challenge to the very nature and existence of Chinese civilization."

By challenging that civilization the Taipings naturally became the targets of those who, sincerely or otherwise, wished this structure preserved. When it became clear that the revolt would go beyond the overthrow of the Manchus, and that in theory at

[9] Skorpileff. *Ibid.*

least it was aimed at the achievement of social and economic changes menacing to the established order, the ranks of those opposed to Hung were augmented by a majority of the wealthy and privileged. It is interesting in this connection to note that the suppression of the Rebellion was in large measure due to the efforts of two very wealthy men, Tseng Kuo-fan and Li-Hung-chang, both of whom were scholars and officials before they became soldiers, and who pretended that they were fighting not so much in defense of the dynasty as "for the preservation of Chinese civilization."

The leader of the Taiping movement, Hung Sui-tsuen, was born in a poor immigrant farmer family, near Canton in 1813. He received enough education to become a village teacher, though not sufficient to pass the State examinations. Some of the biographers regard him as a *penseur,* but it seems more likely he was an inspired neurotic. Hung claimed to have had certain unusual visions, and for a time was looked upon as mad. But he finally recovered and, declaring that he had been commanded to restore the worship of the true God, began the preaching which led to the establishment of several small religious communities called "God-worshippers."

In 1846 Hung and his cousin and fellow worker, Hung Jen, who also later became an important leader in the Taiping movement, received a certain amount of Christian instruction from a missionary called Roberts. They left him, however, without being baptized; though later they claimed to have performed the ceremony by themselves.

The following year Hung Sui-tsuen left Canton for Kwangsi, where he joined Feng Yun-shan, afterwards "Southern King" in the Taiping hierarchy. The congregations, which by then were quite numerous, included a few scholars and men of influence, but were chiefly recruited from the "hakka," or immigrant peasants and Miao tribes. By this time, too, the followers of Hung had achieved a certain amount of military organization, partly as a precaution against bandits, and partly in preparation for possible conflict with authority. The year 1848 found Hung Sui-tsuen already styling himself the "Heavenly King" by command of God, who, he claimed, had ordered all to obey the Taiping leader. It is apparent, says G. E. Taylor, that Hung was working hard to establish his leadership over unruly and rebellious followers by spiritual means, continually emphasizing the duty of obedience on the one hand and his own position as prophet and teacher on the other. "You should work together and dwell in harmony," he preached, "bear no malice for evil words. Be friendly and upright. When you go to a village you should not rob. Never retreat in battle. Ownership of money should not be strictly distinguished; do not divide it among yourselves. Have one heart and one strength, and know and follow the road to Heaven."

Christian though this doctrine sounds, it was not Christianity that the Taiping leader wanted to introduce. Indeed, in spite of the assertion of some students, he knew comparatively little about Christian teaching, as a number of contemporary missionaries who lived in China and knew Hung Sui-tsuen, have pointed out. Rather, he made his appeal through the promise of a new order which, though based to some extent on religious doctrines, was primarily economic, political, and social. If the movement took on a religious character it was partly because of the peculiarities of its leader and the theocratic nature of the government organized by him, and partly because the masses needed a veil of mysticism to cover a scheme for the betterment of their lot which they could instinctively accept but could not understand. This need was supplied by the vague religious teachings of Hung.

It is important to understand that Hung Sui-tsuen drew support from other classes than the poor. Wealthy farmers, merchants, and even gentry had their own grievances and were also among the discontented. The easiest victims of the predatory officials, they suffered keenly from the depredations of bandits, and were often found at the head of anti-bandit organizations; indeed they were the customary local leaders in such rebellions as were not directed against themselves as oppressors of the poor. As for the educated gentry, they complained that their legitimate path to distinction was barred by the Manchu conquerors, who allotted privileges to the Manchus in preference to the Chinese. It is probably true, however, that this participation of the rich and of the aspirants for privileges was at least partly responsible for the eventual failure of the entire movement.

For a dynastic rebellion the psychology of the people and the actual conditions were favorable enough, but for a social revolution the time was apparently not yet ripe. The period of preparation of the psychology of the masses through the teachings of the Taipings was too short, and in the recent history of the country there were no revolutionary precedents on which to build. The only bond, aside from their mutual discontent, which held together the adverse elements in the ranks of the Taipings even temporarily, was the "Ming tradition" of resistance to the Manchu foreigner—in other words, the sentiment of "China for the Chinese." This bond, however, sufficed only to keep together those who were chiefly interested in a change of dynasty; it meant nothing to the impoverished peasant, to whom the fundamental, and indeed the only important issue, was that of a redistribution of wealth to end his misery and subserviency. On that issue, naturally, the rich and poor parted company. Nor did the "Ming tradition" always act as a cement; in one instance, indeed, it was actually a cause of rupture. An important secret society called the "Triad," which strongly favored the restoration of the Mings, was finally rejected as a partner in the Taiping campaign because Hung Sui-tsuen cherished the ambition to establish a new dynasty of his own. But there were other obstacles, too, to the coöperation of the "Triad," such as the iconoclasm of the Taipings, who destroyed the temples and images of the Buddhist religion, to which the "Triad" owed many of its ceremonies and much of its inspiration.

As for the Taipings themselves, they hardly represented the idea of "China for the Chinese" in a popular sense; in one respect at least they were not a part of the great body of Chinese tradition. Not only did they include various races speaking miscellaneous dialects unintelligible in the Central Provinces, but they preached a new religion at once alien and obnoxious to many of their countrymen. In their endeavor to reorganize the country in compliance with their doctrines, the Taipings challenged almost every Chinese institution and thereby alarmed many meek souls. The consequence was that the Taiping movement was forced to alter and afterwards even to abandon most of the phraseology derived from Christian influence. "The Tien-wangs' Christianity is nothing but the rank blasphemy of a lunatic," wrote T. W. Blakiston in his *Five Months on the Yang-Tsze,* published in London in 1862, "and the profession of religion by his followers a laughable mockery and farce." J. L. Nevius, in his *China and the Chinese,* published in London in 1869, noted that "their form of religion became more and more corrupt, and the religious element which was their principal source of strength became weaker and weaker." So it is not surprising that the attitude of the foreigners toward the movement began to change, and that accordingly the anti-foreign phase of the movement, which in the beginning had been strictly anti-Manchu, later became anti-Imperialistic.[10] At

[10] Note a certain resemblance to the evolution of the interpretation of Nationalism in Dr. Sun Yat-sen's teachings.

first the attitude of the Powers was inclined to be approving, but gradually, as individual foreigners awoke to the true import of the Taipings' aspirations, the attitude veered, and eventually the Powers helped Peking in crushing the movement. Besides, there can be little question that the growth of foreign trade and the spread of foreign abuses had been a distinct contributing factor to the rise of the masses under the Taipings, even though it is doubtful if this point entered in any way into Hung Sui-tsuen's program.

The "Heavenly Kingdom of Great Peace," [11] as the Taipings' state was called, came into existence in 1851 in the market town of Yung-An in Kwangsi Province, and ended in 1864 with the fall of Nanking, its capital, and the suicide of Hung Sui-tsuen, who aspired to the throne of the Bogdohans but succeeded only in becoming the "Heavenly King of the Taipings." The five other important monarchs of the strange hierarchy were Yang Hsiu-ch'ing, the Eastern King; Hsiao Ch'ao-kuei, the Western King; Feng Yun-shan, the Southern King; Wei Ch'ang-hiu, the Northern King; and the Assistant King, Shi Ta-k'ai. Yang was next in order and importance to Hung himself; but—as the military and civil systems corresponded—all five were both civil and military chiefs and close in council with the "Heavenly King." It is doubted by the students of this period whether the Taiping administrative system as a whole was ever attempted on any considerable scale outside the territory immediately surrounding Nanking: and in any case the military always took precedence over the civil administration. But in both the military and the civil hierarchy the theocratic principle prevailed. Whatever his other duties, the official was also a leader in religious observances; and this linking together of state and religion was completely in accord with Chinese tradition.

In view of the constant fighting in which the Taipings were

[11] Or Universal Peace.

engaged, it was impossible for their civil government to function adequately. But on paper, at least, a complex and elaborate code was evolved. The entire administrative system was based on the unit of twenty-five families, and graded upward to the largest unit, the "Chun" or army, consisting—since the military and civil system corresponded—of 12,500 families, plus the 656 families of those in command of various units comprising the "Chun." Prompted to revolt by the unbearable agrarian situation and the general economic plight of the masses, the Taipings naturally came out with an agrarian program also, suggesting: (1) the redistribution of land on a basis of equality, and (2) redistribution of wealth in general. The land system of the "Heavenly Kingdom" was set forth in an interesting document which we shall discuss in detail in connection with the agrarian reforms recently introduced in the Sovietized areas of China.

In following the general principle of promotion and degradation, the Taipings were guided by old Chinese ideas. Officials were ordered to obey the "Ten Commandments" and to serve the country. Those serving well were to be promoted; those disobeying the "Ten Commandments" or the Imperial orders, and those receiving bribes, were to be degraded to lower positions. Every year there was to be an official examination to fill vacancies. Any person recommending another for promotion, or the reverse, was to be considered as a guarantor, and if the wrong man was promoted the guarantor as well as the candidate was punished. In this way indiscriminate recommendation and accusation were to be forestalled.

Various other reforms—some of them quite radical—were projected. Women were given a new social status: they held positions in the army administration and played a considerable part in the Taiping scheme. Two of them, Tsiu-Ehr and Sy-San, even became famous on the field of battle. Gambling and the smoking of opium, adultery, killing, robbery, and the practice of witchcraft were all prohibited. But old doctrines of filial piety and certain other classical ideas were upheld.

In the field of international relations the Taipings advocated, in the beginning at least, the conceptions of Brotherhood and Equality. Such ideas were not new to the Chinese: they had been taught by Confucius, who said that "all men have one and the same purpose under the great way." This doctrine was elaborated, presumably by Hung Sui-tsuen himself, in a poem entitled "The Original Way for Saving the World." In the part entitled the "Awakening of the World," along with commentaries on the provincial hatreds of China and international enmity, an appeal was made for the Golden Age of Universal Brotherhood. "We are the light, and should fight against the darkness," says the author of this socio-political poem. "We want to rebuild the fallen society so that the world shall become just, the strong shall not oppress the weak, the wise exploit the ignorant, or the brave impose upon the timid."

Contemporary authorities attest that the government of the Taipings was "administered with remarkable energy," adding that "their order and discipline are no less remarkable than their energy." Hung's army was generally recognized to be not only well organized and trained, but far better than that of the "Son of Heaven," the Bogdohan. Even without this superior organization and training, the army of the Taipings would still have excelled that of the Manchu government, because it possessed an aim comprehensible to the ranks.

Undoubtedly these ranks, like those of the supporters of Dr. Sun Yat-sen and like those of the Red armies of Soviet China today, included numbers of former bandits. This was no exceptional thing in China. Reformed brigands and others who turned to lawlessness through inability to adjust themselves to existing conditions, always constituted at least part of the per-

sonnel on which leaders of economic and political revolts had
to rely.

However, since the Taiping Rebellion was primarily an
agrarian uprising, the greater part of Hung's army was recruited
from the poorer peasantry. Starting in 1850-51 with a band of
about three thousand, Hung increased the forces until, according to some estimates, he had approximately three million
men.[12] In the beginning this army was composed of volunteers; but eventually conscription was introduced, and every
family was expected to contribute one soldier. Consequently
the social composition of the army changed considerably, and to
the poor, naturally sympathetic to the cause, were added the
well-to-do and other elements opposed to the far-reaching economic changes of the Taipings. The spirit of the army was
undermined. Devotion became less ardent, and desertions
drained the ranks, making the struggle more difficult, and finally
rendering further resistance to the united forces of the Peking
government and the Powers impossible. Another factor which
tended to lower the quality of the Taiping army was a growing
discrimination against the young soldiers and in favor of those
who had joined the movement earlier, with the result that a sort
of privileged Revolutionary Guard came into existence.[13] This
aristocracy of the revolution abused its seniority and contributed
in large measure to the demoralization of a once strong and
victorious army.

It had been strong and victorious in spite of many handicaps. In the matter of arms, for instance, the Taipings were
wretchedly equipped. Most of them carried only swords and
lances, while such guns as they had were usually old. They had
no arsenals, and were forced to manufacture such weapons as

[12] Skorpileff, in "The Army of the Taiping Revolution" (Nos. 4-5 of
the *Problemi Kitaia,* Moscow, 1930), questions these figures, but agrees
that the army was quite large.
[13] Veniukov, *Contemporary China.*

they could by the most primitive means, though in the early days of the revolt they were able to buy some equipment from the foreigners. Fabulous prices were paid, and examples are cited of English merchants buying old guns at two or three dollars apiece and selling them to the Taipings for twenty-five to thirty dollars and more.[14] The Taipings' armament and ammunition were always inferior to those of Peking; and their victories were principally due to their fine spirit and enthusiasm for the cause.

The strictest discipline was enforced in the Taiping army. Conduct was elaborately prescribed by all sorts of rules and regulations, of which the basis, curiously enough, was the paraphrased "Ten Commandments." Unlawful requisitions of food and other supplies on the population were severely punished, and every appropriation had to be paid for. Of course "lawful" requisitions were often nothing but confiscation of the property of the wealthy; the idea was to prevent arbitrary interference with property by individual soldiers of any rank.

These regulations, contemporaries report, were actually enforced before those later days when the Taiping discipline waned. Eventually the morale of the army broke down, equality disappeared, the simplicity of the officers' life was replaced by extravagance, and corruption ate into the upper part of the hierarchy. Finally the whole movement degenerated and collapsed before the united onslaught of the forces of Peking and Europe.

"It is the established custom of our nation in no wise to interfere with any contests that may take place in the countries frequented by our subjects for commercial purposes . . . in short, it is our desire to remain perfectly neutral in the conflict between you and the Manchus." Such were the words of Sir George Bonham, once the British Minister, addressed to the

[14] Veniukov. *Ibid.*

Taipings in 1853. These were noble words, but what are words when trade, politics, and—perhaps—Imperialism are subsequently involved? The ruling classes of the Celestial Empire, representing the remnants of feudalism and the beginnings of Capitalism in China, were not averse to receiving the support of well-armed foreigners to put down an "outrageous revolt of the plebeians, the peasants, and the paupers of all kinds," and asking, received it. Franco-British troops entered the territories of China and, despite the avowals of Sir George Bonham eleven years earlier, the demoralized and diminishing forces of the Taipings were finally crushed, in 1864, with the help of English arms under General Gordon, who was later glorified by his compatriots for this very deed. As for the partisans of the Bogdohan, they paid dearly indeed for invoking foreign help; for in so doing they sanctioned that elastic and all-too-frequently invoked principle of foreign intervention through which they themselves were eventually forced to surrender the sovereign rights over which they fancied themselves the guardians.

So ended the "Heavenly Kingdom" of the Taipings. Though this picturesque movement failed, its significance for China was emphatic. "No rebellion in Chinese history has been of such unique importance," writes G. E. Taylor; "it did much to dissolve the superstition among foreigners of Chinese immobility; it served to prove that as in all countries, the power of ideas in China is an immense and incalculable force . . . considered as a chapter in the relations of China and the West, it played a decisive part." As we have just seen, it did much to bring about that unfortunate policy of intervention by the foreign Powers in the internal affairs of China. But especially was it significant for the psychological change it inaugurated in the Chinese masses. In the Taiping Rebellion was born the spirit of revolution, the outgrowth of which we are witnessing today.

Considerable space has been here devoted to this Rebellion,

and not without reason. Without some understanding of its history and purpose it is difficult to comprehend what is taking place in the China of our day. There must be some reason why many students of recent events in China predict a new Taiping Revolution, and one on a much larger scale, growing out of the Communist activities. It may be profitable to learn why, geographically at any rate, the Soviet movement in China Proper is following almost identically the path of the Taipings. And last but not least, there are important analogies to be drawn in the agrarian reforms designed by the Taipings and those taking place in the Sovietized districts of present-day China.

CHAPTER III

THE HISTORICAL BACKGROUND: THE SECRET SOCIETIES

THROUGH many centuries and in many different parts of the globe a profound effect on political, social, and economic life has been exerted by secret societies. The political influence of the societies of the Ancients in Egypt, Persia, Judea, Greece, and Rome has long been recognized. Similarly the activities of the Illuminati in the great French Revolution of 1789, of the Epingle Noire, of the Patriots of 1816, and of the Knights of the Sun in the French Restoration, and of the Carbonari in the Revolution of 1830 seem well established, even if not adequately proved by documents, and hint at a more than superficial connection between the Freemasons and many of the important revolutionary movements of the past. Their participation in more recent uprisings, though doubtless exaggerated, is also considered by Favre [1] as reasonably clear. The French Grand Oriental Lodge of the Freemasons, in his opinion, played a part in the Young Turks' movement and American Masons influenced the Chinese Revolution of 1911. In the Munich Revolution of 1918, he believes, the members of the Order were conspicuously active, for Kurt Eisner was a Mason and "Spartacus" was the Masonic name of Dr. Weisshaupt, the head of the Illuminati of Bavaria.

In the Orient the influence of secret societies has been equally great, if not greater. Indeed, their pervading influence, as well as their picturesque character and ancient lineage, is undoubtedly the reason why the Freemasons and other similar

[1] G. B. Favre, *Sociétés Secrète en Chine*, Paris, 1933.

associations in Europe and America boast an Oriental tinge and proclaim linkage with the East. As for the Chinese, they discovered the axiom that "Union is Strength" long ago, and in the Empire of the Bogdohan numerous secret societies have played an important part in history making from very early days. Unfortunately the insufficiency of thorough research on the subject makes it difficult to define, in the cases of most of the associations, the exact nature of their rôles. However, at least one Chinese society—the "Triad" or "Hung" which, as we have seen, was active in the Taiping Rebellion—has been examined more systematically, and has been found by two such erudite Masonic scholars as Dr. Milne and Stauberg to bear striking resemblances to the Masons of Europe. Their view, however, is not shared by Favre, whose interesting book on the Secret Societies of China has been consulted extensively in the preparation of this chapter.[2]

It is important to note that the secret societies of China have been primarily political rather than religious in character and influence. It is true that in the Orient, as elsewhere, religious doctrine breeds mysticism; and some of the Chinese fraternities have indeed possessed a distinct religious flavor. But this characteristic has been less potent in China than elsewhere, probably because China developed nothing resembling a Church for many centuries. Taoism was not a religion in the orthodox sense, but rather an accumulation of rules for personal behavior with a good dose of occultism. Confucianism was a moral code teaching order and wisdom. Taoism was mystical, appealing to the emotions; Confucianism was decidedly rationalistic, and almost devoid of mysticism. The influence of Buddhism, though, was specific; and religious peculiarities characterized many of

[2] In this discussion of the Secret Societies in China, we have relied almost exclusively on B. Favre's *Les Sociétés Secrètes en Chine*, Paris, 1933; and on De Groot's *Sectarianism and Persecution in China*, Amsterdam, 1903.

the secret societies formed after the introduction of that faith
into China. But in general, the political element was dominant;
and from time immemorial the secret societies of China were
persecuted by the Emperors as hatching places for conspiracies
and plots. Often, too, they were persecuted for professing religious doctrines at variance with the creed of the ruler of the
day. This forced certain religious societies into secrecy, and
later brought about their transformation into purely political
organizations.

In China, where the individual counts for little and the adage
"Union is Strength" is much appreciated, the majority of the
secret societies were naturally modeled on the family or its extension, the clan. For many centuries the family, with its unlimited power and hierarchical structure, was the basis of the
Chinese social system. Hence practically all the Chinese societies looked upon the Emperor (a word synonymous with
"elder," "wiser," and "Heaven-born") as head of the country
by God's mandate. And at the same time they all cherished the
right to revolt against an incompetent leader; for, in the words
of the great sage Mencius, "if a prince loses his people he
loses the Heavenly mandate, and if he is assassinated, it is
therefore not a prince but a bad ruler who is killed." This
typically Chinese idea formed, as we have seen, the foundation
of the teachings of the Taipings, though in other respects they
differed considerably from the other fraternities; with a definite
political and military organization and a religious doctrine to
spread, they had nevertheless none of the rituals, initiations and
similar peculiarities found in secret societies of orthodox type.
But in proclaiming himself a Sovereign after the fall of Nanking in 1853, Hung Sui-tsuen only followed the precedent established by the leaders of revolts fostered by secret societies
in the past, though none of these other societies ever became
a government, as was the case with the Taipings.

Exactly how far back the secret societies go we have not yet been able to discover, for the Chinese Emperors, like the Inquisitors of Europe, were addicted to occasional bonfires of books.[a] Thus there are no known documents through which it has been possible to trace the existence of such organizations in China prior to the "Era of Wide Empire" inaugurated by the Dynasty of Han (100 B.C.-210 A.D.), which itself originated in a secret society. We do know, however, that the secret society was a classical means in China of uniting the discontented and leading them in revolt for "the restoration of justice," and that this latter word has constituted an inseparable part of the slogans of all such organizations in the country. We know, too, how the element of secrecy in these associations appeals to the imagination and makes easy the exploitation of human curiosity and vanity by flattering the desire to be different and to know what others know not. Consequently, in spite of the lack of direct documentary proof, authorities on the subject believe that secret societies in China must have existed well before 100 B.C.

The founder of the first secret society known to historians was a certain Liu Pang, who subsequently established the new dynasty of Han; and his life story is not unlike that of Hung Sui-tsuen, the leader of the Taipings. Of humble origin and scarcely literate, Liu Pang was nevertheless a man of good common sense, strong will power, audacity and adventurous disposition—traits eminently conducive to leadership. The political and economic conditions of his time were such that discontent was general and increasing. The feeble and incompetent Emperor, surrounded by a corrupt bureaucracy, ruled as a tyrant. Agriculture, the main source of livelihood for the masses, was precarious, and commerce languished. Trouble and revolt were daily occurrences. Grasping the situation and know-

[a] *E.g.,* 213 B.C.

ing how to take advantage of it, Liu Pang assembled a small gang of bandits and, later attracting followers from other walks of life, set about "the conquest of the Empire" and establishment of a new dynasty—an objective quite familiar to Chinese leaders of popular revolts. Liu planned wisely. He did not embark on his venture without some ideological preparation of the masses, and he devised a strong organization in the form of a secret society. To justify his ambition to the populace he proclaimed that the design of Heaven that he should become Emperor had been revealed to him when, while crossing a swamp, he had killed a serpent. A mysterious female voice then said, he declared, that "the son she had of the White Emperor had just been killed by the Red Emperor." This was declared by the interpreters to mean that the reigning Emperor should be replaced by Liu-Pang; and the story—resembling that of the visions of Hung Sui-tsuen—gave birth to a complicated legend involving mystical figures, symbols, and the rest of the time-honored paraphernalia for befogging the simple and credulous. The scheme succeeded; and Liu Pang became the ruler of his nation, embarking on that task of establishing the "Great Peace" which most of the Chinese reformers, including Hung Sui-tsuen, have announced as their aim.

About this period a great many new secret societies, such as the "Red Eyelids," the "Celestial Pillards," the "Thieves of Rice," the "Diabolical Soldiers," and the "Yellow Turbans," came into existence. The majority were affiliated in one way or another with Taoism. Some of them originated in gangs of bandits, all of them adopted the slogan of "Justice," and most of them promised "everlasting peace." [*] The members were usually bound by oath, often signed in their own blood. Sometimes, even, the ritual included an actual transfusion, symbol-

---

[*] The idea of "making the World safe for Democracy" might here be found in embryo.

izing fraternization through becoming of the same blood or family, thus demonstrating the all-prevailing dominance of the family idea. Furthermore, a number of the secret societies, such as the "Three Yangs" and the "Three Tchangs," included in their hierarchy such titles as "Sovereign of the Heavens," "Sovereign of Earth," and "Sovereign of Humanity"—all of which, with variations, we find repeated by the Taipings.

Buddhism was introduced into China in 68 A.D. Among the secret societies of Buddhist origin, probably the best known as well as the longest to survive was the so-called society of the "White Lotus" or the "White Lily." [5] Founded in the Fourth Century as a Buddhist sect, it was later transformed into a political association. Still in existence, it has figured—except during a few intervals of eclipse—in almost every political revolt in subsequent Chinese history, and was responsible for the overthrow not only of the Yang or Mongolian dynasty, but also of the purely Chinese Ming dynasty, which followed. Finally, it was instrumental in bringing about the collapse of the last dynasty of all, that of the Tsing (Ch'ing) or Manchus.

The fates of these dynasties were practically identical. Each was founded by an energetic leader who inaugurated, sometimes with recognized authority, a benevolent and efficient rule. His successors, spoiled by the easy life of the parasite and weakened by excesses, would thereafter degenerate and come to neglect their subjects. Then in some way the rumor would spread that Heaven had deprived the ruler of its blessing. The discontented would be credulous, and some new leader or other would be sure to arise, supported by his secret society and glorified in a more or less stereotyped legend of miraculous birth

---

[5] Coöperating with, and sometimes supplanting, the "White Lotus" were the societies of the "White Ocean," the "Purified Waters," the "White Fan," the "Celestial Reason," etc.

and divine blessing, in the character of Heaven-sent savior. After a while an attempt at revolution would follow. If it were successful, a new dynasty would be established. If not, this event would only be temporarily postponed.

These revolts occurred most frequently during the ascendancy of the Manchus (1644-1912), who had to suppress endless insurrections and attempts at dethronements, beginning with that headed by three generals who had helped them to establish their power. These generals, Wu San-Kuei, Keng Ching-chung, and Chang Ko-ri, being dissatisfied with the rewards they received for their services, revolted in 1673 and attempted to establish independent hereditary thrones of their own. Their revolt, in the course of which they occupied six provinces in China, was made successful by the participation of the Mongols, who marched concurrently on Peking. Other rebellions followed throughout the Manchu era, and the secret societies, though often persecuted with extreme cruelty, carried on the struggle and flourished as never before.

It is probable that some of these fraternities, like the Taipings, incorporated certain Christian characteristics, though in most instances no definite proof exists. We do know, however, that the Christians, being aliens, were accused of plotting through certain of the secret societies, and were persecuted, too. Moreover, practically all these organizations incorporated in their doctrines characteristics from every new religion that came into China. Most of them were strongly tinged with Taoism and Buddhism, and many were tinted with Confucianism as well. There is every reason to assume that Christianity contributed something, too.

From an Imperial Decree of 1808, by which persecution of the secret societies was ordered, we learn of the existence of such associations as the "Whip of the Tiger's Tail," the "Hand of Justice," the "Pure Tea," and the "Burners of Incense."

Seven years later, in 1815, the celebrated name of the "Boxers" [6] appears. This famous society, memorable in history for the rebellion it sponsored in 1900, merged teachings from Taoism with those of Buddhism and Confucianism, adding many mystical traits. In a proclamation issued by this fraternity in 1900 we read that "if one repeats incantations and the 'mantras,' if one humbly offers incense and appeals to the 'Shen' (the immortals) and the 'Hsien' (the Spirits), asking them to come out of their caves, they (the latter) will descend from their mountains and help men to exercise Boxing." Like the sect of the "Celestial Reason," with which they were affiliated, the "Boxers" believed that they might become invulnerable through the use of charms and talismans. This accounts for the ferocity of the attacks made by the almost unarmed "Boxers" in the rebellion of 1900, in face of the superior and abundant equipment of the foreigners.

A Chinese proverb says that there are seventy-two sects, each with different principles, but all designed, with slight variations, to fool the masses and when necessary to incite them to fanaticism.

We now come to the society of the "Triad," or the "Hung," and thence, at a step, to the influence of the secret societies on recent occurrences in China in general, and in the Communist areas in particular. Fortunately the "Triad," or "Hung," has been made the subject of thorough study by both Chinese and foreign scholars, and there is even available an elaborate description of its ceremonies, symbols, mystical signs, and ritual. "The Supreme Being charged us to destroy the evil contract between crushing poverty and excessive luxury. Father Heaven and Mother Earth had never given to the few the right to abuse, for their own satisfaction, the properties of the millions. The Supreme Being had never given to the rich and powerful the

[6] A secret society of the same name is also found in Indo-China.

exclusive use of the wealth which was the product of the labour and sweat of millions of oppressed workers. The Sun with its radiant face, the Earth with its treasures, the world with its joys, are a common good that must be taken back out of the hands of the few, in order that it may be universally enjoyed by the millions." [7] From this excerpt from the ritual formula some students deduce that certain Communistic ideas were rife among the "Triad," or "Hung," Societies.

The "Triad," as we have already seen, participated to some extent in the early stages of the Taiping Rebellion. Later, owing to Hung Sui-tsuen's opposition to the stress laid by the "Triad" on the restoration of the Mings and his desire to found his own dynasty, the coöperation was discontinued. The "Triad" also participated in the preliminary stages of the Revolution of 1911, when the society's membership included so many bandits, vagabonds, and other disreputable characters that Dr. Sun Yat-sen felt called upon to explain why his Nationalists had to rely upon support of this type. The Manchus, he declared, had cleverly attracted to their side most of the educated people and the savants, with the result that the Nationalists were forced to turn their hopes toward the less respectable elements. They relied upon the "Triad," moreover, because that particular society was not to be suspected of any serious political aims. [8]

As a matter of fact most of the secret societies consisted of ignorant and even illiterate persons frowned upon by the upper classes of Chinese society. Uneducated and scarcely realizing what their organizations stood for, the members not only did not know how to make use of favorable situations, but were often made tools to carry out policies in direct opposition to

[7] "Political Parties in China under the Empire," an article in the *People's Tribune*, Shanghai, October 1, 1933.
[8] Among the Chinese *émigrés* living abroad, the "Hung" Societies had become little better than mutual aid associations. The political and anti-dynastic aims were more or less forgotten.

their own aims. If Dr. Sun Yat-sen was forced to rely on them
he knew very well, by his own confession, that this association
was compromising and not without danger for the movement
he sponsored. There could be no question, when once the main
goal had been achieved, the Manchu Dynasty overthrown, and
the Republic established, that it would be safer to break with
elements of such a doubtful character. But was it feasible? Is
it feasible today?

In the issue of the Tientsin newspaper *Ta-Kung-Pao* dated
November 4, 1930, there appeared an article entitled "The
Brigands of the Kwang-Ping" which gives an excellent picture
from the Chinese point of view, of the origin, influence, and
tenets of at least one such society active during the last few
years. "In the area where the three provinces of Shantung,
Honan, and Hopei meet," says this article, "many bandit gangs
are ravaging, among them the so-called San-Fan, otherwise
known as the 'Society of the Red and Blue.' They claim that
they are descendants of the three ancient dynasties." It is then
explained that after the fall of the Mings, when the object of
most of the secret fraternities was the overthrow of the Manchus, these organizations gathering around them many vagabonds, founded the society of "Ko-Lo" or the "Old Brethren."
The article goes on to say that at the time of the Emperor Tung
Chih (1862-74), when insufficient food and clothing made
army life particularly miserable, many soldiers deserted and
joined the "Old Brethren" which developed into quite a strong
organization. Later the "Old Brethren" were divided into two
branches, and subsequently formed a sub-group known as the
"Red Spears." This sub-group, it may be added, is primarily
an association of farmers, and has played a prominent rôle in
recent Revolutionary developments in China.

"Most of the owners of junks and sampans are affiliated with
the bandits," declared the contributor to the Tientsin paper.

"Regulations for those engaged in water-transport prescribe that all affiliated members must be united, observe justice, and comply with strict discipline; those delinquent must be brought to book." It is further enjoined that they must be persevering and must refrain from quarrelling or holding others up to ridicule, and that they must have self-respect "that their spirit may be high. All are equal, and there should be nothing to hide from other members." Various other illuminating excerpts from the regulations are quoted. "The Brethren must refrain from debauchery and from stealing. They must accept as passengers those who are poor, but must refuse those who are bad." So runs one of the regulations; and elsewhere it is pointed out that "one must respect the distance between the Master and his disciples. The masters are like fathers to the disciples, they are like the arms and the feet of the body." Furthermore the Brother is commanded to "respect the ancestors of the dynasties" and to "pray for the Sovereign and his family before the tablets of Heaven and Earth. One must respect the sages and the holy." And finally, "a specific secret language is to be used among the watermen. To be mutually recognized the members of the fraternity must ask questions which should be answered in an established manner."

From this we see that secret societies with peculiar statutes are still very much in existence in China, and that their rites and ceremonies resemble those of other secret societies the world over. In their codes we can trace not only the cultivation of the fraternity spirit but also traces of many different religious and moral doctrines. Doubtless today the mystical element is on the wane, and the rituals have probably been simplified and initiation made easier. And it is evident that principles of high moral value are still enjoined, in spite of the fact that many of these societies live by pillage and cruelty. It should be remembered, too, that they are not all alike and that their actions are susceptible of differing interpretations. But some at least of these societies, whether or not they practice brigandage, are clearly more than mere associations of vagabonds preying on rich and poor, and have other aims to accomplish and political goals to reach. They are still factors very much to be reckoned with in the Chinese scene.

CHAPTER IV

THE HISTORICAL BACKGROUND: THE BOXER UPRISING
AND THE REVOLUTION OF 1911

It was not until late in the Seventeenth Century that China was permanently opened up to foreign trade, but the Celestial Empire had entered into intermittent business relations with Europe some hundreds of years earlier. The Russo-Chinese trade and the prolonged visit of Marco Polo, the Venetian, to the court of the mighty Kublai Khan in the Thirteenth Century are proofs of this, and it is very likely that there were other casual contacts even earlier. But by the Sixteenth Century the Portuguese were definitely carrying on trade with Canton, following in the wake of the Spaniards who, though they had arrived earlier, had at first failed to establish any relations. In 1594 several Dutchmen visited Canton, and in 1622 their compatriots occupied some of the Pescador Islands and obtained a foothold on Formosa, subsequently (1655) even sending a mission to Peking. As for the British, they made their first appearance in China in 1637, and by 1670 had already established regular trade with Amoy. Their East India Company obtained permission in 1689 to have its own warehouse at Canton, and in 1715 began regular dealings with the inland of China through that port. In 1784 the first American ship—laden, however, with the merchandise of the British East India Company—arrived at Canton.

The first steps of the Westerners in Asia, though not always either gentle or gracious, were much less arrogant than their later behavior would lead one to expect. But the Chinese, never cordial to intruders, did not hide their unwillingness to cultivate relations,[1] and the foreigners, discovering their own superiority over the Chinese in the matter of firearms, were not long in demanding additional trading privileges. Then followed the long catalogue of forced opening of ports, extorted privileges, concessions of all kinds, and even plans for partitioning the invaded lands of the Bogdohan. In 1842, at the conclusion of the outrageous "Opium War" this process was inaugurated officially by the Treaty of Nanking, whereby Hong Kong was ceded to England. Besides Canton, the ports of Shanghai, Amoy, Foochow, and Ningpo were also opened to foreign trade, and the extraterritoriality of foreigners was established. A long hiatus in the independence of China had begun.

The Powers were not slow to take advantage of the troubled days of the Taipings. As early as 1851, the year of the outbreak of Hung's revolt, the Russians obtained the right to trade in the Ili Province through the Treaty of Kuldja which they forced on Peking; and in 1858 French and English forces engaged in a "War" with China which culminated in the Treaty of Tientsin. This agreement, which elaborated the special rights and privileges obtained through the Nanking Treaty, not only secured them to France and Britain but—through the clever invention of the "most favored nation" clause—extended them to Russia and the United States as well. In 1860 this agreement was "elaborated" still further by the Peking Treaty, and in 1862 France obtained a handsome slice of Chinese territory in Cochin China. Then, in 1864, the Taipings were crushed with the direct participation of British troops under Gordon.

The "peaceful penetration" of the foreigners continued. In 1874 France negotiated the "independence" of Annam, later

---

[1] For which, of course, they had reasons; *e.g.*, the Spanish massacre of the Chinese in the Philippines; the Dutch in Java; the Portuguese brigandage in Canton, etc.

to become a French protectorate. In 1881 Russia added to her possessions a strip of Chinese territory in the far West in the shape of Kuldja and Western Turkestan. Great Britain occupied Lower Burma in 1862 and Upper Burma in 1886. Japan acquired the Liuchiu Islands in 1885 and ten years later captured not only the Pescadores and Formosa but also a part of Liaotung Peninsula, which, though later relinquished, was re-occupied in 1905. Germany seized Kiao-chow in 1897; and the following year Russia acquired a "lease" on Port Arthur and Talien-wan. By the same method England had secured Wei-hai-wei a year earlier and France now "leased" Kuan-chan-wan. The United States refrained from applying for any territorial concessions in China. But by taking over the Philippines from Spain in 1898 she nevertheless acquired, in a different way, a firm foothold close to Chinese territory.

Finally, in 1900, a long postponed and widespread Chinese revolt against the foreigners took place, not without encouragement from the Throne. This uprising was led by the "Boxers," the militant secret society from whose proclamations we have already quoted. The occasion was seized by the Tsar's Government as an excuse to send Russian troops into Manchuria, thus commencing the unhappy adventure which ended in the Russo-Japanese War of 1904-5. The other Powers naturally sent troops too, and the Boxers were easily quelled. The rebellion came to an end, and by the international agreement signed in September, 1901, the "victorious" foreigners imposed on China a heavy indemnity and other penalties.

One of the indirect results of the "Boxer" Uprising was the inauguration by the Peking Government of a systematic colonization of such neglected Eastern Provinces as Manchuria, where the Russians were building their new railroad in accordance with a concession obtained through Li Hung-chang in 1896. This colonization program was, of course, a natural consequence of the opening up of new territory through railroad construction. But it also helped to arouse the greed of the Russians and the envy of the Japanese, thus leading not only to the clash of 1904 but to the Manchurian "situation" of 1931 and its aftermath.

The "Boxer" Uprising failed, and its failure was probably inevitable. Yet it was not without accomplishment. It stands out as the first long step, after the Taiping Rebellion, in the direction of preparing the Chinese masses for a real revolution. This revolution, involving first the overthrow of the monarchy and aiming later at emancipation from the foreign yoke, arrived in 1911.

THE CHINESE REVOLUTION OF 1911

It was at the time of the Sino-Japanese War of 1894-95, when the decay of the Manchu Dynasty was obvious and the Chinese nation smarted under a humiliating defeat, that the late Dr. Sun Yat-sen,[2] subsequently famous throughout the world as the "Father of the Chinese Revolution," first organized a party "for the regeneration of China." Though this secret body, the Hsing-Chung-hui, was quickly detected and dispersed by the police, Sun Yat-sen himself escaped arrest and went abroad, where he continued to study economics and politics and earnestly propagated his ideas among Chinese students and *émigrés*. The late nineties saw a growth of revolutionary activity in China, and Sun's disciples succeeded in attracting a certain following among peasants and workers. Indeed, they even managed to organize a sort of army, and attempted a march on Peking, where the hated Central Government of the alien Manchus ruled. But the revolt was curbed in 1901, the army disbanded, and the party itself was practically annihilated.

The growth of foreign encroachment which followed served

[2] Or Sun-Wen, as he is more often called in China.

to add new elements, mostly from the bourgeoisie, to the ranks of the discontented. The revolutionist spirit was accordingly strengthened, and a new secret organization, the "Ke-ming-tang" or "Party of Revolution" rose to importance in 1905— the year, by the way, of the "abortive" Revolution in Russia. This "Ke-ming-tang," nominally founded by Sun Yat-sen at Tokyo in 1901, was the original nucleus around which the now more celebrated "Kuo-min-tang" was formed in 1912. During the same period, too, a number of other small groups, also anti-Manchu, were formed in different parts of China. None of these, however, played a rôle commensurate with that of the party of Dr. Sun Yat-sen which, after reorganization, was renamed the "Tung-meng-hui" or "Unity League." Here at last was a well-organized political body headed by able leaders devoted to the revolution.[3]

In the meantime the burden of taxation on the Chinese people had been growing heavier, and discontent was spreading. The strength of the Unity League accordingly increased. In 1910 the League, acting through Hu Han-min and Chen Chiung-ming, organized several mutinies in the army. By 1911 almost the entire South of China was in the hands of rebellious soldiery who sympathized with the aims preached by Dr. Sun Yat-sen, even though they might not belong to his party or even be aware of his existence.

The mutiny, on October 10th, 1911, of the Wuchang garrison under that same Colonel Li Yuan-hung who became President of the Republic five years later, was the signal for Revolution. Peking recalled Yuan Shih-kai, the ablest statesman of the Monarchy, who was then in disfavor and exile, and charged him with the task of restoring order. A draft for a Constitution

---

[3] Lenin has stressed the point that the revolutionary wave which was sweeping the world at that period (*e.g.,* Russia in 1905, Turkey in 1908, and Persia in 1909) stimulated the growth of the revolutionary spirit in China as well.

was adopted by the Senate on November 2nd, and made public the next day. On November 4th the Throne issued a manifesto appealing to the loyalty of the people; and on the following day more concessions were offered and a Parliament was promised. On the 8th, Yuan Shih-kai was appointed Prime Minister, and on the 13th he arrived at Peking. On November 26th the Regent took the oath of the new Constitution on behalf of the infant Emperor, that same Pu-I who became in 1934, by the grace of Japan, the puppet Emperor of the "independent state of Manchukuo."

Events in the South were, however, moving so rapidly in the direction of a Republic that the constitutional monarchy had no chance to survive. Early in November many provinces declared their independence from Peking; the Shanghai junta formed a Republican Government at Nanking that was recognized by fourteen provinces. On November 17th, Dr. Wu Ting-fang, Minister of Foreign Affairs in that Government, addressed notes to the Powers explaining that the object of the Revolution was to bring about the abdication of the Manchu Dynasty, and promising protection for the interests of foreigners.

Although on November 27th Wuchang fell into the hands of troops loyal to Peking, on December 3rd an armistice was signed; and on the 18th of the same month a conference was opened at Shanghai. On December 25th Dr. Sun Yat-sen returned to China, and three days later was elected Provisional President of the Chinese Republic, the inauguration taking place on January 1st, 1912. On February 12th, the Emperor abdicated. The next day Yuan Shih-kai was elected President, and Dr. Sun Yat-sen resigned his provisional Presidency and became Vice-President. In the same year the "Tung-Meng-hui" or Unity League was reorganized, and the new party became known as the National People's Party, or, in Chinese, "Kuo-min-tang."

Actually the Revolution of 1911 did not bring to the fore any united class or large, well-organized group to replace the deposed monarchy. For a number of years it continued to fall considerably short of complete success. Eight or nine changes in the Presidency occurred, and two unsuccessful attempts were made to restore the monarchy—one in 1916 by Yuan Shih-kai on his own behalf, and another in 1917 by Chang Hsun for the boy ex-Emperor. Repeated dissolutions of Parliament occurred; and from time to time rival Governments have been established at Canton, with two Parliaments sitting at the same time, each claiming constitutionality. Frequently also, various war lords and military or political parties joined together in different ways to declare independence from the Central Government or to wage war against one another.

For a few years China was at the mercy of these war lords; but at the same time a process of "differentiation of classes" was developing and worked toward the crystallization of leading groups. The activities of the war lords were encouraged at that time by the fact that enormous numbers of people had been impoverished in the years preceding the period. Endless lines of food-seekers, even more numerous than the adventure-seekers, augmented the following of the generals, who in most cases were interested in nothing but their own profit and aggrandizement. But as the process of differentiation of groups or classes continued, several generals of another character came into prominence. These represented not personal interests but the interests of the groups or classes on which they relied.

Nevertheless, along with these destructive factors there appeared certain constructive and unifying forces. The telegraphs, railways, and new roads, introduced by foreigners, all helped to weld together the hitherto isolated parts of China. The development of trade and the coming of foreign manufacturers had, of course, a marked influence on the internal life of the country in general and domestic industries in particular. Slowly but surely these things worked toward unification. They helped to arouse the national consciousness, to intensify the desire to shake off the foreign yoke, and to teach the nation to understand its best interests.

The downfall of Old China continued with acceleration until 1916 when it became clear that all hope of restoring the former régime was gone and that constructive elements were already at work. But the unsuccessful attempt of Yuan Shih-kai to restore the monarchy, back in 1916, was the climax of the fight to check its decay. In April, 1916, a Confederacy had been organized by five Southern provinces, which declared their independence from Peking. Szechwan joined them in May, and on September 10, 1917, a government was set up at Canton with Dr. Sun Yat-sen at the head.

At that time the bourgeoisie was in accord to some extent with the rest of the people through their mutual desire to rid China of the foreigners. Students who returned home after study abroad where they had been influenced by the propaganda carried on in the Occident under the leadership of Dr. Sun Yat-sen, brought with them new ideas which they strove to materialize. Chinese bankers began to organize; Chinese manufacturers were already numerous and self-conscious. These groups to some extent, though in different ways, represented constructive forces with definite programs. All embraced and helped to work out the leading doctrine that Dr. Sun had promulgated.

What was this doctrine and what happened to the party which tried to carry it out? What was its program and to what extent was it put into effect? These questions will be discussed in the chapter following.

CHAPTER V

THE KUO-MIN-TANG, OR THE NATIONALIST PARTY

FROM THE REVOLUTION TO THE WORLD WAR

IN point of fact the Chinese Revolution of 1911 achieved few immediate results beyond the abdication of the Manchu Dynasty of the Chings and the establishment of a Republic of very doubtful stability and character. The masses were by no means ready to assume the intricate duties of government. Indeed it cannot even be said that the country was of one mind as to the kind of régime best suited to its needs, for in the North particularly, the Monarchists were still quite powerful, and, what is more, much better organized than the masses. Thus it was not until fifteen months after the abdication of the last Emperor that such "second rank" powers as Brazil and Peru saw fit to give the Republic its first diplomatic recognition; and it took another six months—and the election of the reactionary Yuan Shih-kai as President in place of that "dangerous dreamer" Sun Yat-sen—to induce the Big Powers to recognize the new order. In the meantime, of course, those Powers did not hesitate to send more troops into Chinese territory. Meanwhile, too, Yuan Shih-kai was openly working for a counter-Revolutionary and "strong man" Government. By November, 1913, he had declared "illegal" the only real political party of the time—namely, the "Kuo-min-tang." In January, 1914, he issued a decree dissolving Parliament, thus making himself a dictator. In March a commission was appointed to revise the Constitution, and by October of the same year a new one was declared in force.

Then came the World War. Its immediate effect upon China was, of course, the infliction of the humiliating Twenty-One Demands by Japan. But its eventual consequence was to check the forces of reaction and to revive the revolutionary spirit of the nation.

THE TWENTY-ONE DEMANDS

On joining the Allies in the early days of the War, Japan was entrusted with the task of "taking over" from the Germans their lease on Kiao-chow. On August 15th, 1914, Japan sent an ultimatum to Germany advising unconditional surrender of her leasehold of that territory on or before September 15th, "with a view of eventual restoration thereof to China." Failing to receive an answer at the appointed time, Japan declared war on Germany and proceeded to military action. On November 7th the fortress of Tsingtau capitulated.[1] When after the Japanese occupation and the liquidation of German jurisdiction, Peking asked Tokyo to withdraw from that Chinese territory, Japan not only refused to comply, but promptly served on her neighbor the imperious document known to the world as the "Twenty-One Demands." Those, if legally accepted, would have made China virtually a vassal state of the Empire of the Rising Sun.

In August, 1917, China also joined the Allies in their war against the Central Powers, but this neither helped her in preserving her rights nor deterred Japan from "acquiring" a new foothold on Chinese territory. The Peace Conference at Versailles proved to China that she had nothing to expect from the Powers, and must rely on herself; indeed, the results of that international conclave did much to precipitate a renewal of

---

[1] Foreseeing the danger to China if Japan should take Kiao-chow over from Germany and so obtain control over Shantung, Yuan Shih-kai offered his country's coöperation in Japan's campaign. His offer was rejected.

revolutionary activities in China. The humiliation suffered by the Chinese at the hands of the Japanese and Westerners worked toward a resurgence of nationalism in China. Her masses began at last to organize and real leaders emerged. Everything pointed toward more decisive action.

When it arrived this action centered in the activities of the Kuo-min-tang. That party, reorganized as we have seen from the Tung-meng-hui in 1912, had been under a cloud. Indeed it was actually suppressed for a time, and in 1913 had been declared illegal by its enemy, Yuan Shih-kai. But in 1919, the very year of the Versailles Treaty, the Nationalist Party resumed open activity in fostering the liberation of China. After the decision of the Peace Conference to put aside the Chinese claims for the return by Japan of the Shantung Peninsula—where Kiao-chow is located—a country-wide demonstration of protest was arranged. A marked growth of the revolutionary spirit was now witnessed. Social support of the Nationalist movement increased materially, and the Kuo-min-tang again became a leading factor in China's life.

Dr. Sun Yat-sen and His Teachings

In the early years of Sun Yat-sen's activity he dreamed of enlisting help from the more advanced nations in the liberation of China, and expected in due course to see foreign capital fertilizing the almost untouched soil of Chinese industry. In those days he neither voiced any suggestion of fighting the foreigners, nor preached any sort of hatred toward them. But realities brought disillusion, and made him change these views.

The political principles of Dr. Sun Yat-sen which are known to the Chinese as San-Min-Chu-I, or the "Three Principles of the People" were in their main outlines of American origin. The immediate inspiration, thinks Professor Holcombe,[2] was

[2] Holcombe, Arthur N., *The Chinese Revolution*, Cambridge, 1930.

Lincoln's "Gettysburg Address." The first of these principles, that of national independence and the equality of the different groups inhabiting China, was originally employed by Sun Yat-sen to promote patriotism among countrymen, for centuries loyal to their family and clan, but with little regard for the State. Eventually the scope of that principle was extended to include ridding the country of the foreign yoke, and Sun's teachings became clearly anti-imperialistic.[a] "The experience of these forty years has convinced me," wrote Sun Yat-sen in his last will, "that to attain this goal (*i.e.,* the Three Principles) the people must be aroused and that we must associate ourselves in a common struggle with all the peoples of the world who treat us as equals." To arouse the Chinese to the efforts and sacrifices necessary for making the State strong, the Father of the Revolution cited the wrongs his country suffered at the hands of foreign Powers. "He dwelt upon the evidence tending to show that the Powers were still bent upon aggression at the cost of China," declares Professor Holcombe in his book quoted above. "He pointed to the foreign possessions on the Chinese coast, to the foreign settlements in her cities, to the foreign consular jurisdiction over her people, to the foreign control of her customs revenue, to the foreign administration of her postal service, to the foreign gunboats on her soil. . . ."

The second principle—that of popular sovereignty or democracy—was given an original interpretation by Sun Yat-sen; though incorporating the usual theories of Liberty, Equality and Fraternity, he made a distinction between sovereignty and political ability. "The Sovereignty, that is the control of public policy, should be vested in all the people, but the public offices should be filled by those only who are able efficiently to perform their duties." His idea of equality was not that all are

---

[a] It was Sun Yat-sen who advanced the slogan "Down with Imperialism," writes Gustav Amann in his *Legacy of Sun Yat-sen,* p. 81.

created equal, but that all should enjoy equality of political status. The kind of liberty he thought his compatriots needed most was that "which is based on the recognition of duty, especially the duty of sacrificing the interests of the individual in order to promote the general welfare."

During his exile, the Father of the Chinese Revolution had learned much about democratic movements in Western countries, and had noted "that people at large had little or no direct control over the conduct of public affairs." Sun thought that "the reconciliation of democracy and efficiency seemed to be a task beyond the powers of Western political science," but that "in Russia a new type of Government had been recently developed which seemed promising." [4]

His third principle—that of the promotion of the general welfare—really meant Socialism, though Sun Yat-sen himself did not use the term and was by no means disposed to accept the teachings of Karl Marx "in toto." He flatly refused to subscribe to the theory of class warfare; he believed that Capitalism would help China to develop industrially and make good for all the long years in which she had remained behind the Westerners. Bitter experience and utter disappointment alone taught him to modify his views in that respect; but he did revise his ideas in the end and altered their interpretation.

THE REORGANIZATION OF THE KUO-MIN-TANG

After repeated but invariably unsuccessful appeals to the Powers for assistance in his revolutionary work, Dr. Sun Yat-sen turned at last to Moscow. Though not in accord with all the views of the famous revolutionary leader of Russia, Dr. Sun nevertheless established contact with Lenin and became his ardent admirer. The remarkable organization of the party led by Lenin, and the iron discipline enforced within it, impressed

[4] Quoted from Holcombe, *ibid.*, pp. 142-143.

Sun Yat-sen so deeply that he lost very little time in attempting to reorganize the Kuo-min-tang on similar lines. Acting in conjunction with several other Chinese leaders, who had visited Moscow—including Chiang Kai-shek, who was at that time his loyal disciple—Dr. Sun Yat-sen invited to China a number of Russian advisers in political and military matters. Michael Borodin became the chief political councilor, and Galen (or Blucher) was appointed head of a military mission that included experts on different branches of warfare.

In its early years the Kuo-min-tang had been mainly composed of intellectuals and bourgeoisie; but eventually its program was revised to attract broader groups, and by 1919 it already had some backing among workingmen and peasants. In 1920, unfortunately, a split occurred in the party; the conservative elements, under General Chen Chiung-ming, parted with the more radical contingent headed by Dr. Sun. This split in its ranks and the lessons offered by the October Revolution of Russia led to further and more radical changes in the program, and in January, 1924, at the First National Convention of that party the Kuo-min-tang was reorganized along the line of the Communists of Russia. Probably the most important change in that respect was to be found in an elaboration of the interpretation of nationalism, one of the three basic principles of Revolution advanced by Dr. Sun Yat-sen. Formerly the words "struggle for nationalism" had been interpreted in the sense of a political status under which persons of any nationality living in China might enjoy equal rights and opportunities; but the term "nationalism" was now stretched to include the struggle of the Chinese nation for liberation from the foreign yoke.

THE COMMUNIST INFLUENCE

Notwithstanding the fact that the Kuo-min-tang had been reorganized along the general lines of the Russian Communist

Party and had adopted some of the latter's tactics, the main difference between the two, their attitude toward class warfare, remained unaltered. The Kuo-min-tang still considered class warfare inessential to the achievement of revolutionary changes in the social structure, though its leader, Sun Yat-sen, under the influence of the Russian Revolution, had greatly modified this part of his doctrine.

Moderate though the alterations were, the new program nevertheless laid distinct stress on the part that workers and peasants were to play in the Revolution. The Kuo-min-tang now made special efforts to extend its membership to these groups, and succeeded in growing very materially. Being then to a great degree under the influence of the Communists, they enlarged at the same time the field of work of the latter. The Communists, both Chinese and the Russian, who were invited by the Southern Government of China, did not fail to welcome such an opportunity to extend their activities; and in a short time the virtual control of the Chinese Revolution fell into their hands.

Participation in military affairs also opened up unusual possibilities, though later on this proved a trap for the Communists themselves. Knowing that without a well-organized and properly trained army the revolutionist South could not expect to curb the reactionary North, Dr. Sun Yat-sen was anxious to organize a force of his own, and decided to establish at Whampoa [5] a modern military training school for officers. Being deeply impressed by the status of the Red Army of the Soviets, he called for Russian advisers to assist him in his endeavor. "Sun Yat-sen had little talent for finding the bayonets," writes Professor Holcombe, "it was the Bolshevists from Russia who showed his followers how to transform his idea into a revolution which could take the field in force and rout its enemies."

[5] Just outside Canton.

The Northern Campaign

Late in 1924 a reliable Nationalist Army under better-trained leaders from Whampoa seemed ready to start a contest with the numerous military leaders of the Old China. The first test of these Revolutionist soldiers was in Canton, where they supplanted the merchant's guards. In the following year they drove out the Yunnanese detachments, and after this success, were reinforced by thousands of new volunteers from the ranks of labor.

But the shift to the left which was brought upon by the participation of the much more radical elements, including the Communists, naturally prompted disagreements. In March, 1925, the great leader, Dr. Sun Yat-sen, passed away. By March, 1926, General Chiang Kai-shek, then the principal of the Whampoa Academy and a member of the Centrist bloc of the Kuo-min-tang, had already staged a *coup* at Canton which resulted in the flight of Wang Ching-wei and several other radical leaders. In less than two months, however, the "Rights" and the "Centrists" were forced to compromise and agree upon many concessions to the "Lefts" in order to gain the support of the masses, so badly needed for carrying on the military campaign which seemed to be the only way to curb the North. In May, therefore, the factions were reconciled; Chiang Kai-shek became the leader of the Kuo-min-tang, taking place of Wang Ching-wei, and as Commander-in-Chief of the Revolutionary Armies, was charged with the task of overthrowing the Peking Government and unifying the country under the Nationalist flag.

About this time Chang Tso-lin, the War Lord of Manchuria, set up a Dictatorship in the North, and secured the coöperation of several other war lords to form a united front against the Nationalists.

In July, 1926, the Southern Armies started their advance. During August, Hunan fell into their hands; Hupeh and Hankow followed; and by October practically the entire Central China was under the Nationalist control. As usual in China, all military activities were suspended during the Winter, but the following Spring the victorious Nationalist Armies occupied Anhwei and Kiangsu provinces, and on March 24th, 1927, they entered Nanking. By the middle of 1927 the greater part of China proper was already in Southern hands.

THE SPLIT OF 1927

In the meanwhile the compromise that allowed Chiang Kai-shek to enlist the support of radicals came to naught; disagreements between factions were revived and necessitated much attention to internal strife. In June, Feng Yu-hsiang, the so-called "Christian General," withdrew his support from the Left-Wing Government then at Wuhan and, in order to fight the Communists, declared allegiance to Chiang Kai-shek. In July, Borodin and most of the other Russian advisers were forced to leave China; and in August, Chiang Kai-shek resigned under pressure from the "Left" and departed for Japan, only to return three months later. In December a Communist *coup* occurred in Canton and the Nanking Government, formed in April, 1927, decreed a break with the Soviets, which lasted till 1933.

During the Spring of 1928 the Nationalists resumed their drive, and though delayed by the "Shantung incident" staged by the Japanese, finally their allies, Feng and Yen, entered Peking early in June of the same year. Thus within two years of the beginning of their advance the Nationalists had routed the reactionary Northerners [6] and could claim control over the

[6] At that time the Nationalists enlisted the coöperation of Feng—"the Christian General"—and Yen—"the Model Governor" and were fighting only Chang Tso-lin.

whole country, thanks to the sympathy of the workers, the peasants and the soldiers who deserted the Northern Armies to join the banners of the Revolution.

The success of this campaign now brought the Revolution to a new stage entailing further social readjustment and a radical regrouping. War lords altered their alignments; and as a consequence the soldiers in their armies were frequently forced to change chiefs. But more important still was the problem of assimilating those who had demonstrated their revolutionary spirit by supporting the campaign to curb the Northern reactionaries, but who now felt compelled to turn their backs upon the Revolution in its new process of social readjustment. That process was affecting every class and group, including the Kuo-min-tang itself.

Social differences had, of course, existed for a long time among the members of the party. But they had been held more or less in abeyance until 1924, when the Kuo-min-tang was reconstructed under the dominating influence of the Communists. This reorganization inevitably split the party ranks. The "Moderates," opposed to class warfare, frowned upon the growing influence of the Communists, and after the death of Dr. Sun started to undermine them. This was the signal for the masses to go to the support of the radicals and to desert the Kuo-min-tang. Chiang was forced to compromise for a while, since his success depended upon the attitude of the masses. Thus the reactionaries—who dared not yet reveal the true trend of their movement—beat a temporary retreat, and in so doing helped to awaken the nation to a realization of its strength in gaining its own liberty. On the other hand, the bourgeoisie, who had started the campaign in order to stop the intolerable and unjustifiable competition of the foreigners and had attained some results, were now afraid of combining forces with the peasants and the proletariat. The latter had shown unmistakably where it believed its interests to lie and the bourgeoisie henceforward turned their backs on the Revolution and started to organize against the masses.

This change in the attitude of different elements of the Chinese society was immediately reflected in the membership of the Kuo-min-tang. As the "differentiation of classes" within the nation proceeded, the strife within the party developed almost to the breaking point. Following the decision arrived at in the plenary session of the Central Executive Committee of the Party held during October, 1926, at Canton, the seat of the Nationalist Government was moved in November of that year to Wuhan.[7] Chiang Kai-shek was at that time in Nan-chang, the capital of Kiangsi, a province destined to play a conspicuous rôle both in his own later career and in the history of the Chinese Soviet Republics. Surrounded by party leaders of "Moderate" persuasion,[8] Chiang now strove to enlist the support of the merchant-banker class of Shanghai in order to strengthen himself in his plans to overthrow the radical elements represented by the Wuhan group, who were relying on the organized workers. In defiance of the Party's plan of campaign, which called for a direct northward advance from Wuhan toward Peking, Chiang decided to move to Shanghai early in 1927. From the political point of view, and possibly from the strategic angle as well, the Party's plan was the more logical. To move on Shanghai meant inviting friction not only with the Chinese, and especially the foreign, capitalists in that city, but also with the Japanese in Shantung and elsewhere. Moreover it involved delay in effecting a junction with the forces of the "Christian General," Feng.

[7] The three cities Hankow, Hanyang, and Wuchang were merged and named Wuhan.
[8] Officers who were sons of landlords, merchants, etc.

THE NANKING GOVERNMENT

On March 22nd, 1927, the troops of Chiang Kai-shek occupied the Chinese section of Shanghai, which was virtually in the hands of organized labor. On arrival the General immediately ordered the suppression of the activities of the labor unions, in appreciation of which the Shanghai Chinese Bankers' Association arranged for a thirty-million-dollar silver loan for the innocent purpose of setting up an anti-Wuhan government at Nanking. This Chiang achieved after the so-called "Nanking incident" in which six foreigners lost their lives during the city-wide looting. This was attributed, of course, to Chiang's supporters by the Hankow troops, and to their own opponents by the Northerners. Eventually, with the joint coöperation of the foreign police,[9] and of secret societies described by Mr. George Sokolsky in the *China Year Book* of 1928 as consisting of "racketeering gangsters of Shanghai who specialized in the profitable enterprises of opium-selling, kidnaping and prostitution," Chiang "restored law and order," suppressed the radicals and on April 18th formally inaugurated the new régime since known as the "Nanking Government."

One day before this formal inauguration of the Nanking Government, the Central Executive Committee of the Kuo-min-tang issued a manifesto by which Chiang and his collaborators in the *coup d'état* were expelled from the Party as traitors. But the Nanking group was not without support in Wuhan; for the feudal elements, which had entered the army during the organization of the Northern campaign, now took alarm at the increasing menace of their interests from the rebellious peasantry. These reactionary elements now began to disassociate themselves from the radical "leftists," and finally succeeded in

[9] *Foreign Policy Association Report,* February 15, 1933.

acquiring dominant influence, as a result of which the Wuhan
Government capitulated in June.

At that juncture Madame Sun Yat-sen, herself a leader of
the Left-wing Kuo-min-tang, issued a statement emphasizing
the gravity of the crisis. "Whether the present Kuo-min-tang
at this moment rises to the height of its ideals, and courageously
finds a revolutionary corrective for its mistakes," said the widow
of the great leader, "or whether it slumps into the shameful-
ness of reaction and compromise, the Three Principles of Dr.
Sun Yat-sen will conquer in the end. Revolution in China is
inevitable. At the moment I feel that we are turning aside
from Dr. Sun's policy of leading and strengthening the people."
Elsewhere she added: "Dr. Sun's policies are clear. If leaders
of the party do not carry them out consistently then they are no
longer Dr. Sun's true followers, and the party is no longer a
revolutionary party, but merely a tool in the hands of this or
that militarist. . . ."

Degeneration of the Kuo-min-tang

Chiang's group neither rose "to the height of Dr. Sun's
ideals," nor found "a revolutionary corrective for its mistakes,"
for it never considered its acts as mistakes. Backed by the bankers and landlords, and relying on the foreign Powers, it was
compelled to suppress radical labor and peasant movements; and
having lost the support of the masses it became almost totally
impotent to stamp out the militarism on which it now had to
rely.

From the moment when Chiang decided to desert Wuhan
and defy the Party, he himself acted as a feudal militarist,
asserting his own will, and neglecting the constituted civilian
political authorities. Deserted by the radicals, by the organized
workers and peasants, and by many of the intellectuals, the

Nanking régime had no choice but to rely on the elements opposed to all that embodied the revolutionary hopes of the nation.

Toward the end of 1931, when Japan's Manchurian adventure had just begun, and was still unopposed by the Nanking régime, Madame Sun issued a new statement which admirably summarizes the conditions of the Kuo-min-tang at that time. "It is no longer possible to hide the fact that the Kuo-min-tang as a political power, has ceased to exist," said Madame Sun. "It has been liquidated not by its opponents outside the party, but by its own leaders within the party. With the death of Dr. Sun Yat-sen in Peiping in 1925, the national revolution suddenly lost its leadership and broke midway to its completion. The party comrades in Canton at that time, however, adhered strictly to his doctrine by which the masses were made the foundation of the revolution, enabling the Northern Expedition to be successful in the Yangtze Valley within a short period of time. But soon after came the split between Nanking and Wuhan, caused by the personal dictatorship of Chiang Kai-shek and mutual conflicts among militarists and politicians, deepening the gulf between the party and the people daily. The Revolution was driven underground by frightful slaughter and terrorism. Using anti-communism as a screen for its treachery, the Kuo-min-tang continued its reactionary activities. In the central government, party members strove for the highest and most lucrative posts, forming personal cliques to fortify their positions, while in their local districts they likewise exploited the masses to satisfy their personal greed. By allying themselves with one militarist after another, they have been able to jump to high positions in the party and government. But faithful and true revolutionaries have been deliberately tortured to death in many cruel ways, the latest example of which is the murder of Teng Yen-ta. . . .

"I for one, cannot bear to witness the work of forty years by Sun Yat-sen being destroyed by a handful of self-seeking and scheming Kuo-min-tang militarists and politicians. Still more unbearable is it for me to see the subjection of a nation of four hundred million to imperialism, brought about by the Kuo-min-tang betrayal of its own doctrine. I, therefore, am compelled to declare frankly, that since the Kuo-min-tang was organized as a machine for the revolution, and since it failed to carry out the tasks for which it was created, we need express no sorrow for its downfall. I firmly believe that only a revolution built on mass support and for the masses can break the power of militarists, of politicians, and throw off the yoke of foreign imperialism and truly realize socialism. I am convinced that, despite the terroristic activities carried on by the reactionary forces in power today, millions of true revolutionaries in China will not shrink from their duty, but, urged by the critical situation facing the country, will intensify their work and march on triumphantly toward the goal set by the revolution." [10]

There seems no doubt that the prestige of the Kuo-min-tang has been rapidly waning during the past few years. This is evidenced not alone by the general loss of public confidence in this party, which enlisted so much popular enthusiasm in the early years of its existence; it is reflected also in the widespread student agitation, strikes, and criticism by the intelligentsia. Last, but not least, it is closely reflected in the expanding influence of the Communist movement, the progress of which in the agrarian areas of China proper is well recognized in every quarter.

[10] Cited from the *Foreign Policy Association Report*, February 15, 1933, by T. A. Bisson.

CHAPTER VI

THE CHINESE COMMUNIST PARTY

Its Origin

COMMUNISM, as a socio-economic theory, is said by some writers to have been tried in its primitive form in China almost one thousand years ago.[1] Under the rule of Shen Tsung of the Sung Dynasty, the Prime Minister, Wang An-shih was given full power to introduce political and legal reforms. These reforms were so radical that they provoked his colleagues to rise in opposition. The Imperial Court was therefore split into two camps: the New Party, consisting of the reformers on the side of the Prime Minister, and the Old Party of conservatives on the opposite side. Wang An-shih proposed the following reforms, some of which were actually put into effect.[2]

(1) FINANCES:

(*a*) The appointment of an official commission to draw up a uniform budget of revenue and expenditures;

(*b*) the introduction of "Green Sprout" loan system which was to provide the peasants with sufficient capital at the time of the spring sowing for the efficient cultivation of the land;

(*c*) the abolition of compulsory labor and the institution of a regular system of employment on public works;

(*d*) the initiation of regular land-survey system with a view to supplying an accurate basis for land taxation;

(*e*) the nationalization of commerce;

[1] Camille Aymard, "Une expérience bolsheviste en Chine il y a milles ans," in *Revue de France*. Paris, 1922.

[2] "Political Parties in China under the Empire," in the *People's Tribune*. Shanghai, October 1, 1933, pp. 230-231.

(*f*) the equal distribution of surplus products by means of transportation;

(*g*) the adoption of the system of common responsibility for families residing in the same district.

(2) MILITARY AND POLITICAL AFFAIRS:

(*a*) Drastic reduction in the army, thus lightening the general financial burden;

(*b*) the creation of the militia system;

(3) EDUCATION:

(*a*) The reorganization of the civil service examination system;

(*b*) the establishment of institutes of schools for critical study of the Classics;

(*c*) the encouragement of the study of law, military science and medicine.

With the death of the Emperor Shen Tsung all this was discarded; Wang An-shih was replaced by his opponents and the entire experiment came to naught. To call his program communistic is hardly accurate. Nor is it correct to say that his experiment failed, and to use it as a proof of the inapplicability of Communism to China is simply naïve. Even if the ideas of Wang An-shih were somewhat similar to those of Communism they were by no means native to China. His experiment took place almost one thousand years after Christ, whose teachings certainly incorporated most of the main features of Communism.

As a political factor in our own times Chinese Communism clearly derives from the Russian example, and as a party force is generally traced back to a literary and political movement inaugurated among Chinese students in 1919. In that year, as we know, the Versailles Peace Conference was held, and its cavalier disregard of China's rights brought profound and widespread disillusionment regarding Western civilization. The youth of the country, holding the old tradition responsible for China's helplessness and stagnation, now began to work for emancipation of thought in the Chinese people, and to this end encouraged the publication of literature and periodicals advocating the "rejuvenation" of China, such as *The Masses,* the *Pioneer,* the *Vanguard,* and also *La Jeunesse,* which had been founded by Chen Tu-hsiu in 1916. In the year following the Peace Conference, moreover, two professors at Peking University—one of them this same Chen Tu-hsiu and the other Li Ta-chao—having been attracted by the Marxian theories, founded a Society for the Study of Marxism at Peking, and another organization of the same kind—the "Young Socialist League"—was established at Shanghai. Both these societies attracted numerous students and may probably be considered the true nuclei of a group movement which subsequently saw people from all classes join its ranks, and after undergoing various influences, including that of anarchists, finally crystallized into a Communist Party. Another important factor was the so-called declaration of Karakhan, the Vice-Commissar for the Foreign Affairs of the Soviet Russia, addressed in 1919 to the Chinese nation.[3] In this message Soviet Russia expressed its willingness to renounce all the advantages, privileges, and concessions extorted from China by the Tsarist régime—an offer which naturally played a conspicuous rôle in enlisting Chinese sympathizers and paving the road for Communism.

Birth of the Chinese Communist Party

The first communist group in China appears to have been formed at Shanghai in 1920. In the following May, soon after the election of Dr. Sun Yat-sen as President of the Chinese Republic for a new term, and the formation of a government at Canton, rivaling that of Peking, the Chen Tu-hsiu group summoned its members to a general conference at Shanghai. At

[3] See its text in *Russia and the Soviet Union in the Far East by* V. A. Yakhontoff, pp. 381-387.

that conference the Communist Party of China appears to have been officially formed.[4] Soon afterwards the Chinese Communists sent representatives to Moscow and their young party became a member of the Third International, or Comintern, as it is commonly known. Though as yet insignificant in numbers, it was strong in able leaders. Besides Chen Tu-hsiu and Li Ta-chao, it already included Tan Ping-shan, Tsai Shih-siang, Chang Tai-lai, Peng Pai and others, many of whom were highly educated intellectuals, energetically and enthusiastically working for the cause. This little group started at once to play a conspicuous rôle in the Chinese Revolution.

CONTACT WITH SOVIET RUSSIA

Late in 1922 a mission from Soviet Russia arrived in the Far East. After a series of meetings in January, 1923, between Dr. Sun Yat-sen and the head of that mission, Dr. Joffe, a declaration was published to the effect that both Dr. Sun and Dr. Joffe "considered that neither communist organization nor the system of Soviets can be introduced into China at present because the necessary conditions for their success do not exist there," and that "the most important and most pressing problem of China is to achieve her national unification and to realize her complete national independence.[5]

In the Autumn of the same year Michael Borodin and other Russian advisers, invited by Dr. Sun to assist the Nationalists in organizing their civil and military forces, arrived at Canton.

COMMUNISTS IN THE KUO-MIN-TANG

Among the many tasks confronting Dr. Sun was the reorganization of the Kuo-min-tang. Its activities were lagging and

[4] Other sources give 1922 as the year of the official foundation of the Chinese Communist Party. In that year the Communist Party was formally inaugurated in Canton.
[5] Cited from Wellington Koo, *Memoranda,* presented to the Lytton Commission, p. 731.

no longer satisfied either the President or the other revolutionists. In January of the next year, 1924, the party was reorganized to resemble the Russian Communist Party in so far as a definite body of party principles, unity of organization and strict discipline were concerned. In March, at the First National Congress of the Kuo-min-tang, the principle of admission of Communists (as individuals) into that party was favorably voted upon, and a number of Communists, including a few Russians, entered the Kuo-min-tang.

For almost a year thereafter the Kuo-min-tang worked smoothly, experiencing only minor disagreements among its members; but shortly after the death of Dr. Sun Yat-sen, the factional struggle became acute, especially because the labor movement in China definitely took on a more radical coloring.[6] The position of the radical "Left-Wing" nevertheless continued to be very strong.

THE RUSSIAN INFLUENCE

During 1925 Borodin was in the zenith of his influence over the Nationalist Government, then still at Canton. The Russian adviser had the complete confidence of Dr. Sun, was trusted and backed by the revolutionists, and enjoyed the coöperation of the Kuo-min-tang and its leaders. Wang Ching-wei was then the head of the Government, and after the death of Dr. Sun also the head of the Kuo-min-tang; General Chiang Kai-shek was still his docile subordinate. Nevertheless the process of disintegration had begun. After the decision to admit Communists into the party was passed by its Congress, the "Moderates" drifted more and more toward the "right." Finally in March, 1926, about a year after the death of Dr. Sun, Chiang took advantage of Borodin's temporary absence from Canton to

---

[6] Lee-Lih-San (Li Li-San) *Report to the Pan Pacific Trade Union Conference* (held in Hankow in 1927).

stage a *coup d'état,* and forced Wang Ching-wei, the head of the government, to leave the country. Furthermore he disarmed a number of troops loyal to the Communists, and deported several Russian advisers.

Chiang's triumph was short-lived, as we have seen; in less than two months he had to compromise with the "Lefts" because he needed the support of the masses to carry on the war against the Northerners, and the masses were behind Borodin and his followers. The Communists were reinstated, the alliance with Soviet Russia was reaffirmed, and a number of Russian advisers were attached to the Army in order to assure a better control over Chiang and his co-plotters. Borodin's position continued paramount, and the Communist influence reached its peak.

THE GROWTH OF THE CHINESE COMMUNIST PARTY

"From the original centers of Shanghai and Canton, the Communist propaganda had now extended to the whole country so that numerous groups were soon formed, divided in three regions consisting of central, northern and southern China," reports Dr. Wellington Koo in the *Memoranda* quoted above. "The central group was composed of six sub-divisions: the northern of four and the southern of six. Regional organizations remained very loose and the groups themselves could not agree either upon a common program or upon a method to be followed. They were divided, and quarrelled on many questions as regards principles and personnel. Nevertheless, certain groups exerted considerable influence, as for instance the extremists of the south, whose leader, Chiang Yi-mien,[7] Secretary-General of the Kwangtung and Kwangsi regions, was supported by the all powerful Borodin."[8]

[7] Peng Pai gave the name of that secretary as Chang Tai-lei. (?)
[8] Very obviously this statement of Dr. W. Koo was far from being impartial and correct.

As a matter of fact, early in 1927, or prior to the break with the Kuo-min-tang, the Communists had almost 60,000 adult members and a junior enrollment over 35,000 besides the trade-union workers estimated at 2,800,000, who were under Communist influence. In addition, the peasant-unions organized under Communist auspices numbered 9,720,000.[9]

SPLIT OF THE NATIONALISTS

As we have seen, the compromise with the "Lefts" allowed Chiang to continue successfully the Northern Campaign, but along with military success he regained his lust for power. He quickly showed again his desire to be independent of the Party's control, and occasionally made known his disapproval of its tactics.

After the Nationalist Government moved from Canton to Wuhan a series of grave clashes with foreigners occurred, the most serious being the "Nanking Incident" of March 24th. This unfortunate occurrence served, as we have seen, to justify Chiang Kai-shek in forming in April, 1927, a new "Moderate" Government at Nanking, with the support of the Shanghai bankers and the blessing of the Powers.

END OF COÖPERATION OF THE KUO-MIN-TANG AND THE COMMUNISTS

The new Nanking Government immediately issued a proclamation condemning Communism and ordering the "purification" of the Army and the civil services. In one of the numerous manifestoes that followed, Chiang declared that: (1) The Revolutionary Party [10] wishes to emancipate the Chinese people as a whole, that is to say all classes including farmers, workers,

[9] These figures, given in the *Foreign Policy Association Report*, April 20, 1933, by T. A. Bisson, almost check with those given by Dr. W. Koo, in his *Memoranda*, though in the latter they are somewhat larger.
[10] *I.e.*, the Kuo-min-tang.

merchants and soldiers. It does not wish therefore that only one class should dominate. Especially it does not desire the dictatorship of the proletariat. (2) The Revolutionary Party wishes to assure every Chinese of his entire liberty of thought and action. It will not therefore admit a super-government under Borodin. It only admits a Government of a liberated China enjoying a full measure of freedom. (3) The Revolutionary Party wishes to assure the welfare and the progress of the entire nation. It cannot therefore allow 390 millions of Chinese citizens to be treated at will by 10 millions of Communists (supposing that there are as many as that). Dr. Sun admitted the Communists into the Party as collaborators and the Russians as friends. If the Communists wish to dominate and the Russians desire to ill-treat us that means the end of their activity." [11]

Three months later the Wuhan group capitulated. Borodin and other Russians departed. And with the inauguration by Chiang of a terror against the Communists the latter were forced underground.

On July 13th the Executive Committee of the Chinese Communist Party issued a manifesto, declaring that it had withdrawn its representatives from the National Government, but would continue to collaborate with the truly revolutionary elements of the Kuo-min-tang. The acts of the Wuhan group were denounced by the Comintern, as they were considered as amounting to a betrayal of the cause of the agrarian revolution and a sabotage virtually aiding Nanking. [12]

Borodin's task was extremely difficult. On one hand, he was handicapped by the mere fact that as a foreigner he was opposed by certain Chinese, particularly those unscrupulous opponents who were willing to use any and every weapon against

[11] Quoted from the text as given by Dr. Wellington Koo in his *Memoranda*, presented to the Lytton Commission, p. 739.
[12] Wellington Koo. *Ibid.*, pp. 740-741.

him and, on the other hand, he was hampered by conflicting trends among Communists. One group urged immediate dissociation from the Kuo-min-tang and at once setting up a strict Communist régime at Wuhan, to take the leadership of the Revolution, with the aid of an armed force of workers and peasants. The other group considered it proper to continue loyal coöperation with the Chinese bourgeoisie as represented in the Kuo-min-tang, and to adhere to the policy of assisting the Chinese leaders to achieve a national revolution, taking care only that an adequate basis should be laid through a strongly organized mass-movement.[13]

By the end of July the pressure became unbearable and Borodin, feeling himself disowned by his comrades in Moscow, decided to leave China. On July 27th, despite the pleadings of the Left-Wing Kuo-min-tang leaders [14] he left Hankow, and started his homeward journey via Mongolia.

Shortly after Borodin's departure the Chinese Communists under Generals Yeh Ting, Ho Lung (who was in command of the 20th Army of the Kuo-min-tang) and Chu Teh, carried out at Nanchang, in Kiangsi province, a successful revolt among the "Ironsides," the best army corps of the Kuo-min-tang. By so doing they brought into the ranks of Communists an armed force of about fifteen thousand men, which served as the nucleus for the Red Armies organized later. In the same Summer of 1927, however, these troops were frustrated in an effort to acquire an outlet to the sea by occupying the port of Swatow, and they were forced to retreat into the mountains, where they had established their footholds. But other Communists remained in that area and under Peng Pai formed at Haifong and Lafong what became known as the First Chinese Soviets which continued till April, 1928, or about five months.

[13] *Foreign Policy Association Report* of February 15, 1933, by T. A. Bisson.
[14] Louis Fischer, *The Soviets in World Affairs*, p. 676.

The Communist Coup-d'état at Canton

On December 11th a group of Communists, led by Wang Ping,[15] Su Chao-jen and others, with the participation of Yeh Ting, staged a *coup-d'état* at Canton and established a Soviet Government in that city. But this Commune was easily curbed by the Nanking troops, acting with the assistance of foreigners, after a short existence of only three days. This was taken as pretext by Chiang for the final and now official separation of the Kuo-min-tang and the Communists. This separation was followed by an unprecedented "white terror," and a break with Moscow, which was accused of plotting the revolt. On these occurrences the well-informed writer on China, Gustav Amann, commented in his *Legacy of Sun Yat-Sen* as follows: "Everything that others had done for the glorious rise of the cause and of Chiang Kai-Shek, everything that had given his army victory, was forgotten. . . . The worst had happened. The very thing had happened which Sun Yat-Sen had always called the danger which threatened his work. The militarists of his own party got ready to exploit the victory of the Revolution."

The Communists Go Underground

At the close of the year 1927 the Chinese Communist movement reached a low ebb and went into hiding. In the cities the militant unions had been crushed and the workers were being reorganized into unions closely regulated by the Nanking Government. In the universities from which Communists were banned, the radically inclined students kept under cover. In the rural areas the peasant unions had been wiped out in a series of frightful massacres. Only in South-Central China, where a few Communist leaders were operating with small bodies of troops, was Communism still openly active.

[15] The former Secretary-General of the All-China Trade Union Federation.

Certain students claim that during the first two years of the new phase of the Chinese Communist movement created by Chiang's "terror," a falling-off in party membership and influence of Communism were registered.[16] Others disagree, saying that if at the end of 1927 the membership of that Party was about 60,000, early in 1929 it was already over 130,000.[17] But all agree that beginning with 1929 the movement once more assumed large and increasing power. "It has reëmerged," says Bisson,[18] "as an indigenous agrarian revolution, centered chiefly in the interior areas of South and Central China, with its own political institutions and economic and social objectives."

The propagation of Communism in China is strictly prohibited by law. By virtue of the "Regulations for the Enforcement of Martial Law and the Emergency Law regarding the Safety of the Republic," persons engaged in Communistic activities can be arrested and summarily dealt with. "Since the split of the Kuo-min-tang and the Communists in 1927 the execution of Communist agitators has become almost a daily occurrence," writes Mr. Lowe Chuan-hua, "and the number of persons killed on the charge of having participated in Communist activities has increased by leaps and bounds. In some places, persons who are by no means Red but have in one way or another displeased the Government authorities have also been silenced without due process of law. The execution of Liu Yu-sen, editor of the Kiang Sen *Daily News* in Chikiang in the beginning of 1933 is an illustration that can be easily multiplied. The suppression of 'Dangerous thoughts' in Republican China has become as rigid as in Imperial Japan. Under these

[16] The official Japanese *Document on Communism* prepared for the Lytton Commission claimed that in May, 1930, the membership of the Chinese C. P. was only 17,000.
[17] *Pravda,* June 25, 1929.
[18] *Foreign Policy Association Report* of April, 1933, by T. A. Bisson.

circumstances, the Communists cannot but adopt desperate methods to spread their influence among the Chinese masses." [19]

But in spite of such restrictions, and even of the terror practiced by Chiang Kai-shek and his mercenaries, the outlawed Communist Party of China continues to grow, and its membership at the opening of the year 1934 was over 400,000 not to mention numerous sympathizers and aspirants to membership in its ranks. The influence it wields on the Chinese masses today is considerable and rapidly increasing.

The mere existence of the Sovietized areas, spread over a large part of China proper, and of the Central Soviet Government and the Red Armies, which seem invincible in face of attack by Nanking, are strengthening the popularity of the Communists all over China. For the latter are credited with these achievements, and are actually the leaders of this movement.

[19] Lowe Chuan-hua, *Facing Labor Issues in China,* China Institute of Pacific Relations publication, Shanghai, 1933.

CHAPTER VII

SOVIETIZATION OF CERTAIN AREAS OF CHINA

THE CANTON COMMUNE AND THE SOVIET REPUBLIC OF HAILOFONG

SOON after the formation of the Nanking régime, several army units, as we have seen, revolted against the self-styled successor to the Nationalist Government. Being out of sympathy with the "less-revolutionary" group, these units remained loyal to the Wuhan Government, and by deciding to stand behind their Communist comrades, laid the foundation of that Red Army which has become such an important factor in the Sovietization of China.

In the period between 1924 and 1927, when the Communists were still not only tolerated but looked upon as the best friends of the nation and leaders in the Revolution, two classes of Chinese were noticeably attracted by their doctrines.[1] These were the peasants, particularly of the South, and the soldiers, especially those who participated in the Northern Campaign. In the case of the peasants this trend toward Communism is explained by the fact that the discontent in the Southern provinces was widespread and the misery acute. The numerous associations existing among them such as the secret societies described in Chapter III, and especially the newly formed peasants' unions, made them all the more ready to organize for the struggle. As for soldiers, they were influenced by those Communists who had been attached to most of the units of the Expeditionary Forces for their "political enlightenment." As

[1] Aside from the workers who entered the Communist Party in numbers and were spreading its teachings among the others.

the result of these efforts of the Communist propagandists, many farmers and numerous army units were won over to Soviet doctrines and not only supplied the material from which the Soviets were first organized but later helped to direct their policies.

After the revolt at Nanchang the troops of Ho Lung, Yeh Ting and Chu Teh, were forced, under pressure by the soldiers of the Nanking régime, to seek refuge in the mountains. One detachment, under Yeh Ting and Chu Teh, was instrumental in laying the foundation of the first soviets in Kiangsi, where in November, 1927, the First Soviet Republic of China, that of Hailofong, was set up. They also participated in the Canton *coup-d'état*, which was staged on December 11th, only to be crushed after three days by Nanking forces aided by the for-eigners.

Orthodox members of the Party believe that the Canton Commune, short-lived though it was, contributed much to the cause of Communism in China. At least its government had time enough to proclaim its revolutionary policy, which included the eight-hour day for workers; increase of wages; social insurance; control of industries by workers; nationalization of large enterprises and banks, and confiscation of the land of the wealthy and its distribution among the poor, as well as confiscation of other property of the rich and its distribution among the needy. Furthermore it proclaimed complete freedom of assembly and speech "for the toiling masses."

In connection with this policy, however, it is well to note at once that actually neither nationalization of land nor the expropriation of the capitalists enters into the present plans of the Provisional Government of Soviet China, and that both are opposed by the Communist leaders.[2] If there are some areas

[2] Safaroff, G., "Revolution and Counter-Revolution in China," in the *Problemi Kitaia*, Nos. 3 and 4, pp. 25-30.

where this was actually achieved it was not in accord with the "general line" of policy and was disapproved by the Center. As a matter of fact in most of the Sovietized areas manufacturers are left unmolested and allowed to continue their business, provided they abide by the newly established order. The stress seems to be laid by the leaders not on the intensification of the Revolution but on its extensification. The larger the area affected and the more peasants there are involved in this agrarian revolution, the stronger, they feel, will be the Soviet cause. In other words, in this way more can be accomplished of a lasting nature and with a minimum of errors due to haste. That is why the leadership had strongly opposed any so-called "putsches," when the situation is not actually favorable for revolt and when success is not even probable.

Considering the prevalence of rural population in the South, the appeal of the Canton Commune was virtually an appeal for agrarian revolution, and this revolution was in fact advanced thereby. The idea of a Soviet régime, wherein the poor must rule, was sweeping the masses. Naturally the rural populace proved most enthusiastic, for they expected through the Soviets to obtain land which was, of course, their main concern. As for the rest of the program, and especially the intricacies of Communism as an abstract doctrine, most of them neither heeded nor understood it.

Starting in Kiangsi and in the Canton district of Kwangtung, the Soviets rapidly spread to the neighboring provinces of Fukien, Hupeh and Kwangsi. From these three provinces they expanded westward to Szechwan and Kweichow, to Chekiang and Kiangsu in the North-East, and to Anhwei and Honan in the North, eventually penetrating as far as Kirin province in Manchuria.

Even the official investigator, Yang Chien, has been compelled to admit that "the activities of the Communist Party of

China after its repudiation by the Kuo-min-tang have been as a whole very successful." [8] The story of these activities is yet to be told in a manner at once systematic and exhaustive. At present well-correlated and authenticated material on the subject is very sparse; and the substance of the following survey has had to be pieced together from the study of a very large number of personal letters from Soviet China in dependable translations, the few books so far written on the topic, and from information scattered through various newspapers and magazines. Taken together, however, these sources afford a fairly reliable picture of the ways in which the Sovietization of China proceeds.

THE AGRARIAN REVOLUTION

Peng Pai, the young revolutionist whose activities resulted in the organization of the first Chinese Soviet Republic, was curiously enough born in a well-to-do family of landlords. A well-educated man, he started his revolutionary activity in 1919, when indignation at the injustice of Versailles and the cruelty of certain domestic rulers were combining to revive the revolutionary spirit of the nation. His work among the peasants was centered first at Haifong, in Kwangtung province, where he started in 1921 to organize the groups which later developed into the now powerful peasant unions. In the beginning the peasants were reluctant to join him. They expected nothing but trouble to come out of his activities. But his personality and eloquence gradually gained adherents and eventually he became one of the most trusted, influential and beloved leaders of the Chinese peasants. Starting with a mutual aid society, he proceeded to organize consumers' coöperatives, and then schools and hospitals, controlled by peasants themselves. With this

[8] Yang Chien has since been murdered (by Chiang Kai-shek's thugs, as rumors persisted) because of his activities in connection with the China League for Civil Rights.

support he succeeded in staging a well-organized campaign against the exploiting landlords, first demanding lower rents, then the redistribution of land; and eventually he had tens of thousands of poor farmers behind him in a well-organized, large-scale peasant movement, which spread over a considerable part of several provinces in the South. Nor did Peng Pai permit himself at any time to cease striving for his goal. Always he was actively engaged, in one way or another, in fostering his ideas among the people and working toward their realization. At times, when Wuhan needed him, he would work with the Government. At other times, such as the years following the advent of the Nanking régime, he would continue to labor in strict secrecy, and in the face of persecution, until in 1929, the fiery revolutionist and brilliant leader was caught by his enemies, imprisoned, and shot after a mock trial. But his work has born fruit. The movement he inaugurated, spreading from his own little village to cover its entire district, and from that district to the next and the next, may well be regarded as the inception of the Chinese Agrarian Revolution of today, with Sovietization as its form.

It so happened that in the self-same district where Peng Pai began his work—namely in Haifong and its neighboring town Loofong—the first Chinese Soviet Republic was organized. It was known as the Hailofong Republic, and though it endured for only about five months between November, 1927, and April, 1928, it naturally prompted imitations. One of the first among them was the Soviet régime established in the Jen-hua (?) county of Southern Hunan. Most of the land in that county belonged to the rich and the well-to-do, who constituted about ten per cent of the entire population. About ten per cent were paupers, and of the remainder more than sixty per cent, though owning some land, were compelled to rent more to keep body and soul together. This situation was duplicated in most of the

Southern provinces. To return to Jen-hua, however, agrarian unrest developed in this county early in 1925, and was evidenced by the organization of peasants in unions. These unions struggled for the betterment of the lot of the husbandmen, and for lowering of rents, and achieved a certain amount of success. But in 1927 the landlords and the well-to-do farmers, united by fear of losing what they possessed, forced the authorities to declare these unions illegal. This proscription actually went into effect in April, 1927, or about the time of the inauguration of the Nanking régime, and was accomplished by the ingenious method of declaring all the members of these unions to be Communists, and as such, naturally, "advocates of free-love, nationalization of women, and wholesale destruction!" As a consequence, some of the more active among the peasant unionists of the Jen-hua district left their villages and went to the hills, where they quickly assembled an armed force of over 1,500.

At about that time Chu Teh, who was one of the leaders of the Nanchang rebellion, was invited to unite his force with the provincial army of Fang Shi-shen, and with the approval of the Communist Party, did so. These revolutionists began to spread their propaganda in the region. A number of volunteers joined their ranks, and various groups were founded for the purpose of guerrilla warfare. Under pressure of the reactionaries, General Fang was compelled quickly to "discharge" Chu Teh, but accompanied the dismissal with a present of 40,000 Mexican dollars and 70,000 rounds of ammunition. Chu Teh, now independent, moved freely over the province and intensified his propaganda work among the peasants. By the beginning of 1928, the Soviet régime had already established itself in a number of communities of Northern Kwangtung, *i.e.,* in the area adjacent to Hunan and Kiangsi. The peasant movement was swiftly developing. Among the first things which inevitably followed the formation of the Soviets were confiscation of land of the wealthy, abolition of border-marks on the fields, and burning of the deeds and other documents establishing title to land. The redistribution of land was accomplished in different counties in different ways as we shall see in a subsequent chapter. In some places this redistribution was repeated again and again, as being unsatisfactory in the previous form; in a number of cases, naturally, all sorts of errors were made; in some places the unscrupulous elements took advantage of this or that situation. After the establishment of the Soviets, many villages organized public feeding, opened schools, started public health work, et cetera.

Though the Soviet régimes described above did not last long —five months in Hailofong, and only forty days in Jen-hua county—they nevertheless served to show that most of the poor peasants were not only in favor of, but willing to fight for Communism, and that the local forces were quite capable of establishing Soviets and even of running them effectively. The Agrarian Revolution had begun.

The Process of Sovietization

The process of Sovietization in China did not vary greatly in different parts of the country, and the case of certain districts of Fukien may therefore be taken as fairly typical. By piecing together passages in numerous letters coming from this locality it is possible to form a fairly clear picture of what went on. Before forming and studying this picture, though, it might be well to explain that the word "Soviet" is used in China in a somewhat corrupted form. When expressed in Chinese ideograms a foreign word must sound like the ideograms used for its transcription. Thus, instead of "soviet" the Chinese say "soo-wei-ai," which happens to sound rather like "she-wei-yo," which means "this is mine." Some people jokingly suggest that this consonance may explain the success of the movement.

Soon after the Nanchang revolt, the revolutionary troops under Ho Lung and Yeh Ting were a short while in Fukien. Most of them were forced to leave that province after reverses at Swatow, but some remained scattered over the region. The result of their sojourn was the establishment of Soviets in several counties of the province. In February, 1928, they succeeded in organizing at Yudin (?) a district Committee of the Communist Party and a number of new Soviets, which started energetically to prepare for the general revolt. The first attempt was made in May at Tingchow. Though it failed, similar revolts quickly occurred in several other places. At the end of the year the unrest grew to such dimensions that the Nationalist Government sent a whole army division to suppress it. The Communists were forced to flee and the "white terror" soon inaugurated by the government forces at first indicated that the Soviet movement could not revive. But soon the "Red" troops led by Chu Teh and Mao Tse-tung [4] reappeared in Fukien. The peasant leaders who had fled to the hills returned, and the brief interval of complete demoralization that had followed the terrible blows of the reaction gave place to a rallying time for the revolutionary forces under these leaders. Warring for their lives, these groups, though small at first, were soon able to organize into belligerent units and to develop fighting tactics uniquely suited to the mountainous areas in which they operated. "Their guerrilla tactics made punitive expeditions helpless and futile," declared *China Forum* in May, 1932. Town after town was occupied by the "Reds." The government troops fell back and soon the entire Judin county was ablaze with revolution. Wherever the "Red partisans" ap-

[4] In 1931 Mao Tse-tung became Chairman of the Provisional Government of the Soviet Republic of China.

peared, the peasants rallied to their side and in most of the villages immediately established Soviets. For above all else the "Red troops" were good propagandists, who rarely needed to resort to arms to gain the results they sought. To occupy this place or that they had merely to send their representatives to the peasants, and usually after a chat the rest of them were invited to come and stay in the village.

When Chu Teh and Mao Tse-tung arrived in Fukien, their 4th Corps consisted of only three or four thousand men, but a year or so later they had under their command over 40,000 men, a considerable number of whom were deserters from the government ranks. These troops now formed an Army of four Corps.[5]

By the Spring of 1930 practically all the counties of the western Fukien had their own Soviets under a central Government headed by Ten Tsi-huei. A Chinese letter, written in the early Spring of 1930, described the situation in that area as follows:

"As the result of the uprising of May, 1929, the workers and peasants of western Fukien, after having overthrown the power of the gentry and the police (tuhao), organized Soviets and accomplished the agrarian revolution. At the present time Sovietized western Fukien is an entirely different world from the rest of the province where the Kuo-min-tang is still in control. After the victorious revolt the peasants divided the land among themselves and the wages of the workers were raised. The standard of living of the toiling masses has been changed drastically. If, previously, the poor peasants dreamed of being sons of the rich, the rich ones now would prefer the lot of the poor.

"Deeds on land, promissory notes, mortgages and the like all were burned. The slogan 'no rent to the landlord, no taxes to

[5] The 3rd, 4th, 5th and 6th.

the Kuo-min-tang authorities, no payments to the usurers,' now became realized. The old collecting agencies are gone, the tax-collectors are shot. Now we are doing our best to help other counties to get rid of the reactionaries, and to start constructive work; to increase production, to improve the irrigation system of the rice-fields, to repair the roads, to open schools, etc.

"In every county of western Fukien there are Soviets, and the elected deputies, forming executive committees, are taking charge of all the affairs concerning workers and peasants. The elections are held on the occupational basis . . . to be elected in the Soviet district one must first be passed by the local and the county Soviets. Everybody of 16 years of age or over, of both sexes, can vote and be elected. Only those who belong to the exploiter class are disfranchised. . . . At this moment all the deputies are from the poor peasants, workers, soldiers, revolutionary students and tradesmen. . . . From a population of over one million, now under the Soviet régime in our district, there are over 200,000 able-bodied men, on which the Red Army may count. . . .

"The Soviet Government has started reclamation work. Every peasant now receives enough water for the irrigation of his fields; there are no more quarrels over scarcity of water here. . . . In every village we have coöperative societies of consumers and also of producers in some fields. . . . Some of the Soviets have founded banks or rather credit-associations, where we, the peasants, can borrow money without being robbed by the money-lenders. Usurers are gone. . . . In every county 'Lenin' schools are opened, and in some villages also. The lack of qualified teachers naturally is a serious handicap to the increase of their number. . . . Night courses for adults are organized. . . . Among the delegates elected to the Soviets there are women; women have become equal with men in every respect. Their revolutionary zeal is not inferior either . . . you may see them even in the Red Army.

"The Soviet Government passed a labor law, protecting the workers; it established the eight-hour day, raised wages. . . .

"We have no thieves, no beggars in our territory. Everyone can work. . . . Those who are disabled are taken care of by the Soviets . . . we opened hospitals and pharmacies with no charge for their services; if previously the peasants had no place to turn when ill, except to Pusa, the Buddhist god, now they come to the Soviet institutions. . . . Every community now has its own club, which serves not for recreation alone but for enlightenment as well. They are quite different from the dancing halls, indeed. . . .

"In the Soviet territories all taxes are abolished except the land tax, which is 20% of the crop. Before the Revolution the farmers had to give 50% and more to the landlords alone, but there were taxes besides. . . ."

This picture, in its essentials, is reproduced again and again in the numerous letters from different parts of Soviet China. In Kiangsi province, for instance, 70 out of 85 counties [6] were under the Soviet régime by the early part of 1931, and not only had their local Soviets but looked up to the Provisional Government for the whole of Soviet China, with its site at Juichin [7] in the South of that province. According to the figures given by Dr. Wellington Koo to the Lytton Commission there were 181 districts in the interior of China under Soviet administration in 1930. Of this total the largest percentage was found in the Kiangsi province; with Hupeh, Kwangtung, Hunan, Fukien next in order, and Kwangsi, Szechwan, Honan and Anhwei closing the list. Naturally this success did not mean that after establishing the Soviet régime all the troubles were over, and

[6] Or "hsien," as they are called in the Chinese.
[7] Also spelled Shaikin.

no difficulties were experienced. Quite the contrary; in most of the Sovietized areas serious economic difficulties were felt; sooner or later the new régime had to show its ability to provide for the needs of the population. A virtual blockade of the Sovietized areas by the Kuo-min-tang intensified their difficulties.

CAPTURE OF CHANGSHA

In the Summer of 1930 the success of the Sovietization of Hunan led to the capture by the Red Army of Changsha, a large metropolitan center, where a Soviet régime was established and lasted for some ten days. An interesting description of this campaign is to be found in the special issue of the *China Forum,* dated May, 1932:

"In the Spring of 1930 Peng Teh-huei started his forces moving into Central Kiangsi and turned westward toward Hunan. Chu-Teh followed him, made an unsuccessful stab at Nanchang, then joined Peng. . . . Ho Lung, who had in the meantime gathered about him a considerable force, estimated at about 20,000 men, had been operating extensively in Western Hunan and in the Hupeh border regions, using Hung Lake as his center. While Chu, Mao and Peng were moving into Hunan, Ho Lung swooped down and in June captured Yochow, an important river port. On July 27th Changsha fell before the armies of the red generals."

According to a Special Bulletin published by the Communist Party of China, there were 17,000 Red Soldiers and about 50,000 "Red Guards" of Hunan and Kwangsi behind them. General Ho-Chien's provincial troops fell back. "Immediately after the troops defending Changsha had retreated," reported Reuter in the *North China Daily News* of July 30, 1930, "the city became a mass of red flags. . . . The reds entered the town wearing straw hats and flaunting red rosettes." British,

Japanese and American gunboats had evacuated almost all foreigners! There was a note of alarmed surprise in some of the foreign press reports. Said one United Press dispatch from Hankow, on July 29: "The band that has captured Changsha is an army organized on typically Communist lines and equipped with up-to-date arms. Reports arriving from the captured city tell of wholesale confiscation of private properties and persecution of landlords, shop proprietors and others classified in the category of 'capitalists.' Red flags are hoisted everywhere and the city flooded with pamphlets and handbills denouncing capitalism and imperialism."

Although Changsha was held only about five days a Chinese merchant fleeing from the city was reported by Rengo [8] as saying that with the advent of the new régime various labor unions, including railway employees and seamen unions, were formally organized under the leadership of the Communists.

"While C. T. Wang, Foreign Minister of Nanking Government, was expressing his 'profound regrets' over the burning of foreign consulates and property and making fulsome promises that the Government would 'curb' the reds, the foreign gunboats went into action. . . . 'The foreign gunboats,' said the *China Weekly Review* on September 6, 1930, 'in this particular case performed a good service for the Chinese Government by helping to drive the Communists out of Changsha.'

"Following the red evacuation of Changsha the revolutionary forces moved out along two routes. Chu Teh and Mao Tse-tung marched their men due eastward toward Nanchang in Kiangsi. Peng Teh-huei moved first southward in Hunan and then East across the border into Kiangsi. . . . Later Chu and Mao joined Peng, and on October 5, they captured the key city of Kian.

"One of the sequels of this campaign was the development

[8] Rengo is the name of the Japanese News-agency.

of a large red army,[9] and the establishment of important Soviet districts in the Honan-Hupeh-Anhwei border area. So the Sovietized area was tended still further."

The extent of the Sovietization movement at that time may be judged by the following extract from one of the letters examined in connection with this book: "With the insignia of the Soviets," says the letter in question, "one can easily cross safely from Kwangtung, through Fukien and Kiangsi, to Hupeh and he need not even take money with him, for his board and lodging are gladly given free everywhere if he is on some Soviet business. . . ."

Naturally, the majority of those living in these Sovietized areas did not technically belong to the Communist Party, though members of the peasants' unions frequently took pride in calling themselves Communists, usually, according to one of the letters in our collection, out of "respect and admiration for that party as something which is inseparably connected with the idea of emancipation from exploiters and hope for the better life to come."

THE CASE OF THE INDUSTRIAL WORKERS

The Chinese student of the labor movement, Mr. Lowe, who is an official of the Chinese Young Men's Christian Association, has testified that the labor movement became more definitely radical after 1919,[10] when the student movement was intensified and the Communist Party was formed. Since that time the Chinese working class has begun to participate more actively in the National Revolution and in the anti-Imperialist struggle; for, as the workers displayed unprecedented activity,

[9] According to the special issue of the *Chinese Communist Party Bulletin* describing the Changsha affair, the "Reds" captured there quite a considerable number of arms, requisitioned large stores of food and other supplies, and collected over 400,000 dollars from the local Chamber of Commerce.

[10] In the opinion of others the organized labor movement was inaugurated in China only in 1920.

the proletariat became more conscious of its strength. Thus, as the result of coöperation between the Kuo-min-tang and the Communists, Red Labor Unions began to grow by leaps and bounds, particularly in Kwangtung province. In this period four National Labor Conferences were held.

Dr. Sun Yat-sen had encouraged the formation of labor unions as early as in 1919, and had even given an appropriation to the well-known Communist labor leader, Tan Ping-san, to conduct propaganda activities and to secure the support of the labor organizations in the Nationalist Revolution. Labor unions, however, could not function freely at that time, and did not acquire any centralized leadership until the Communists were admitted into the Kuo-min-tang.

Russian-trained labor organizers, such as Li Li-san, former Chairman of the All-China Labor Federation, and Hsiang Chung-fa (Chan Chung-fa), once Secretary General of the Central Executive Committee of the Chinese Communist Party, were sent to Shanghai, Hankow, Tientsin, Tangshan, and other industrial centers of China to organize trade unions and "cells," and to stir up the workers to a sense of the country's wrongs. There was a marked increase in the number of political strikes, the most famous being that of the Hong Kong seamen in 1925-26.

"With the eviction of the Communists from the Kuo-min-tang most of the Red Labor Unions in China were dissolved and many of their leaders killed," writes Mr. Lowe, adding that "over 470 labor organizations in Canton alone were ordered closed while only 30 others (in Canton) were left undisturbed." [11] Since they can no longer conduct their activities openly, the Red Labor Unions have suffered serious reverses in recent years. At a secret plenary session held in February, 1928, they adopted a number of measures among

[11]Lowe Chuan-hua. *Ibid.*, pp. 149-150.

which the overthrow of the Kuo-min-tang and the abolition of the "Yellow" labor unions, created by the Nationalist régime, were perhaps, the most important. The membership of the Red Labor Unions was reported in 1930 at 114,525, more than 50% of which was in the Sovietized areas.

In May, 1930 the Soviet authorities adopted a code providing for the eight-hour day, fixing of a minimum wage, labor protection for women and children, social insurance, and the establishment of trade-unions. Accordingly, wages were increased, the eight-hour day has been introduced, the contractor's system abolished, and night work for women and children stopped. In addition, the trade-unions were given the right to organize and to declare strikes, to negotiate and conclude agreements with employers and to participate in the running of factories. Members of the Labor Commission of the Provisional Soviet Government and the labor inspectorates of the various Soviet districts are directly recommended and nominated by the trade-unions. However, only a few industries exist within the Soviet sphere in China. But, numerous or not, the industrial workers are, apparently, important in the Soviet movement and, as we shall see, are even expected to lead the rest of the population toward the goal of the proletarian revolution.

WHY THE SOVIETIZATION OF CERTAIN PARTS OF CHINA BECAME POSSIBLE

It is, of course, insufficient to describe, as we have done, the events and the process of the Sovietization of certain areas in China without at least attempting to find its logical sequel. On this point we cannot do better than turn to an interpretation by Soviet students of the Chinese situation writing in *Problemi Kitaia*. This very valuable magazine published by the Research Institute on China, which is attached to the Communist Academy at Moscow, printed in 1931 an illuminating article on

"The Soviet Movement in China," by E. Yolk and O. Tark-hanov [12] which reads in part as follows:

"What is the explanation of the Soviet movement in Southern and Central China? What made it possible to bring together under the banner of the Soviets millions of struggling peasants, led by the proletarian party of the Communists in China? The advance of the Chinese Revolution into its Soviet stage was necessitated by the new factors which are shaping the development of the revolutionary process. . . . The first, and the most important, peculiarity of the present stage of the Chinese Revolution is found in the fact that it is developing at a time when the conflict of various interests is deepening owing to the world-wide crisis of Capitalism and when the Capitalist system has to struggle for its life side by side with the socialist system, which is successfully operating and opposing the capitalists. . . .

"The world-wide economic crisis inevitably is followed by the lowering of prices on agricultural products. The usual tendency of the Imperialists to lay most of the burden produced by the crisis on the colonial and semi-colonial nations has at this time exposed with unprecedented clarity the parasitic character of the exploitation of China by the capitalists of the world.[13]

"This crisis tends in every way to intensify the most barbaric exploitation of the colonies by the Imperialists, in the hope of super-profits to check the losses incurred through the crisis. Imperialism cannot allow itself to grant concessions to the colonial countries. It stubbornly sticks to its positions, it struggles for every extra dollar obtainable from China, India and other colonial and semi-colonial states. These extra dollars are coming from the forced labor and cruel exploitation of peas-

[12] *Problemi Kitaia* (*Problems of China*), Nos. 6-7, 1931.
[13] A very interesting illustration of this is found in an article by Tadao Tanaka in the Japanese magazine *To-A Keizai Kenkyu*, July, 1933, under the title: "The Formidable Lowering of Prices on Cereals and the Future of Chinese Agriculture," pp. 54-69.

ants, enslaved by the system of feudalism, combined with usury and commercial robbery, which are part and parcel of this economic system and the result of political privileges possessed by the Imperialists.

"This leads quite naturally to the unification into one revolutionary movement of the anti-Imperialist and the anti-feudal struggle of the colonials. Here is the explanation why every blow directed at the feudal landlords is at the same time a blow at the foreign exporters, at the banks, the Stock-exchanges, etc. . . .

"The other peculiarity of the present stage of the Chinese Revolution lies in the fact that it has already reached the point in its development where it cannot advance any further while continuing as a bourgeois-democratic, anti-imperialistic revolution. It must now direct its blows not only against the domestic feudals, not only against the foreign Imperialists and their servants, the *compradores,* but also against the Chinese bourgeoisie; and that means against the Kuo-min-tang as representing only the bourgeoisie and the landlords.

"During its four years in office the Kuo-min-tang has demonstrated its utter incompetence to solve the basic problems advanced by the Revolution. The agrarian question, which stirred for the struggle tens of millions of China's peasants, proved insoluble to the bourgeois Kuo-min-tang. Even under the pressure of the Soviet movement undermining the very foundation of its power, the Kuo-min-tang did not dare to go further than to offer the agrarian law, issued by the Nanking Government last Summer. Actually this law is an attempt to give relief to the 'kulaks' and to encourage the landlords to replace the parasitic system of renting small parcels to the tenants by large-scale farming on a capitalistic basis. But the law failed to achieve even those results. The lowering of rent to 37.5%, the abolition of subtenants, the right of perpetual lease—all this, though in that law, remained in force on paper only. Where the landlords feel themselves strong enough, they grab from the peasants all that they possibly can, and the Chinese landlords have been used to receiving as much as 70% of the whole crop. On the other hand, where the peasants feel themselves strong enough to raise their voices in protest, they prefer now not to pay the 37.5% recommended by the Kuo-min-tang, and even not to pay anything at all. . . . Furthermore, the Kuo-min-tang has not been able to solve the problem of unification of the country or to stop the dictatorship of militarists in their various feudal possessions in China, the latter continuing in saddle. Nor did the Kuo-min-tang show any progress in the emancipation of the country from foreign control, political and economic. All the talk about the abolition of foreign jurisdiction, extraterritoriality, and other privileges remains merely talk. At the same time there is a marked process of denationalization of the Chinese industrial enterprises, which are passing more and more into foreign hands . . . depression affected China badly . . . prices on silver continue to fall . . . famine is ravaging the country . . . in spite of these the tax-burden has been increased . . . in their attempt to escape bankruptcy many foreign businesses are introducing increasingly rigid 'rationalization,' which spells a further drop in the already ridiculously inadequate earnings of the Chinese workers. . . . All these are factors in making the present Soviet movement in China not only possible but inevitable. . . . Its success could not be properly understood, of course, without seeing it in the light of the victory of the Soviet Revolution in Russia and the successful building of socialism in the USSR. . . . As adopted by the Chinese masses, Sovietism serves not only as the culminating point of the bourgeois-democratic revolution, but also as the form through which the bourgeois-democratic revolution is being transformed into a social revolution. . . .

"The Revolution in China is not developing uniformly throughout the country . . . the Imperialists control the seaports, railways, and certain waterways where they can, and sometimes do, suppress any revolutionary activities; and therefore the Soviets are established in spots, here and there, and not over the whole of China. . . ."

In short, in spite of economic and other variations in different parts of the country, the Soviet movement was advancing—though unevenly—at a notable pace. Over Southern China it had already spread with astonishing success. And up to the present all the efforts of the Kuo-min-tang Government to subdue it have met with failure. For this failure there are a multitude of reasons, some of which we shall endeavor to present in the succeeding chapters.

CHAPTER VIII

THE ANTI-COMMUNIST CAMPAIGNS

The First Campaign

Alarmed by the recrudescence of the Communist movement in China, the spread of the Sovietized areas and the growth of the Red Armies, the Nanking Government decided late in 1930 that the time had come to eradicate Communism by force.

The First Anti-Communist Campaign was inaugurated at the meeting of the Central Executive Committee of the Kuo-min-tang, held at Nanking in November of that year, soon after the termination of the war between Chiang Kai-shek and the Northern Coalition of Feng and Yen. This First Campaign began in December and lasted till the end of February, 1931. Altogether about one hundred thousand Nanking troops participated, yet the result was complete failure; the expeditionary force was defeated, many of the government soldiers deserted to the "Reds," and the rest were withdrawn from the field.

It was in this campaign that the ingenuity and effectiveness of the strategy employed by the Communist military commanders were first revealed. Effecting a preconceived retreat from Kian (in Kiangsi province), the Reds decoyed the 50th Division of the Nanking Army into the Southern Kiangsi mountains where they completely lost their way. By a similar device, on December 31, the 18th Division under General Chang Hui-tsan was tricked into entering Tungku. Then, in the words of T. A. Bisson: "Overcome by the effects of its celebration of this easy victory, the division was defeated and disarmed by a rapid counter-attack of the Red forces carried out under cover of darkness. Dressed in the uniforms of this division and carrying its banners, the Communist force then sought out the strayed 50th Division and virtually annihilated it before it had realized what was happening. These crushing blows, coming in rapid succession, demoralized the regular troops and led to their withdrawal." [1]

Describing this campaign, the Chinese official observer, Yang Chien, wrote as follows: "After the suppression of the Yen-Feng Rebellion, the government was able to release many divisions from the Honan and Shantung front for service in Kiangsi, which was already badly overrun by Communists. In addition to the return of the 12th and 50th Divisions many other divisions were sent, with a strength exceeding 100,000. They were all placed under the command of General Lu Ti-ping. The result of this campaign was very disappointing. Although the important city of Kian was recaptured, the 18th Division ventured too far into the Soviet territory, and lost half of its effectiveness, and its Commander, General Chang Hwei-tsai, was captured and killed. The 50th Division also suffered heavily, losing half of its strength. The rising tide of Communist-bandits instead of being staved off, rose higher."

Commenting on these events, General Tai Yueh, one of the brigadiers under Lu Ti-ping, lists half a dozen striking reasons for the Nanking defeat. "There are six reasons," he writes, "for the failure of the campaign: (1) The government forces engaged in fighting them were ordered away before the territory was cleared of Communist-bandits, giving them opportunity to come up again; (2) the government forces were unacquainted with the geography of the territory, the organization of the Soviets, and the strength of the Soviet forces; (3) the different units of government forces were reluctant to coöperate with

[1] T. A. Bisson, *Foreign Policy Association Report*, April, 1933.

each other, each trying to pass the responsibility to others; (4) the mismanagement and incompetence of the hsien,[2] magistrates; the inefficiency of the police who disturbed people instead of protecting them; the local gentry who fatten themselves on the people by oppressing them, combined to drive the people to the arms of the Communists; (5) the lack of coöperation among the party, government, military authorities and people in their common effort to put down the Communist-bandits; (6) the bankrupt condition of the peasantry, unemployment among the artisans and workers and the general economic distress among the people supply inexhaustible fuel to the growth of Communism."

THE SECOND CAMPAIGN

Alive to the seriousness of their task, and prodded by the attitude of the Powers who were intent on seeing the "Red menace" crushed, Nanking decided in February, 1931, to enlarge the expeditionary force. Consequently, in March of the same year, an army of about two hundred thousand men,[3] under the command of the Minister of War, Ho Ying-ching, embarked upon the Second Campaign, only to meet practically the same fate as in the First. "Ho adopted the conservative tactics of consolidating the territory first recovered before advancing further into enemy territory," writes Yang Chien, "and also carried out measures of rehabilitation in the devastated areas, organizing militia, and giving relief to returned refugees." To this, however, we can add that the rehabilitation was meant for the well-to-do, not for the masses; as before, the lost territory was partly recovered. But once again the Red Armies dissipated the forces of Ho Ying-ching in the mountain regions and then

[2] *I.e.,* county.
[3] The Communist sources assert that in the Second Campaign Nanking had in the field twenty divisions.

readily massed for crushing attacks on isolated divisions. Near Tungku, the Government Fifth Army was cut to pieces; two of its divisions lost much of their equipment, and thousands of dead and wounded. The Nineteenth Route Army, destined to win international fame only a year later by its valiant resistance to the Japanese attacks on Shanghai, was outflanked and turned back with heavy losses at Ningtu, where Chu Teh, the Commander of the Red Armies of the Kiangsi Soviet area had his base. Having taken Nanfeng, Chu Teh then moved rapidly eastward to the Fukien border, and there defeated also the 56th Division and captured two regiments. Nanking officials attributed the defeat in the Second Campaign partly to the fact that during its progress Canton suddenly declared its independence, which shook the morale at the front and encouraged the Communists. Wellington Koo had a different apology. In his *Memoranda* for the Lytton Commission he explained that "the configuration of the territory which afforded excellent natural defence, and the clever strategy employed by the Red Army . . . prevented General Ho from obtaining any real success. The situation remained unchanged." In point of fact, however, it was a new and shaking defeat, so damaging that Chiang Kai-shek and his lieutenants were forced to plan a new campaign which lasted from June to September of 1931, and involved the use of over three hundred thousand men, one hundred and fifty to two hundred cannon, and over one hundred airplanes, some with foreign pilots. This new campaign was considered by Nanking as the continuation of the Second Campaign, but is called by the Communists the Third Campaign, which seems to be correct.

THE THIRD CAMPAIGN

Before starting on this new offensive, Chiang Kai-shek undertook various measures of a political nature. He convoked the so-called National Assembly at Nanking on May 1st, promulgated a law regulating certain problems of labor, issued a decree by which taxes in the areas "infested by the Red-bandits" were suspended or annulled, and a Manifesto in which he flirted with the idea of wresting the Chinese Customs from foreign control. The latter was intended as a sort of earnest of his determination to fight the Imperialists. In spite of all this, the new anti-Communist Campaign, like its predecessors, was a failure.

In his report before the National Assembly in May, General Ho Ying-ching declared that the Communist-bandit movement had spread all over the country. He asserted that the question of liquidating them was one of life or death for China. Impressed by the seriousness of the situation, the Assembly voted its approval of the new offensive, this time on a much larger scale, and appropriated necessary funds. Chiang Kai-shek was asked to lead the armies himself, and to direct the operations.

The first two campaigns had been waged in the Kiangsi, Hupeh, Hunan, and Fukien provinces. In the Third, Chiang decided to concentrate the main blow on the province of Kiangsi, which was the heart of Soviet China, and to keep only small forces to guard himself against the First and Third Red Armies, advancing along the borders between Kiangsi on the one hand, Fukien and Hunan on the other, and to keep the remaining force in the center. The object was to close in on the enemy in the southern part of the province of Kiangsi, near Kanchow and Yutu. In case this plan did not succeed, he hoped to force the First and Third Red Armies to cross the southern border of Kiangsi and to retreat into Kwangtung, and to defeat both the "Red" and the Cantonese "rebels" in that province.

The main assault was to be executed by the left-wing column, led by the Minister of War, Ho, in whose command there were twenty-three divisions,[4] numbering about two hundred fifty thousand men, of which eleven divisions had joined the Expeditionary Army since the beginning of May, and were hence quite fresh. Facing General Ho were the forces of the First Red Army under Chu Teh and Mao Tse-tung, fifty or sixty thousand strong. The Third Red Army, of about forty thousand men, under Peng Teh-hwei, confronted the other two columns, namely, the Right under Chen Min-su with about one hundred thousand men, and the Middle commanded by Sun Lien-chun, who had formerly served under Feng Yu-hsiang, with about thirty thousand very weak and unreliable troops.

On June 22nd, Chiang Kai-shek arrived at Nanchang with his numerous German advisers. On July 2nd the armies started their advance. After the first encounter of Ho Ying-ching's advance-guard with the Reds near Kwangchan, one of his brigades went over to the enemy and the rest retreated toward Nanfeng. After almost two weeks of fighting in the neighborhood of Tungku-Kwanchan, with the Nanking air-forces participating, the Reds retreated, abandoning Kwangchan. On July 25th the troops, under the command of Peng Teh-hwei, evacuated Tungku also, and by order of Chiang Kai-shek this city was burned to the ground and most of its population massacred. The First Red Army, leaving only a small detachment to face Ho Ying-ching, now marched into the province of Fukien, where they won a victory over the insignificant Nanking forces, left to protect their main column from that side. This caused General Ho to change his plan, and to turn part of his forces toward Fukien, in order to prevent an attack by the Reds in the rear. August 1st was the climax of the Nanking's advance. On this date, its right-wing column succeeded in occupying Hsinkuo, and Ho Ying-ching's troops finally captured Yuitu.

[4] Nineteen in the left-wing column and four more divisions in the special detachments to resist attack from Fukien and Chekiang.

After that time no further advance was possible for Chiang Kai-shek's forces. Heavy rains made any progress in the practically roadless mountain district very difficult. Transportation of food and other supplies became almost impossible. The stubbornness of the Reds, offering resistance on every front, exhausted their enemies and the Campaign came to a standstill. Not long afterwards it was abandoned entirely under the convenient excuse that the Japanese invasion of Manchuria made the defense of the country against the foreigners a matter of greater concern to Nanking.

Indeed, by the second half of July, the Japanese news agency, Shimbun Rengo, was quoting an English officer who had visited Kiangsi, to the effect that in his opinion "the Nanking troops had a very slim chance of defeating the Reds, since they were demoralized, their commanding officers were corrupt and wages were in arrears, with the consequence that the soldiers were marauding and terrorizing the local population." Even early in July the *Peking and Tientsin Times* had declared that nobody seemed to believe in a victory, neither the generals nor the soldiers. Rumor claimed that even the commanders, including General Ho Ying-ching opposed continuation of the campaign. Consequently Chiang Kai-shek issued an order censoring defeatist talk of all kinds, but it was too late. The Reds seized the opportunity and started an advance of their own, and during August they re-occupied Ningtu, Kwangchan and Hsinkuo. Before the end of September they were in Tungku and continuing the advance toward Nanchang. These successes of the Red Armies were reported by the Japanese and English-language press in the Orient at the time.

The net result of the campaign was that the Reds defeated seventeen out of Chiang Kai-shek's thirty-three divisions; and to make matters worse, the entire 50th Nanking Division and a part of the 14th deserted to the Reds, increasing the strength of the latter by some thirty or possibly forty thousand men. More than twenty-five thousand rifles, numbers of machine-guns, several cannon and a large supply of ammunition were taken as booty. In addition, practically the entire territory taken by the Nanking troops in the first stages of the offensive was recaptured by the Reds in the final few days. For Nanking the Third Campaign had been as futile as its two predecessors.

Actually during this Third Campaign many new Soviet districts were organized, some in the rear of the Nanking troops, some in the more Northern provinces, where none existed before.

The *Memoranda* of Wellington Koo, who had first stated in describing that campaign that "the efforts were crowned with success," included the following lines: "The reds, thus made bold, launched a counter-offensive. The conquered regions had to be evacuated and the gains realized in the course of the campaign were almost completely lost."

THE FOURTH CAMPAIGN

After the very disappointing outcome of the Third Campaign to eradicate Communism in China the Powers became alarmed. The native bourgeoisie and the foreigners in China both insisted that the Government must now do everything in its power to bring to an end this growing menace. The Press devoted much space to the Communist problem, and depicted the situation in gloomy colors. One prominent Chinese newspaper, *Junanjibao*, declared in December, 1931, that the majority of the population of Kiangsi was under the influence of the Communists, especially the youth; and a similar opinion about Fukien was expressed by an English-language paper, the *Hongkong Telegraph*. The *North China Daily News* repeatedly sounded the alarm, incessantly urging Nanking to act, and the foreign Powers to interfere on behalf of the interests of the foreign population living under constant fear of Communist onslaught.

Under such pressure Nanking decided to prepare for a new attack and, by February, 1932, the Fourth Campaign was started. As for the activities of the Japanese army in Manchuria, they were practically disregarded and no official resistance was ever offered to the attack on Shanghai, the famous 19th Route Army acting against the wishes of Chiang,[5] who was only forced later on to render the most insignificant assistance. In other words, Nanking preferred to desert those Chinese who continued fighting the Japanese invaders, and to concentrate almost 500,000 troops in a new attempt to annihilate the Red Armies. This time Chiang succeeded in obtaining the coöperation of the Cantonese; and while their efforts were not coordinated or placed under a single command, they, nevertheless, managed to make a good deal of trouble for the Reds.

In March the Communists, relying on the support of the masses, launched a counter-offensive. The Second Red Army, under Ho Lung, defeated three brigades of Government troops; and eight regiments of the 34th and the 48th Kuo-min-tang Divisions deserted to the enemy. A month later the Red Army of the Central region managed to break the Government front and to defeat a few regiments, capturing 6,000 rifles, a number of machine-guns, two airplanes, and other booty. On April 20th it occupied the important town of Chanchow in Fukien, not far from Amoy, and retained it for a month and a half. As for the Fourth Red Army, it had defeated the 21st Division in March, and during the three months of the campaign (March-May) captured 15,000 rifles, 300 machine-guns, and one airplane.

In May this Fourth Campaign came, like the others, to a

---

[5] There were rumors that Chiang even ordered the 19th Route Army to withdraw, but with no avail.

disastrous end for Nanking. The Kuo-min-tang troops lost in this offensive more than 25,000 rifles, hundreds of machine-guns, several airplanes, and an enormous quantity of other war-material.

THE FIFTH ANTI-RED CAMPAIGN

After all these reverses on the battlefields, Chiang and his entourage, including the so-called Leftist, Wang Ching-wei, finally awoke to the fact that the Communist evil could not be cured by force alone. Though somewhat late in the day, they came to the conclusion that the injustices inflicted by the out-moded agrarian system and the national calamities had reduced the Chinese masses to a state of discontent that could no longer be ignored. In other words, they realized the gravity of the situation at last, and determined to do the utmost to re-habilitate the peasantry. For this stupendous task Nanking accordingly established a special organ called the Rural Rehabilitation Commission. Unfortunately for the Government, however, its finances did not allow much to be done, aside from drawing plans and discovering the appalling needs.

In the meantime the misrule and neglect on the part of the local administrations, and the exorbitant taxes imposed on the farmers by the landlords, officials and the constantly quarreling war lords, continued to aggravate the situation. Patient beyond belief, satisfied with an extremely low standard of living, the exasperated Chinese peasant now seemed at the end of his endurance. "We see in China a peasant village civilization which must find a way to live in the modern life. This is the key to the great revolution which is going on in China," writes C. F. Remer in his new book, *Foreign Investments in China."* In other words, the peasant is at last definitely resolved to change the old unbearable conditions by his own initiative and to

* Remer, C. F., *Foreign Investments in China,* Macmillan, 1933.

enable himself henceforth to live as every human being is entitled to live.

With no money to float a serious plan for rehabilitation or to improve the lot of the peasants, though one may doubt that he ever sincerely contemplated it, Chiang finally turned to a continuance of his attempts at eradicating the "Red menace" by machine-guns.

Simultaneously with his eloquent announcement of wonderful plans for economic miracles, he busied himself with a new anti-Communist Campaign, where "only three-tenths belong to the military and seven-tenths to the political measures."

After the disappointing results of the Fourth Campaign, from which the Nanking troops were withdrawn in May, a new offensive was quietly planned. As early as June, 1932, the Fifth or the Fourth—according to Chiang's system of calculation —campaign was started with an enormous display of arms involving more than 700,000 soldiers on the Government side.

During the latter part of July and the first days of August a Conference was in session at Looshan, with Wang Ching-wei, Sun Fo, and most of the other prominent leaders of the Kuo-min-tang participating, and a number of foreign "observers" in attendance. At this Conference plans for the new campaign were discussed and approved. These plans included first the formation for each community of a peculiar police system based on the family unit, with the purposes of espionage and strict control over the "thoughts" of the people; secondly, an "improvement" of the local administration, meaning its subordination to the Nanking régime; thirdly, an adjustment of the agrarian situation through the creation of farmers' banks and coöperative societies; fourthly, a stiffening of the blockades of the Sovietized areas, with capital punishment for those breaking it; [7] fifthly, road construction in the regions adjoining the Soviet areas, in order to facilitate the movement of troops; and finally, the extension of all methods of political provocation which might possibly help to corrupt the Communist Party and the Red Armies. These methods included propaganda designed to discredit the Communists in the eyes of the population and to present them as plotting in the rear of the Kuo-min-tang troops to prevent their resistance to the Japanese invaders; the offering of bribes and other attractions to the ex-Communists who had been expelled from the Party with the object of using them and their writings to "expose" the Soviets. [8] These political, economic, and cultural "measures" represented the "seven-tenths" already mentioned, while the three-tenths left to the military part were represented, as we have seen, by more than 700,000 soldiers and plenty of ammunition and modern arms, lavishly supplied by the "neutral" foreigners.

What were the results? In July, the First Canton Division was defeated by the Reds, its commander wounded, and about one-half of its personnel captured; another Canton division, the Fourth, was also defeated and lost a great number of men; and still another was withdrawn from the front because suspected of sympathy with the Communists. In August, also in Kiangsi, the 8th, the 27th, and the 90th Nanking Divisions were badly beaten, while the 6th was defeated and withdrawn with serious loss of equipment. In the Hupeh-Honan-Anhwei area most of the 30th and 31st Nanking Divisions deserted and joined the Reds. In the same area the 3rd, 35th, 75th, and 83rd, Nanking

[7] This point included measures for controlling all business in the regions adjoining the Soviet areas, especially the selling of salt and certain other articles, the scarcity of which in those areas constituted a serious problem for the Soviets.

[8] See in the Appendices the "Proclamation" issued by Chiang inviting the Red soldiers to desert their ranks, and offering rewards for assassinations of their commanders.

Divisions suffered partial defeat. In the Hunan-Hupeh district the 51st Division was defeated and the 5th Brigade met with almost complete annihilation. In Kiangsi during September, the 28th and the 33rd Nanking Divisions were defeated, and part of the latter deserted to join the Reds. In October also in Kiangsi, the old 56th and the new 2nd Nanking Divisions and the 4th Nanking Brigade all suffered serious reverses, and at the same time the Red Army repulsed the attack of the Nanking forces in the Hunan-Hupeh district. During November the Red Army in Hupeh-Hunan-Anhwei area repulsed the attack of two divisions of Government troops. In the Hunan-Hupei district, not far from Shensi, the 42nd Nanking Division was routed. In January, 1933, in Kiangsi, the 5th, 11th, 14th, 53rd, 56th, and 57th Nanking Divisions were defeated. In Szechwan, the Reds, who retreated there under the pressure of the over-whelming forces of Nanking in the early part of that Campaign, defeated four out of the six local divisions, partly disarmed them, and captured a great number of men. Later, between February and May of 1933, four Nanking divisions were completely defeated in Kiangsi, five suffered partial defeat; and two of the division commanders were captured by the Reds.

In other words, the results of the Fifth Campaign were very like those of the previous four. In the beginning the Communists lost part of their territory, and some of their troops were forced to retreat and moved into Szechwan; but eventually the Red Armies reoccupied part of the lost territories, occupied new districts and succeeded in establishing themselves in Szechwan and in the Southern part of Shensi. The Chinese Communists claim that as the result of the Fifth Campaign they obtained control of a larger territory than they had before, and in every case they acquired much ammunition and were able to equip more troops with the material captured from the Government units. The reports of the foreign Press in March, 1933,

indicated that sweeping Communist successes had largely nulli-
fied the results of Nanking's campaign in 1932 [9]

THE 1933 CAMPAIGN AND THE FUKIEN REVOLT

With as little publicity as possible the Nanking troops were
once again gradually withdrawn from fighting the Communists
and remained inactive till the late Fall of 1933. In the Spring
and Summer of last year, Chiang had trouble enough with
the Japanese on his hands, with the problem of finding some
way out of the unbearable situation created by the Manchurian
affair and the expansion of the Japanese occupation beyond the
Great Wall. By May, indeed, the Japanese forces were within·
one-day's marching distance of Peiping,[10] and Chiang decided
to seek a truce, and on May 31st the armistice was signed at
Tangku. Thus the Japanese question was "settled" for a while,
leaving Chiang free again to fight his main enemy—the Soviets.

By August the Chinese press was again devoting considerable
space to the Reds and to the discussion of the preparations for a
new campaign "to annihilate the Communists," for Nanking
now became really busy in mobilizing additional resources for
that exploit. The American "Wheat and Cotton Loan" of $50,-
000,000, arranged for by T. V. Soong, while in the United
States on his mission to Geneva and back, came in very handy.
Soong was bound, of course, by the terms of the contract, but
his brother-in-law, Chiang Kai-shek, did not consider that a
serious obstacle. Soong resigned from the Ministry of Finance,
but the other brother-in-law, Dr. Kung, was available and became the new Minister of Finance. The money question was
arranged to some extent: 50,000,000 American dollars would
stretch to almost 200,000,000 when converted into the Nanking
dollar, but even 200,000,000 were not enough for the enormous
scheme of the Generalissimo. Of course the economic and

[9] *E.g., New York Times,* April 10, 1933.   [10] *E.g.,* Peking.

political reforms he promised to introduce could wait, but even the military expenses loomed large, and those who know more about money than generals usually do, advised Chiang to be careful. It was useless. Chiang wanted to fight and fighting was on the program. Again the troubadours announced that the last day of the Soviets was in sight, that Chiang was going to lead the campaign, and promised "not to return to Nanking alive unless he succeeded in exterminating the Red-bandits." These servile admirers failed to remember that this had been the refrain in all the previous campaigns and that their idol had returned from all of them, alive, and, even though defeated, still pretending that he was successful.

The finances of Chiang needed support very badly. Contributions, large and small, were eagerly sought from every source and from the very beginning of the campaign. At the end of October the standing Committee of the Central Executive Committee met under the chairmanship of Wang Ching-wei, and decided that a sum of one hundred thousand Mexican dollars should be appropriated by the Central Treasury as a gift to the bandit-suppression forces. Thus the Government tried to appease the soldiers whose pay was in arrears, by offering them gifts from the Treasury.

Chiang himself again went to Nanchang, the capital of Kiangsi, where his headquarters was located. From there he directed the operations of his armies. About 200,000 of his troops were concentrated on a front of some 125 miles stretching from Lichwan to Kian, on the Kan River, alone, while others were stationed in Fukien and other areas. The Red Armies on that front were commanded by Chu Teh, numbered about 70,000, and had plenty of machine-guns. According to Reuter's the Red soldiers were always paid promptly and in full, at the rate of eight dollars a month, and were well fed through the efforts of the local population. This was in striking contrast to the Government troops in Kiangsi, who "for the last three years have only received an average of two dollars a month."

Interviewed at Nanking on October 20th, after his return from Kiangsi, Yu Fei-pang, Vice-Minister of Communications, declared that Generalissimo Chiang Kai-shek had already ordered a general offensive against the "Reds," and the "complete suppression of the Communists within three years." The troops were making good progress, he said, and General Chiang had addressed a manifesto to the Red combatants, guaranteeing safety and liberal treatment to all deserters from the ranks of the Communists.

But Kiangsi was not the only territory which had to be cleared of "Reds." The latter were getting stronger and stronger in their newly acquired area of Szechwan; indeed, the *China Weekly Review* reported in its issue of October 28, 1933, that "in spite of optimistic official reports to the contrary, the Communists in Northern Szechwan are gaining ground every day and the troops under General Liu Tsun-hou show themselves unable to put up an effective resistance against the onrushing Red forces. At present the total strength of the Communists is estimated at 60,000 men. They are moving steadily eastward, with the object of capturing Suiting and thus joining up with the Communist forces in Western Hupeh under Ho Lung."

At about the same time the *China Times* commented: "It cannot be denied that Communism in China is, to some extent, encouraged by our corrupt administration. If we want to stamp out Communism for good we must lose no time in reforming our administration. At the present moment there are numerous factors which compel law-abiding citizens to turn to the Communist-bandits. We cannot overlook the cause and yet insist on removing the effect. This would be a hopeless task." As for the Hankow correspondent of the *China Weekly Review*, he declared in the opening sentences of a despatch to his periodical, that "disquieting though it may be, nevertheless it is true that the areas are increasing in size in most places where the Reds operate. No wonder that General Chiang Kai-shek and his colleagues have determined to root them out once and for all. But this is easier said than done."

As a matter of fact it was not long before all of these gloomy comments and prognostications were vindicated. In November a revolt began in Fukien, and those who were supposedly coöperating with Chiang, turned against him, and proclaimed the province independent. A Provisional Government was set up. General Tsai Ting-kai, Commander of the Nineteenth Route Army (of Shanghai fame), who had been fighting the Communists for a long time and almost continuously since May, 1932, suspended operations against the "Reds." Rumor spread that an understanding of some kind had been reached with the latter, if not for coöperation, at least for neutrality. This neutrality was of advantage to the "Reds" since they were able to acquire in the interim considerable amounts of supplies from the Fukien coast, especially of salt and other goods, the scarcity of which made their subsistence rather insecure.

This new development, naturally, forced Chiang to concentrate his attention on the Fukien group, and to shift part of his troops from fighting the Communists to suppressing the new rebels. The latter task was accomplished in less than two months. By the middle of January, 1934, the Nanking forces were in a position to oust the Fukien Independent Government. Foochow, the capital of the latter, was occupied on January 13th, by the Nanking marine force, and the army captured a number of other important points, making further resistance futile. The Nineteenth Route Army was withdrawn southward even earlier and before the end of January the whole affair was considered as settled. The Nanking Vice-Minister of War was made head of a new provisional government for

Fukien, and usual negotiations were opened with the rebel-leaders to define their further status, including that of the Nineteenth Route Army, which had to be reorganized and "purified."

How the Communists Explained Their Successes

Let us conclude with the opinion of the Communists regarding their successes. In an article published in June, 1933,[11] Wang Ming, representative of the Chinese Communist Party in the Comintern, wrote on this subject as follows:

"What is the basic explanation of the victory attained by the Red Army over the Army of the Kuo-min-tang, with its strength of one million men and its partially modern equipment? First of all the explanation lies in the very substance of the Red Army, which is the anti-Imperialist, anti-landlord, anti-bourgeois army, composed of workers and peasants . . . its strength does not rely on the soldiers and their arms only, but on the energetic coöperation and support of the masses, who even go so far as to take part in the fighting also. Millions of the people were able to find out for themselves, while fighting in these years of civil war, what the Soviet revolution means as compared with the Kuo-min-tang counter-revolution; they learned, as well, what the programs of the Communist Party of China and of the Kuo-min-tang are in regard to each and every problem of politics and economics in China. . . . For instance, the Kuo-min-tang declared that it is the sole defender against Japanese aggression. But what are the facts? The Japanese Imperialists occupied Manchuria, and the Kuo-min-tang met it by advocating a policy of calm and nonresistance. The Japanese Imperialists bombarded Shanghai, and the Kuo-min-tang met it by betrayal of the defense of Shanghai staged by the heroic 19th Route Army, who fought together with the revolutionary

[11] In the *Communistichesky Internazional*, June 20, 1933. Moscow.

workers against the invaders. Japan occupied Shanhaikwan, and the Kuo-min-tang patiently awaited the interference of the League of Nations. Then Japan occupied Jehol and a considerable part of Northern China. The Kuo-min-tang not only failed to offer any resistance but even openly capitulated to Japanese Imperialism, by concluding the so-called truce. The masses of the Chinese people are carrying on a heroic struggle with the Japanese Imperialists in Manchuria, and the Kuo-min-tang was and is sabotaging it by passivity and secret negotiations with Japan. The Chinese people were and are staging strikes, arranging meetings, demonstrations and conferences against the Imperialists, which the Kuo-min-tang meets by arrests, executions and massacres of the workers, peasants, soldiers, students, and all the anti-Imperialist elements.

"The Soviet Government of China declared war on Japanese Imperialism early in 1932 . . . it offered the coöperation of the Red Army with any other armed forces to fight the Japanese Imperialists . . . but the realities proved that the Kuo-min-tang Government is the government which betrayed and brought disgrace upon the nation. . . . The Chinese Communist Party and the Soviet régimes directed by it, are the only real fighters for the emancipation of the Chinese people from the yoke of the Japanese and other Imperialists. . . . The Kuo-min-tang declares, as a matter of demagogy, that it is defending the interests of the workers and the peasants, not only in its own territory, but also in that of the Soviets. In practice something different occurs to the peasants and workers of the Soviet areas when they come temporarily in the hands of the Kuo-min-tang. The very first thing they see is mass-slaughtering . . . in the Tianmin county alone there were massacred over ten thousand "red-bandits"; in the Chantsian county, on suspicion of sympathizing with the Reds, more than 16,000 people were killed.[12]. . . . After the Kuo-min-tang troops enter a territory the restoration of landlords to their proprietorship follows. . . . Another factor which contributes to the successes of the Reds is the victorious completion of the First Five Year Plan by the USSR . . . it served to increase the prestige of the Chinese Communist Party . . . which, following the example of the Russian Bolsheviks, will transform China from a semi-colony of the Imperialists . . . into an independent, sovereign, mighty state, similar to the USSR. . . ."

In his report before the XVII Congress of the Communist Party, held in February, 1934, at Moscow, Mr. Manuilsky had this to say about the successes of the Chinese Communists:

"The first place among the Communist Parties of the world after the Bolsheviks of USSR belongs to that of China. . . . That Party is in control already of a territory larger than France or Germany or any other Imperialist country outside of the U. S. A. . . . The Red Armies of Soviet China, well experienced in civil war, have already repulsed five campaigns led against them by Chiang Kai-shek. During the Fifth Campaign the Reds captured about 80,000 soldiers of the Kuo-min-tang, and from January to April, 1933, seized 140,000 rifles, 1,390 machine-guns, 6 airplanes . . . and occupied 79 new counties. . . . Such an Army, and such a Party . . . are serious factors in the balance of power in the Far East. . . . Now these Armies are resisting the sixth campaign of Chiang Kai-shek, facing superior forces of the adversary, who is operating under the plan designed by the German General von Seeckt, and equipped with modern arms with American airplanes, English tanks, and armored cars, and French artillery. But this campaign has so far brought 15 new counties in Szechwan into the hands of the Chinese comrades, and they hope that it will end

[12] Both of these counties are in the province of Hupeh.

in a new defeat, for Chiang Kai-shek and 'a fresh supply of modern arms for the Reds,' at the expense of the Kuo-min-tang. . . . It must end by the defeat of Chiang Kai-shek, for the Chinese Communist Party and the Red Armies of China possess what its enemy does not possess, namely, the ever-victorious idea of Communism and the enthusiastic support of the masses, ready for boundless sacrifices."

CHAPTER IX

THE INTRA-PARTY AND INTER-PARTY STRUGGLES

THE Communist Party of China, like most young political organizations, covered a wide range of opinion in its membership and contained many divergent elements. Indeed, from the very time of its inception there was apparent the usual tendency toward the formation of "Right" and "Left" Wings, from which the "Right" and "Left" oppositions were later on recruited. The "Right" Wing, of course, originated in the tendency of certain members to underestimate the opportunities for emancipation offered by the Revolution, and at the same time to overestimate the nationalist feeling in such a country as China, which has been essentially a semi-colonial state. As for the "Left" Opposition, it was, on the other hand, born of an unduly optimistic estimate of the revolutionary possibilities, and of an underestimate of the need for coöperation between the working classes and the revolutionary bourgeoisie, during the struggle against foreign Imperialism. Such, at any rate, was Stalin's analysis of the Chinese trend as given in his *Voprosi Leninisma*.[1]

In the beginning, of course, the trend was merely latent. It was not until the revolutionary process began to pass from one stage to another, forcing distinct alignments on projected courses of action, that it began to take pronounced form, causing the formation of groups which would from time to time split with the main party, and eventually leading to more serious schisms. As a matter of fact it was the temporary defeat of the Com-

[1] Quoted from an article by G. K. in No. 11 of the *Problemi Kitaia*, 1933, p. 80.

munists in China in 1927, culminating in the formation of the
Nanking régime, that but accentuated the differences between
the various groups which were incorporated in it. The weaker
elements, whose roots were not yet deep in the soil of Com-
munst faith, and who did not whole-heartedly belong to the
Party, but who were rather coöperating or were "on probation"
as coöperators started to shift in one direction or another. Some
went to the Right, others to the Left. Some joined parties and
associations already in existence, while others tried to organize
their own groups.

Chen Tu-hsiu and His Teachings

Curiously enough, the first considerable rift in the Com-·
munist Party of China was created by Professor Chen Tu-hsiu,
who is generally regarded as its founder as well as one of the
leading pioneers of the movement in the former Celestial Empire. It was also probably the most important schism for the
various other divergences from party orthodoxy which occurred
later, guided by leaders of less erudition and brilliance than
Professor Chen, who lacked his power to attract a wide following, and whose teachings, being less scholarly and sophisti-
cated, were easier to combat. Though he himself is now held
in prison at Nanking by the unappreciative Kuo-min-tang, his
following is still active and to a certain extent influential; therefore the questions of the origin, character, and future of his
doctrines are matters of considerably more than mere academic
interest.

It was Chen Tu-hsiu's opinion that the Chinese Revolution
was essentially a bourgeois-democratic movement in a semi-
colonial country, and that its first aim should therefore be emancipation from the yoke of Imperialism. In other words, he believed in liberation of the country from the foreign yoke first,
and serious reforms in the country itself only afterwards. He

considered that in the first stage of the Chinese Revolution the proletariat ought to coöperate with the bourgeoisie in the struggle against the foreign Imperialists and the war lords or other domestic militarists, and almost completely neglected the question of agrarian reform, which the Comintern regards as the greatest and most urgent of all China's problems. In short, Chen Tu-hsiu apparently failed to take into consideration the remnants of feudalism in his country, and this brought him into disagreement with his erstwhile comrades. In the opinion of Chen Tu-hsiu, the bourgeoisie must play the leading rôle in the first stage of the revolution so long as it is a bourgeois-revolution. On this point again he was in opposition to the "general line," which while approving coöperation with the bourgeoisie, asserted that the hegemony even at that period should belong to the workers closely coöperating with the peasants.

Considering the insignificant size of the industrial proletariat in China, and the political backwardness of the majority of its members, Chen Tu-hsiu came to the conclusion that this group was scarcely able to lead the revolutionary movement. The backwardness and political passivity of the farmers made them, in Chen Tu-hsiu's opinion, practically valueless for the revolution. Hence he arrived at the point of practically denying the necessity for class struggle, and so, eventually, became quite estranged from the Communists. Gradually concentrating in the bourgeoisie his hopes for revolutionary changes and forgetting how easily a paramount bourgeoisie will slide down to reaction, Chen steered a middle course, trying to evade extremes and to reconcile the irreconcilable, he followed the usual road of liberals and finally developed, so said his former comrades, into a mere opportunist.

Chen Tu-hsiu was opposed to the Communists remaining in the Kuo-min-tang (1925-27), and advocated their withdrawal long before they were expelled by Chiang Kai-shek. The Comintern condemned Chen Tu-hsiu's stand on this and other questions, and voiced the opinion that he was "following, and on certain points even going ahead of, Trotzky." At a discussion held in 1930 in the Communist Academy at Moscow, several orators expressed the view that Chen Tu-hsiu, who was one of the foremost leaders in China's progressive movement, and an advocate of Western civilization, was at the same time a believer in Capitalism as a step forward for China, and remained through his entire career a defender of Capitalism and an opponent of the idea of class struggle. His opposition to the "radicalism" of the masses and his preference for gradual changes made it inevitable for Chen Tu-hsiu, the intellectual *par excellence,* to part company with the Communists, and so he became one of the leaders of the "Right-Wing Opposition," a liquidator of revolution, a "menshevik," in the opinion of certain of his critics. Chen pointed to his belief in gradual revolutionization of the Chinese bourgeoisie along with the development of industries in their country, growing under Capitalism; and therefore his belief in the inevitability of the Capitalist stage of economic growth of China.

Utterly disagreeing with these interpretations of Chen Tu-hsiu, the Communists of China, in accord with the Comintern, condemned their former comrade and founder of the Party, accusing him of underestimating the rôle of the proletariat and of discouraging the farmers from carrying on the agrarian revolution, which, in their opinion, should be the foremost aim of the present-day China.

Asserting that the Chinese farmer is a staunch believer in private property, Chen wrote: "It goes without saying that the Communist social revolution easily contradicts the interests of the farmers and even the landless-tenant. Their struggle with the landlord is the struggle for their property, and against the property of the landlord.". . . And again: "Only when industry will go on vigorously developing in China, and when it will be in the Capitalist stage, will the rural proletariat start growing and organizing itself. Only then a social revolution will be possible in the Chinese village. If we advance now the slogans which do not correspond to the present situation, we shall greatly damage and hinder the national revolution." The expulsion of Chen Tu-hsiu, naturally, did not end the dissensions. Intra-party disagreements and quarrels continued to develop in other quarters and "opposition" factions continued to crystallize. For example an "Ultra Left" group was formed by Li Li-san and his followers, who advocated an immediate armed uprising to be led by the Communists. Paying no due attention to the actual situation, they preached a sort of "putschism," favored pretentious demonstrations, and attempted to seize power without any solid backing. Their efforts, therefore, were not only destined to be abortive and futile in achievements, but also distinctly troublesome to the Party, as a political organization striving for leadership.

Chen Tu-hsiu'ism began its oppositionist tactics as early as 1923. At that time, said M. Borodin at the discussion in the Communist Academy at Moscow (and from the proceedings of which much of the material in this chapter is derived), the Communist Party of China already had two different wings, one represented by Canton and M. Borodin himself, and the other, with its center in Shanghai, led by Chen Tu-hsiu and others. The Canton group asserted that the Chinese Revolution must and will win through the agrarian revolution, and therefore encouraged the organization of peasant-unions. The Shanghai group of Chen Tu-hsiu and his followers placed the anti-Imperialist aspect of the revolution first and foremost. As a matter of fact, the Canton group was not quite determined to achieve hegemony of the proletariat, and the Shanghai group worked for coöperation with the Left-Wing of the Kuo-min-tang, neglecting the question of leadership. In the opinion of M. Borodin, one of the principal errors of the Chinese Communists was that they did not follow any clear-cut policy and that they had no proper theoretical foundation to their program, since one of their foremost theoreticians, Chen Tu-hsiu himself, was in error.

Other Communists reject this explanation, seeing no justification for such overemphasis on the rôle of individuals. On the contrary, they declare that the main error lay in the failure to organize the peasants or to place the proletariat in the leadership of the revolution. It is true that Chen Tu-hsiu did neglect this phase of the problem, but, apparently, the Canton group also failed to do its part any more vigorously. So 1927 saw a disintegration of the Communist Party in China, brought about by the natural irreconcilability of those inclined to coöperate with the bourgeoisie and those who considered this not only futile but even detrimental to the cause for which they were struggling.

More recently Chen Tu-hsiu and his followers suggested convening a National Constituent Assembly on democratic lines, as advocated by Trotzky in his recent writings on China.[2] The Comintern naturally denounced this idea as an attempt at retrogression, for it meant slowing down the revolutionary process to conciliate the reactionary elements. The orthodox Communists classified this stand as definitely counter-revolutionary, in spite of certain revolutionary phrases "still used by Chen Tu-hsiu and the others, supporting his views."

THE LI LI-SAN SCHISM

The other important deviation from the main body of the Chinese Communist Party was the "Left" schism started by an-

[2] His article of September 4, 1928.

other prominent member, Li Li-san. After a marked success of Sovietization of certain areas and a number of victories of the Red Armies over the Kuo-min-tang troops, a group of Communists, headed by Li Li-san "considering the moment ripe for the overthrow of the Nanking régime, organized local uprisings and armed insurrections in a number of cities, as a prelude to a general offensive of the Red Armies." [8]

Li Li-san and his group were of the opinion that the situation called for active revolutionary measures, contrary to the policy of the Party's Central Executive Committee and the general directives of the Comintern, who strongly condemned at its Sixth Congress any "toying with insurrection." The Comintern at that stage favored organizing the masses and carrying on propaganda in order to enlighten them; it understood the actual situation in China and opposed any revolutionary adventures.

At that time Li Li-san was in Wuhan, and more or less out of direct touch with the Central Executive Committee, then at Shanghai. However, he considered himself well versed in the actual situation and decided to act on his own responsibility. He tried to organize the "Central Committee of Action" at Wuhan, when the Party launched an insurrection in Changsha against the Nanking régime. The Red Army attacked and occupied that city but was driven out by the foreign gunboats. Simultaneously Li Li-san was ejected from the Communist Party. This insurrection caused a general "purging" of the rank and file of the Party, resulting in the elimination of some 25% of the followers of Li Li-san. The rest recanted, and remained in the Party, promising strictly to follow the orthodox "line." In January, 1931, the Communist Party of China held its Fifth Plenary Conference, condemning this "putschist" schism most severely and affecting a certain amount of reconstruction of the Party and its auxiliary organizations.

[8] Wellington Koo. *Ibid.,* p. 747.

Since Li Li-san believed in the theory of "permanent revolution," he was often classed as a follower of Trotzky, which seems hardly reasonable. He ignored the bourgeois-democratic stage of the Chinese Revolution and was blind to the need for systematic preparation of the masses. He forced socialization, when the actual situation was not ripe for it, and he disregarded the difference between the various groups of peasantry and the class struggle existing between these groups. Generally speaking, he followed a policy of adventure.

The Anti-Bolshevik League

Besides the intra-party differences which, as we have seen, gradually led to the formation of the "Right" and "Left" Oppositions, and the natural inter-party struggle with the Kuomin-tang, the Communists of China had also to deal with certain groups who, remaining in the ranks of the Party, plotted against it by "boring from within." One such organization, known as the "A-B" or "Anti-Bolshevik League," was discovered in one of the Red Armies. This led to the exposure of most of its branches, and, soon afterwards, to the elimination of these enemies and the frustration of their plans.

The well-known revolutionist, Peng Pai, who was active in the Hailofong Republic and was known as one of the first organizers of the peasants' unions, was credited with the discovery of the "A-B" plot and the raid on their headquarters. It happened that one day on his arrival at Juichin he met a young student, a son of a wealthy landlord, who was complaining indignantly about the activity of the peasant-unions and dropping vague hints that plans were under way to suppress them. From further conversation Peng Pai sensed that there was danger for his movement in the making. A search in the house of the boy who revealed something of this plan, produced certain documentary proof and by inducing the boy to talk further, Peng

Pai finally learned where the headquarters of the A-B League was located. With a group of Red soldiers he surrounded the house, arrested those inside, and obtained all the information he wanted. The dissolution of the League quickly followed.[4]

The "A-B" League was an organization composed of and controlled by the well-to-do peasants' sons of the landlords and the gentry, who were bitterly opposed to the idea of redistribution of land and to the entire Communist scheme, and were therefore planning open revolt against the Soviets after a brief period of agitation in the ranks of the Red Armies, where they strove to organize groups of supporters. These plans failed owing to the timely discovery made by Peng Pai.

[4] This episode is described by Emi-Siao, a friend of the late Peng Pai, in the *Red Haifong,* p. 77, Moscow, 1932.

CHAPTER X

THE FIRST CONGRESS OF SOVIETS IN CHINA

Composition and Origin of the First Congress

On November 7, 1931, the anniversary of the Russian "October Revolution," the First Congress of Soviets in China was convened at Juichin, in Kiangsi province, which is the heart of the main Soviet area. Altogether six hundred and ten delegates were present from the various Soviet regions of Kiangsi, Fukien, and the border areas of Hunan-Hupeh-Kiangsi and other provinces, as well as a number of delegates from the Red Armies, the All-Chinese Federation of Labor, the Seamen's Union, and the Chinese Communist Party.

This Congress was the outgrowth of the work started by the Communist Party of China in 1930, which had convoked at Shanghai on May 31st of that year a Conference of delegates from the various Soviet areas and all China. At that Conference a special Committee was elected and charged with the task of making all the necessary preparations for the First All-China Congress of Soviets, which was scheduled to assemble on December 11th of the same year, but which did not actually meet until nearly eleven months later.

The First Conference of Soviets

This preliminary conference was convoked at a time of growing economic unrest and in the deepest shadow of reaction. Delegates arrived from the Soviet area of Kiangsi, Hupeh, Hunan, Kwangtung, and Kwangsi, and were joined by others

representing the Red Armies and the "volunteers," the Red
Trade Unions of Shanghai, Nanking, and Wuhan, and other
revolutionary organizations. During the sessions a study was
made of the status of the Revolution at the moment; the main
problems confronting the Soviets were outlined; various drafts
for laws, both agrarian and labor, were submitted; and a number of interesting resolutions were passed. The great significance of the Conference, however, lay in the attempt made to
bring together all the scattered Soviet areas, and so to put into
motion their unification under a general central government.
As the next step to this end the Conference voted to convene
that First Congress of Soviets which actually met a year and a
half later. The Conference adjourned after having elected a
special Committee for its preparation.

The laws drafted, accepted, and codified by the Conference
provided, among other things, for the introduction of the eight-
hour working day, social insurance, and confirmation of civil
liberties; the emancipation of women; abolition of taxes imposed by the feudal and military authorities; cancellation of
debts to the usurers; and liquidation of land ownership by the
large landlords. In all, five resolutions were passed by the Conference. Of these five one dealt in a general way with the
political situation, one with the provisional land law, one with
labor, and one with the defense of the USSR. One took the
form of a Manifesto summoning the First Congress of Soviets.

These resolutions were severely criticized by certain special-
ists in Moscow.[1] First of all, the analysis of the political situation was criticized for failure to appreciate the unevenness of
the revolutionary process in different parts of China, and the
lagging of the industrial population behind the more thoroughly revolutionized agrarian elements. Actually there were
considerable territories where the landlords had been practically

[1] *Problemi Kitaia*, Nos. 4-5, 1930.

eliminated, and in which the Soviets were set up and the Red Armies in existence; but at the same time there were still larger areas, especially in the North, where reaction was triumphant and the masses had only begun their struggle for emancipation. Disregarding these realities the Conference passed resolutions presupposing the situation favorable for immediate armed uprising all over China and even over the entire world. The critics asserted that in the face of actualities the appeal for an all-Chinese uprising will be nothing but empty words; the first needs they saw were the organization of the masses; fostering of the economic struggle in the areas outside of the Soviet jurisdiction; strengthening of the sovietized communities; and a thorough preparation for eventual uprisings. In short, the resolutions failed to give proper emphasis to the most important aspect of the Revolution, namely, the necessity of stirring up the lagging revolutionary spirit of the industrial workers. The critics also disapproved the stand of the Conference on such an important matter as the composition of the Red Armies, insisting that they should be purged of such "undesirable elements" as the well-to-do, the formerly privileged classes, and all others who supposedly could not be trusted implicitly in affairs predominantly proletarian. Severe condemnation was visited upon the light-hearted way in which the Conference suggested the beginning of a struggle for Socialism, for which the time was not yet ripe. In the field of agrarian reform, the attempt of the Conference to keep intact the large holdings of the former landlords in order to create state-farms and collective-farms was even more bitterly challenged since, in the opinion of the Moscow critics, the peculiarities of the Chinese farming methods, the family ties, and so forth, made these projected reforms not only untimely but very dangerous.[2]

[2] The materials on the Conference of the Delegates of the Soviet Areas published in the *Problemi Kitaia,* Nos. 4-5, 1930, Moscow, pp. 172-198.

THE FIRST CONGRESS

Between the time of the Conference on May 31, 1930, and the Congress which was postponed and eventually convened only in November, 1931, a number of important events took place. The Nanking régime lost three of its campaigns "to eradicate the Reds," and in the Summer of 1930, indeed, the Communists even succeeded in capturing the large and important city of Changsha, though they had to evacuate it about a week later. In September, 1931, the Japanese started their occupation of Manchuria. The economic crisis meanwhile continued to grow more serious the world over, and China was profoundly affected.

The denationalization of the Chinese industries and the depreciation of silver—the basis of China's monetary system— served to strengthen further the Imperialist grip on that country. In 1930 domestic capital was represented in the iron and steel industry of China only to the extent of 5%, and even in the textile industry where it was much more prominent, the percentage of Chinese capital fell to 44%, instead of 52% in 1925. A number of Chinese enterprises were forced to close down owing to the economic crisis. The depreciation of silver automatically brought an increase of the Chinese foreign indebtedness, and this, in its turn, offered the foreigners new opportunities for extending their control over China. The foreign trade of the country went further into the "red," the passive balance increasing. Bankruptcies mounted, and an increasing number of farmers lost their meager holdings by foreclosure. The civil wars continued to drain the country's resources. The taxes became steadily more oppressive, and reached fabulous figures; indeed, certain European economists estimated them as twenty-two times as large as they were under the Manchus before the Revolution, and six times as large as at the time of the World War. Unemployment was extremely high, in certain industries as high as 70%, compared with normal times.[3] The harvest of 1931 was poor, and coupled with the flood,[4] added to the widespread misery.

In such circumstances the First Congress of Soviets in China became an event of real importance, and the enemies of the Soviets, domestic and foreign, although trying to minimize its significance, grew distinctly alarmed. It was obvious that a new force had developed which must be reckoned with. In place of the old division of China into a number of semi-independent provinces, controlled by Governors, more or less representing the Emperor in the past or the war lords in the more recent years, there was now the entirely independent and irritatingly different government of the Soviets, which not only defied the "legitimate" Nanking régime but seemed invincible. Of the two régimes, that at Nanking—representing the Kuo-min-tang, and dependent on the foreigners—and the second at Juichin—controlled by the Communists and bitterly opposed to the Imperialist dominance over their country—one must eventually dominate. The struggle was, and still is, on, and upon its outcome depends the future of the country.

THE ACHIEVEMENTS OF THE FIRST CONGRESS

The Congress voted upon the provisional Constitution for the All China Soviet Republic and elected Mao Tse-tung its president.[5] The Congress also discussed a number of impor-

---

[3] *Sovieti v Kitaie* (in Russian), Moscow, 1933, p. 46.

[4] "In August, 1931, there came the disastrous Yangtze floods, which inundated the entire valley, brought death to unknown hundreds of thousands, and destitution to the millions who survived." (*China Forum*, May, 1932.)

[5] Mao Tse-tung, born in Hunan, was formerly a student in Peking University, later continuing his education in Europe, especially in France. He organized the trade union of coal-miners at Pinghsiang, which was the center of Communist activity in Kiangsi and Hunan. He has assumed the political control of the Red Armies of Hunan, Kiangsi, and Fukien since 1928. (W. Koo, *ibid.*, p. 771.)

tant measures, such as a Labor Law and a Land Law, drafted by the Communist Party of China.

Article 1 of the Constitution of Soviet China defined the tasks of the Soviet régime as follows:

"The aim of the democratic dictatorship of the proletariat and peasants is the abolition of all remnants of feudalism; cancellation of the power of the Imperialists in China; unification of the country; systematic restriction of growth of capitalism; the building of national economy; development of class-consciousness, and organization of the proletariat; and the bringing together of the masses of the poor, peasants, and the proletarians, with the eventual dictatorship of proletariat in mind."

In other words, the national anti-feudal and anti-Imperialist revolutions were regarded as the immediate concern, while the social revolution was looked upon as the second stage to be deferred to the future. The Constitution itself was designed, naturally, for the Sovietized areas only, but the aim of the régime, as declared in the preamble, was to be accepted eventually by the whole of China.

The second Article declared that all power is concentrated in the hands of the toiling classes, represented by the Soviets; while Article 3 assigns the supreme power in the Republic to the Congress of the Soviets. The goals marked out by the Constitution were regarded as attainable only through the hegemony of the proletariat, led by the Communist Party. In the first stage of the Revolution, it was expected that a road would be paved to further socialization by gradual restriction of the capitalistic development.

The immediate objects of the Soviet régime were listed in four subsequent sections. Article 5 prescribed radical improvement of the standard of living for the toiling masses; the inauguration of labor laws; the introduction of the eight-hour working day; the establishment of the minimum wage, and organization of social insurance and unemployment relief, as well as recognition of the right of Labor to control production. Article 6 dealt with the abolition of the feudal system, radical improvement of the standard of living of the peasants, and codification of the land law, and this included confiscation of holdings of the landlords and consequent distribution of this property among the poor and the "middle" class of peasants and pointed to the eventual nationalization of land all over China. Article 7 protected the interests of the workers and peasants, restricted the development of Capitalism, advanced the idea of economic emancipation from the control of Capital, with socialization as the final goal, abolished the unreasonable taxes imposed by the former governments, and introduced a uniform progressive tax. The fourth aim, as defined by Article 8 of the Constitution was the emancipation of China from the Imperialist yoke.

THE AGRARIAN REFORM

Agrarian unrest had been the starting point of the evolution of the Soviets in China. The establishment of the Soviets almost without exception followed the path of peasant revolts and armed uprisings, sometimes with participation of the Red Armies, sometimes without. One of the first measures introduced by the Soviets ordered destruction of title deeds, mortgages, and all other documents establishing ownership of land, as well as of all documents proving indebtedness, such as promissory notes.

Article 1 of the Land Law provided for confiscation of lands belonging to the feudal lords, landlords, militarists, "tuhao," gentry, monasteries and other large holders, but not those belonging to the "middle-class" farmers; [6] and Article 2 specified that a certain amount of lands should be reserved in each dis-

[6] Meaning "middle," between the well-to-do and the poor.

trict and cultivated by the Communists to provide for the subsistence of soldiers in the "Red" Army; Article 5 recognized that equalized redistribution of land would be the most thorough and satisfactory method of putting an end to feudal and semi-feudal ownership and to the unjust relations between the landlords and the enslaved peasants, but established the view that it was not proper to impose these measures forcibly, by command of the authorities. Such measures, it was explained, should be introduced only with the approval of the majority of peasants and should be preceded by thorough clarification of their meaning to the masses.

Article 7 established that the well-to-do peasants were insisting on redistribution of land in accordance with the means of production, but the Congress, considering this as an attempt to sabotage the agrarian revolution while taking advantage of it, declared itself vigorously opposed. In Article 12 of the Land Law the Congress favored the nationalization of land and waters as the best way to improve the standard of living of the peasants and a step necessary for further advancement toward socialist development. It conceded, however, that this can be realized only if the agrarian revolution is successful in most of the important parts of China and is supported by the majority of the peasants. In the meantime the Soviets must explain to the peasants why the nationalization is desirable, but not to deprive them of the right of buying, selling, or renting their holdings, unless these would involve speculation or attempts by former landlords to re-acquire their confiscated possessions.

THE COMINTERN'S OPINIONS

In consideration of the actual distribution of social forces the Comintern took the view that it would not be justifiable to press such measures as nation-wide confiscation of industries, complete abolition of private proprietorship of the means of production in the villages, collectivization of farming, prohibition of leasing land and hiring help for farm purposes, abolition of private internal trade, or the establishment of a monopoly of foreign trade. To launch such a wide program at once, the Comintern believed, would mean alienating many sympathizers, and by making the coöperation between workers and peasants ineffective, would place the Soviets in a most unfavorable position.

The first and foremost task of this first stage of the Revolution was to emancipate the toiling masses of China from the yoke of the feudal economic system and from the privileges and monopolies of the Imperialists, which were held responsible for the hardships and pauperization of the Chinese masses. A certain amount of leniency toward the Capitalistic elements, especially in the villages, and the toleration of the petty merchants and others was considered unavoidable at this stage, and even, in the opinion of certain students, desirable as stimuli for the standard of living.

EXTENSIFICATION OR INTENSIFICATION?

In the years 1925-27, when the Nationalist Party was coöperating with the Communists, the future of the Revolution was a frequent topic of discussion in the Kuo-min-tang. Should the Revolution be extensified or intensified? Should it branch out, embracing new territories and involving new elements at once? Or should it be first intensified by consolidating its achievements in the regions already occupied by the revolutionary elements? That was the dilemma. Now, in the opinion of the Communists, no such dilemma exists, for extensification and intensification must be, they say, attained simultaneously. Extension of the Soviet movement directly depends on thorough penetration of the masses, its success depends on the extent to which it involves the masses and actually engages them in propagation of the Soviet ideal. In other words, the larger the groups involved and deeper the revolutionist process in those groups, the more rapidly will it expand to broader areas. Without extending the process to the urban centers, without involving the industrial workers, the success of the Sovietization cannot be complete. However great its victories in the agrarian field may be, it must still be extended to embrace the city-dwellers. Indeed, it cannot develop properly until it comes under the leadership of the industrial proletariat.

At its present stage the Soviet movement in China accumulates momentum chiefly through agrarian revolts, through the exploits of the Red Army supported by the so-called "partisans" or volunteers from the villages, and through strikes and uprisings by the industrial workers. From village to village, from one "hsien" or county to the next, from one province to another, this movement is spreading, slowly and not without reverses, to be sure, but still spreading in spite of all the "vigorous" anti-Communist campaigns of Chiang Kai-shek, and in spite of all the up-to-the-minute arms and other devices of destruction generously imported from the more civilized Westerners and employed for the "annihilation of the Reds."

THE LABOR LAW

The draft for a Labor Law prepared by the Communist Party of China and presented to the First Congress of Soviets, included the eight-hour working day for adults; a six-hour day for adolescents between 16 and 18; and one of no more than four hours for those between 14 and 16. In the mining and other industries dangerous to health, where the handling of lead, zinc, and similar material was involved, the working day was limited to six hours. It was stipulated also that night work, between 9 P.M. and 6 A.M., must be shorter by one hour than day work. No overtime was to be allowed except with the special approval of the inspectors of industries. The length of the working day included half an hour for lunch, and every working person was to be guaranteed at least 42 hours of rest each week. After six months' work in the same place, everyone was to be entitled to a two weeks' yearly vacation with pay. Wages were to be fixed by the employees together with the management, or proprietors, by agreement. Women were paid at the same rate as men, and all must be paid in cash. For overtime work, if approved by the inspectorate, the wage is doubled. No fines or any other deductions from wages were allowed.

Women are exempt from unhealthy occupations. They cannot be employed on any work where the carrying of heavy weights is necessary. No women under 18 years of age, nor the expectant or nursing mothers, are allowed to work on night shifts. Every working woman is entitled to be excused from work for eight weeks before and eight weeks after confinement in the case of those occupied in manual work and six weeks for clerical workers, always with pay. Collective bargaining is recognized as the normal basis of employment and contracts may stand for no longer than one year. Special sections of the Labor Law are devoted to industrial hygiene and to social-insurance. Another is devoted to the trade-unions, and the last of all deals with the enforcement of the Labor Law and the inspectorate of industries.

OTHER BILLS AND RESOLUTIONS PASSED BY THE CONGRESS

In addition to the measures already mentioned the Congress considered a law of economic character dealing with industry, trade, finances, taxes, and communal policies. Another law was passed enumerating ways and means of building up the Soviets, including regulations for elections, for the organization of the Soviets and the routine of their work, and for the functions of various organs of the new régime. A resolution concerning the Red Army outlined the problems confronting the armed forces of Revolution and authorized the Central Executive Committee of the Congress to form a Supreme Military Council. This Council was charged with the task of purging the Red Armies of undesirable elements, and of enhancing the fighting ability of the Red forces both in regard to number and quality. The establishment of arsenals and other factories and shops engaged in manufacturing arms and war materials, of military training academies and hospitals, was provided for in this resolution as well.

A resolution concerning national "minorities" recommended the legal equalization of the Mongols, Thibetans, Annamites, the Miao tribes, and other similar groups inhabiting China. It established the opposition of the Soviets to granting to the Chinese any privileges denied to the others. It approved the idea of self-determination and stressed the fallacy of the assertion so often advanced by enemies of the Soviets, that the Russians intended to subjugate the Chinese. In connection with this the resolution emphasized adherence to the idea of independence or autonomy of certain parts of the country, if the population of those places expressed a desire for independence or autonomy, specifically establishing the right of Outer Mongolia to retain its present independence.

Finally, the Congress issued a Manifesto addressed to the toiling masses and the governments of the whole world announcing the foundation of the Chinese Soviet Republic, and the establishment of its government and that government's program. This Manifesto declared for immediate abrogation of all the unequal treaties, concluded with the Powers by the previous Chinese governments; for annulment of all the foreign debts incurred by the ruling classes and used for the oppression of the masses; for the immediate evacuation of all the settlements occupied by foreigners and the withdrawal of the foreign troops from the Chinese territories; and for confiscation of all the foreign banks, business enterprises, mines and railways, and so forth, held by foreign capitalists. In the final paragraph the Congress declared its indignation at and willingness to fight against the Japanese invasion of Manchuria, and closed with an appeal to the toiling masses of the world to prepare themselves for the civil war against world-wide reaction.

THE KUO-MIN-TANG CONGRESS IN SESSION

On November 12th, simultaneously with the Congress of Soviets, the Fourth Congress of the Kuo-min-tang opened at Nanking. In the course of its sessions it was stated that "the extermination of the Red Menace" was the major task of the Nanking Government, Japanese aggression in Manchuria notwithstanding.

The Minister of War, General Ho Ying-ching, rendered his report on the outcome of the anti-Red campaign, of which he was the commander. "The menace has not been entirely removed," he declared, and attributed the difficulty in dealing with that menace to the fact that "the Reds all hide in the mountains." He stated frankly that "the inhabitants in the bandit-infested regions are giving their support to the outlaw bands and government troops find it extremely difficult to obtain the assistance of the people in securing food or in the transportation of their ammunition and military equipment." Speakers at the Kuo-min-tang Congress expressed optimism not over the future victories of the forces of reaction, said an article in the *China Forum* of May, 1932, but over the fact that "diseases of epidemic proportions have broken out in their (*i.e.,* the Red's) camps, and because of the lack of medical help, many are perishing. With the approach of the cold Winter their hardships are steadily growing worse as very few of the bandits have winter clothing."

As a matter of fact we are now in a position to see that

neither the epidemics, nor the cold Winter, and even several cold Winters, helped the Nankingites, for the Soviet régimes continued to exist, and, as we know, the anti-Communist campaigns of Chiang Kai-shek and his generals achieved little or nothing.

CALL FOR SECOND SOVIET CONGRESS

The *Red Banner,* the organ of the Chinese Communist Party, published in the Summer of 1933 a call for the Second National Soviet Congress to be held at Juichin, the Soviet Capital in Kiangsi. The Congress was expected to convene on December 11, 1933, the sixth anniversary of the Canton Commune, but apparently because of the new anti-Red campaign, was postponed, and actually came into session on January 22, 1934.

The Second Congress was called "to make a general survey of the Soviets during the past two years." [7] The Manifesto, signed by Mao Tse-tung, president of the Provisional Soviet Government, "reviews the betrayals of the Kuo-min-tang in the face of the Imperialist attack, recalls the offers of the Red Armies to join the fight against the invaders, and points out that in the Soviet districts the forces of Imperialism and exploitation are things of the past. It declares that two ways only are open to the masses of China: one way leading to colonial subjection under the Imperialists and the Kuo-min-tang, the other to the power of the Soviets; and that under Imperialist-Kuo-min-tang rule the worker-peasant masses and soldiers suffer from hunger and death, from the brutalities of exploitation by landlords, capitalists and militarists. Under the power of the Soviets, says the Manifesto, this exploitation has been done away with. Toiling peasants share their lands with the fighters of the Red Armies. Workers are protected by the

[7] *China Forum,* Shanghai, October 4, 1933, pp. 9-10.

Soviet Labor Act. Economic reconstruction has greatly improved the standard of living of the worker-peasant masses.

"Under Soviet rule," continues the Manifesto, "workers and peasants enjoy complete political freedom. They have wrenched political control from their exploiters. For the first time in the history of China, workers and peasants are governing themselves. They have become the ruling classes, with the working class in command. These facts plainly indicate that the road to the power of the Soviets is the only road to salvation of the Chinese masses. They also explain why the Kuo-min-tang and the Imperialists are desperately attacking the Red Armies and the Soviet districts with all their strength. The heroic Red Armies have smashed successive drives of the Kuo-min-tang and Imperialists who are now preparing a sixth offensive, on an even larger and more brutal scale. The smashing of the Red Armies is a necessary prerequisite to the complete colonial subjection of China. That is why the Imperialists and their Kuo-min-tang puppets are concentrating their forces toward this end."

The Manifesto concluded with an appeal to the Chinese masses to coöperate in crushing the new Kuo-min-tang offensive and carrying the struggle forward to the overthrow of the Kuo-min-tang régime.[8]

[8] See in the Appendices the Report of Mao Tse-tung before the 2nd Congress, on January 22, 1934.

CHAPTER XI

THE PRESENT-DAY STATUS

EXTENT OF SOVIETIZATION

IT is difficult to define accurately the area of the Soviet régimes in China, at any given moment. Their boundaries are constantly shifting. The Red Armies advance as rapidly in one direction as they retreat in another under the pressure of their enemies from Nanking. Accordingly the so-called Soviet areas are Soviet in fact only so long as they remain in the rear of their own troops. This does not mean, of course, that with every withdrawal of a Red detachment the Soviet influence disappears from the area previously occupied. Often enough the sympathy for the Soviets will be strong enough to survive a more or less temporary occupation by the government troops. This fact, however, makes it still more difficult to make precise territorial definition. The Sovietized areas accordingly must be regarded as including certain districts temporarily occupied by Nanking, as well as those entirely controlled by the Communists.

However their actual borders may shift, these districts admittedly occupy a large territory, variously estimated as covering from one-sixth to one-fifth of the entire area of China proper. They include (1) the Central Soviet area in Kiangsi; (2) the scattered districts in the provinces of Honan, Hupeh, and Anhwei, to the North of the Yangtze River, and in Hunan to the South; and (3) lesser areas in Kwangsi and Kwangtung.

To these may be added remnants in Fukien, dispersed after the suppression of the recent Fukien rebellion by Nanking; a new and, apparently, rapidly expanding area in Szechwan; and a few smaller areas scattered through other provinces.

With the formation of the Central Government, declares Wellington Koo, six sectional or regional governments were created for the following areas:

(1) South-West of Kiangsi;
(2) The border districts of Fukien, Kiangsi and Kwangtung;
(3) North-East of Kiangsi;
(4) The border districts of Hupeh, Hunan and Anhwei;
(5) The border districts of Hunan, Hupeh and Kiangsi;
(6) The border districts of Hunan and Hupeh.

Three years later, at the end of 1933, one of the Chinese Communist leaders, Wang Ming,[1] was already able to recognize two large Soviet areas: (1) a Central region, to which belonged the Soviets of the Southern Kiangsi, Western Fukien, Northern Kwangtung and the border district of Kiangsi-Hunan-Hupeh, totaling about 50 hsiens, with a population of approximately fifteen million;[2] and (2) another large area in which are merged the Soviet districts of the Western Honan-Hupeh and of the Anhwei-Honan-Hupeh borders. Besides these two, he said, there were eight smaller areas.

Population: In all, the Soviet areas have a population of from sixty to eighty million[3] according to various estimates. Nor, most probably, is the higher of these figures exaggerated, for the provinces where the Soviets are found are very densely populated. According to G. Cressey[4] in 1926 there were:

[1] *Problemi Kitaia,* No. 11, 1933, p. 5.
[2] *Soviets in China,* 1933, p. 21.
[3] The *Soviets in China* gives the first and the article by Yolk in the *Problemi Kitaia,* No. 11, 1933, p. 27, the second figure.
[4] George Cressey, *China's Geographic Foundations.* McGraw-Hill, New York, 1934, p. 55.

In Anhwei .... over 20 mil.	In Kiangsi .... over 27 mil.
In Honan 35	In Fukien 14
In Hupeh 28	In Kwangtung 36
In Hunan 40	In Szechwan 52

The density of population in these provinces and their economic plight do much to explain the success of Sovietization, and in this connection it may be interesting to quote a few lines written by Dr. Sun Yat-sen to Li Hung-chang in 1894. "At present," wrote Dr. Sun, "China is already suffering from over-population, which will bring impending danger in its wake. She is confronted with a great many hidden uprisings and frequent famines. It is extremely difficult for the populous masses to make a living even during good years, and in time of great drought and famine, many people will starve to death. Our food problem is already very acute. The situation will be much worse as times goes on. . . ." [5]

CHARACTERISTICS OF THE AREAS

Up to the Summer of 1934, at least, practically all the Soviet areas were to be found in the South of China, which is, generally speaking, a land of green hills and wooded mountains, varied by goodly amount of level land suitable for cultivation. It is famous for its elaborate system of canals providing irrigation for the rice-fields and the bamboo woods. The abundant rainfall of these provinces usually guarantees them from drought, but the mighty rivers are always menacing with floods. The growing season here is from nine to twelve months, and therefore two or even three crops a year are raised. The teeming population of these provinces is crowded into cities, characterized by their narrow streets in marked contrast with the broad thoroughfares in the North. Here the people are shorter in stature than in the North. They speak a number of dialects, and are considered more radical and revolutionary

[5] As quoted by G. Cressey in his *China's Geographic Foundations*.

in their tendencies than the stolid and conservative Northerners.

The Central Soviet region, in Kiangsi, is predominantly agricultural. No large industries are found there; but the manufacture of textiles, paper and camphor—not to mention the mining industry—is carried on after a primitive fashion in the form of small enterprises. The South-Western part of this area is mountainous, covered with forests, and almost roadless, which makes the region not only exceedingly well adapted to guerrilla warfare but a practically impregnable fortress for the Red Armies. The second large area, that in Hupeh, is highly important to the "Reds" because it commands the middle course of the Yangtze, making possible a threat to Nanking and the control of the vast hinterland whose trade concentrates at Shanghai. That explains, says Dr. Wellington Koo, "the desperate efforts which the Red Armies have never ceased to exert to cut the Peiping-Hankow Railway, and to seize Wuchang, Hankow and Hanyang"—the three cities jointly known as Wuhan. This area too is primarily agricultural; the neighborhood of the Tung-ting Lake being one of the richest granaries of China, with rice, cotton and tea as staple crops. There is also some mining of coal and iron-ores. Among the smaller areas those in North-Eastern Kiangsi and Southern Anhwei and Chekiang are known for the porcelain manufactures and the mining of iron ores at Yufon and Paoshin in Anhwei, and of coal at Pingsiang, in Kiangsi. The province of Szechwan is richly endowed with a variety of natural resources. Coal and iron ores are widely distributed, and the production of salt in that province dates back to a period prior to the Christian era.

The average acreage per person in these provinces was estimated by D. K. Lieu and Chen Cheng-min [6] as follows:

[6] Statistics of Farm Land in China in the *Chinese Economic Journal*, March, 1928.

in Kiangsi ....3.5 mou [7] of farmland per person;
in Hunan 3.3
in Hupeh 5.4
in Fukien 2.2
in Anhwei 5.0
in Szechwan 2.5

In the opinion of G. Cressey almost all land suitable for cultivation in these regions is already utilized to the limit, but others contend that a certain amount of arable land is still not fully utilized.

GOVERNMENT

The supreme authority in the Chinese Soviet Republic is vested in the Congress of Soviets, and the government consists of the Central Executive Committee, representing the Congress of Soviets when the latter is not in session, and a Cabinet or Council of Commissars, which include the Commissars of the Interior, Foreign Affairs, Agriculture, Labor, Education, Finance and Defense. Most of the delegates to the Congress, and consequently of its Executive Committee and the higher officials, are members of the Communist Party of China. The head of the Central Government is Mao Tse-tung.

The industrial workers have the strongest representation in the Soviets, as they are considered the leaders of the Revolution. It is difficult to ascertain if all the departments of the Soviet Government are actually functioning, and if so with what success, but such documents as the Constitution of the Chinese Soviet Republic and the Land and Labor Laws give a fairly adequate idea of the programs and policy. They may be regarded as the blue-prints of an elaborate machine not yet completed but already partly in operation. A number of resolutions of the Comintern relating to the situation in China and

[7] One mou is approximately equal to one-sixth of an acre.

suggesting remedies for its shortcomings are also of great
assistance in forming some idea of what is actually taking place
in China and what is planned for the future. They make clear
the nature of the errors already made in the execution of the
plans of the Chinese Soviet Government, and offer suggestions
for the straightening of the course of events in accordance with
the "general line" of policy, drawn not only with regard to the
general principles of revolutionary theory and practice but also
with careful consideration of the peculiarities of China. Finally,
a large number of letters from the Chinese Soviet areas enables
us to some extent to compare the theory with the actual situation and so to judge to what extent the practice differs from the
plan.

Agrarian Situation

Under pressure of unrest among the peasants the Kuo-min-
tang adopted in the Summer of 1930 a new Land Law promising agrarian reforms. This law had been under consideration
for more than two years—the Nanking régime having had the
original draft ready as early as 1928. Before the 1911 Revolution the agrarian reform scheme outlined in Dr. Sun Yat-sen's
program actually advocated the nationalization of land. It was
based in general on the single-tax idea of Henry George, as the
purpose was to concentrate rent in the hands of the State. But
when the Revolution actually took place Yuan Shi-kai and those
whom he represented had opposed this far-reaching change as
affecting their property rights. Dr. Sun Yat-sen had no choice
but to withdraw his scheme, as an open revolt of the peasants
was no part of his plan. Soon afterwards Dr. Sun resigned,
and his party, the Kuo-min-tang, did not insist either then
or later on putting into effect the agrarian part of his program.
Even when Dr. Sun himself returned to power, he did not
renew his recommendation for the nationalization of land,

and it never reappeared in the Kuo-min-tang's pledges. In his famous "Lectures" Dr. Sun advocated the slogan "Land to those who work it," but did not advance the principle of confiscation from the landlords. He did not even regard confiscation with compensation as feasible, but went no further than to favor the purchase of those lands, though prices were so high as to make any such transactions impossible for the overwhelming majority of peasants.

Dr. Sun was, indeed, mainly interested in the urban real estate with their sky-rocketing rentals; he wanted to transfer the control over them to the State as a means of increasing the income of the Treasury.[8] But that was in the period of 1923-25. Later on the agrarian program of the Kuo-min-tang underwent certain modifications, for the Revolution was entering a more advanced stage. It was necessary to do something to tempt the masses, whose support was so essential to the success of the Northern Campaign. Borodin and other advisers, naturally, were advocating a more radical policy, and so, finally, the Kuo-min-tang compromised on a 25% reduction of the rents, accompanied by a limitation of the rate of interest chargeable by moneylenders to 24%. That was the limit of the concessions acceptable to the propertied classes in control of the Kuo-min-tang. The more radical elements of the Wuhan Government were discussing in the Spring of 1927 the confiscation of "larger" estates, but that régime was already dying, and actually passed away before accomplishing anything of that kind even on paper. The "Lefts" of the Kuo-min-tang were inclined for a while to support the idea of wholesale confiscation of estates larger than 100 mou. But, after the defeat of the Wuhan group, the inauguration of the Nanking régime and suppression by the latter of a number of agrarian revolts,

[8] A. Eisenstadt, "Nationalization in the Theory of Sun Yat-sen." In the *Problemi Kitaia*, Nos. 4-5, 1930, pp. 119-145.

they changed their minds, and this radical measure ceased to carry weight in the Kuo-min-tang deliberations.

The Land Law of June, 1930, was no more, in the opinion of L. Madjar, than a codification of perpetual lease of land from the landlord by the tenants, who however, had no right to sublease it to other tenants. The maximum rent now allowed by the Law was 37.5% of the crop, which was no improvement on the 25% reduction introduced by the Kuo-min-tang earlier —for the rents were often 50% and more of the crop. Commenting on this Law, the author quoted above expressed the opinion that such a cut in rent could not satisfy the husbandmen, yet at the same time it appears to be the limit that the landlords are prepared to concede.

The principle of taxation adopted by the Kuo-min-tang, by which lands of better quality or under cultivation are less severely taxed than the inferior and untilled ground, seems to indicate that this law discriminates in favor of the rich, since they are the owners of the better lands. It is true that real estate in the cities is taxed on a progressive scale, since the greater the increase of the price on land may be the higher becomes the rate of the tax. This, however, is about all that remains of the Henry George program which originally inspired Dr. Sun Yat-sen and was included in the Kuo-min-tang creed.

At present the problem of redistribution of land seems the main concern of the leaders of the Chinese Revolution. On the proper solution of the agrarian question in the Sovietized areas, they believe, depends the future course of the entire movement. If successful in this, the Soviets will certainly attract more adherents from the neighboring provinces. On the other hand, if they fail in this cardinal problem, they will be forced into a prolonged struggle of uncertain outcome. As a matter of fact, a bitter struggle between the poor and the formerly well-to-do is even now being waged in the Sovietized areas, for the formerly prosperous are insisting that land should be distributed on the basis of ability to cultivate with the necessary machinery, implements, and so forth. "They are not fighting against Communism—nobody is dreaming of introducing Communism in China at once, right now," remarks Safaroff, "they oppose equalization." [9] The idea of confiscating the lands of the rich is approved even by the Chinese "kulaks," [10] who are willing enough to receive more land for themselves, but who oppose giving equal parts to all. The Communists, on the other hand, insist that the only proper way to solve the problem is to divide the land equally, and that any other form of redistribution will be useless.

In contrast to the Kuo-min-tang Land Law of 1930 the Communist Land Law of 1931 is directed toward a complete overhauling of the agrarian system. As a first step it prescribes confiscation of grounds belonging to the landlords, gentry, tuhao, and so forth, or the monasteries and the like, eventually leading to nationalization of land. Immediate nationalization is opposed for various reasons, including the fact that since Sovietization is not yet accomplished in most of China nationalization can as yet be only local and only partially effective. After confiscation, redistribution on an equal basis is indicated, for without this second step the well-to-do peasants—who are usually the usurers as well—and the "kulaks" are likely to regain control. As we have seen in Chapter X, the project of agrarian reform passed by the First Conference, in May, 1930, suggested redistributing only those lands confiscated from the landlords, and excepting those belonging to the well-to-do peasants. The Land Law approved by the First Congress of Soviets, on the

[9] G. Safaroff, "Revolution and Counter-Revolution in China," in the *Problemi Kitaia*, Nos. 4-5, 1930, p. 26.
[10] This term is borrowed from the Russian terminology, and means "feast"—*i.e.*, the peasant who by all sorts of ingenuity acquires the control over his co-villagers, and becomes an exploiter of them.

other hand, frowned upon this discrimination and extended the same principle to the lands of the well-to-do peasants, in order to avoid inequality and to prevent the transformation of the wealthier peasantry into landlords of a new type.

It is realized that confiscation and redistribution of land will not suffice to settle the agrarian problem to the complete satisfaction of the peasants. Land remains scarce. Consequently the next measures are directed toward amelioration of the peasant's lot and toward improved methods of cultivation by the introduction of modern agricultural machinery, improved irrigation and drainage, the selection of seeds, fertilizers, and above all the establishment of cheap credit facilities. Without advocating immediate collectivization or the creation of state-farms, the leaders nevertheless consider it the only proper way in the future and look on it as the system best adapted to contemporary conditions.

Equalitarian redistribution of land, they say, normally leads to the growth of Capitalistic ideology in the village. But this state of affairs is merely transitory; it meets the demands of the peasants at this juncture, and has one good compensatory feature in strengthening the rural population and making it a more valuable ally for the urban or industrial proletariat. Only through the coöperation of the industrial proletariat and the peasantry can the Revolution advance from the bourgeois-democratic to the socialistic stage which is its goal.

At present the peasants are chiefly interested in obtaining more land provided by the confiscated holdings of the landlords. But these peasants are well aware that when the Government troops arrive, and the Soviets are forced out, their lands must be returned to the former owners. The Nanking program for "economic and political reconstruction of the areas rehabilitated from the Soviets," include the following points: (1) All lands pertaining to which titles or other documents still exist shall be returned to their former owners, and (2) in cases when the documents and boundary-marks are destroyed the question of restoration of the property shall be discussed by the conference of the landlords and gentry." [11] For this reason alone the peasantry would be ill disposed to support Chiang Kai-shek.

Opposed to equalitarian redistribution, especially if it means redistribution of cattle and machinery as well, the "kulaks" have tried, sometimes successfully, to enlist the support of the middle-class peasants, particularly those who feared that redistribution might deprive them of their extra cattle, beasts of burden, and so forth. As the result of such coöperation certain "kulaks" have not only managed to gather into their own hands more and better land than they possessed before the Revolution, but have resumed their old control of the poorer and the less successful peasants.

The Communists must face this organized and very often quite stubborn opposition to the new order, and in doing so must proceed with much tact in order to avoid making enemies.

A number of counter-revolutionary plots, mostly led by "kulaks," have been exposed and frustrated. Among these was the Futian affair at Kiangsi in December, 1930, which was headed by the A-B's, or Anti-Bolsheviks' League. Others were the counter-revolutionary movement of the Social-Democrats in Fukien in March-April, 1931, and the plot of the "reorganizationists" in September of the same year in the Hupeh-Honan-Anhwei border area. All these plots were supported, if not actually led, by the "kulaks," coöperating with the landlords, gentry, tuhao, and other "counter-revolutionary" elements.[12]

[11] "Sin-wen-bao," October 7, 1932. Quoted from the *Problemi Kitaia,* No. 11, 1933, p. 34. It is true that there was some discussion at Nanking to the effect that lands redistributed by the Soviets ought to remain in the hands of the new owners after the rehabilitation of those regions, but these were hardly anything more than mere words.
[12] *Soviets in China,* p. 16.

As we have seen in Chapter II, the Taipings were opposed to inequality in distribution of wealth. In drafting their agrarian reforms, they took cognizance of the different interests of rich and poor, and advanced the idea of redistribution of land, coupled with communal ownership of movable property. The land system of the Heavenly Kingdom was set forth in a document published in the third year of the Taipings' rule. According to this document land was to be divided into nine classes, graded according to the fertility of the soil, in such proportions that one mou of the first quality land should be equal to three mou of the ninth. Land was to be allotted according to the number of the mouths in the family, and in each case a fair division of good and bad land was to be made. Particular attention was given to the famine problem and the principle was established that famine areas must be helped by more fortunate places, where grain was in abundance. The document also embodied an interesting declaration to the effect that "all shall eat food, all shall have clothes, money shall be shared, and in all things there shall be equality; no man shall be without food or warmth." [13]

Such was the program, but there is no evidence that a redistribution of land was effected along these lines. Some of these reforms, however, were at least partially instituted while the Taipings were in Nanking; for it is known that the titles on land were destroyed then as they are destroyed in the Sovietized areas now.

INDUSTRY, TRADE, FINANCES

Large-scale industries, as we have seen, never existed in most of the Sovietized areas; and with the arrival of the "Reds" even the smaller industries in these localities discontinued activity, since their proprietors could neither feel security nor

[13] G. E. Taylor, *ibid.*, pp. 597-598.

vision the process of readjusting their work to the newly created order. In other words, the abandoned shops remained abandoned until such time as the new administration could find people to take care of them and to renew the production—in some cases not an easy task. There were, of course, additional reasons why certain industries had to stop production; in some cases it was impossible to secure the raw materials, formerly imported from other provinces, since the Sovietized areas were cut off from these sources by the blockade of the Nanking troops. In some instances, too, the obstacle was found at the other end, as the blockade prevented the exporting of many articles manufactured in Sovietized areas, for which there was no demand in the Communist provinces.

The nationalization of industrial, transport, trade and banking enterprises by the Soviets is now theoretically applied only to foreign firms. Even the foreigners are allowed to continue in trade, since their businesses, though technically nationalized, may be left in their hands as concessions to be run in accordance with the new laws and regulations. As for the enterprises of Chinese manufacturers they are not even nationalized, though strict industrial control by the workers is instituted in some of them, and the others are waiting for it, pending the attempts of the Government to find and prepare the personnel for building the administrative machine. If one can rely on the information coming from the Soviet regions—and it is probably reliable— the workers' lot has been considerably improved through the introduction of the eight-hour day, an increase in wages, the abolition of the contract system,[14] encouragement of the Red trade-unions' activities, inauguration of social insurance, en-

[14] Employment in factories in China is usually secured through a middleman or contractor, who, after securing a definite understanding with the employers directly, makes an arrangement with the workers. The contractor has full freedom in respect of employment and is empowered to hire whomsoever he pleases at the lowest possible wages, the difference going to him as "commission."

forcement of rules of industrial hygiene, and protection of working women and others.

China had no properly formulated organ of labor of any consequence until the foundation of the Secretariat of Chinese Labor at Shanghai in 1920. In the first year of the Republic, 1912, there had been some labor unrest at Changsha resulting in an attempt at organized effort, but this "labor movement" soon expired. Further attempts were made in 1913 and in 1916, but with no avail. The first considerable organized labor demonstrations occurring in 1917, simultaneously with the Russion Revolution. By 1922, however, the First Labor Conference was held at Canton "to promote friendly relations among the workers throughout the Republic, and to devise ways and means to raise the general standard of life of working people.[15]

The Second Labor Conference was held in 1925, also at Canton, and adopted resolutions dealing with political action, economic emancipation, problems of organization, and labor-farmer coöperation. With regard to political action the belief was expressed at this Conference that "the only way by which the workers could improve their economic status was by securing the control of the Government" for "the economic power of the Capitalists was such that they could control the governmental machinery and abuse the army, police and law courts to restrict the freedom of the workers in their struggle for economic equality. Furthermore, the interests of the working class being in conflict with those of the imperialists, militarists, and capitalists a class struggle must necessarily ensue. The political struggle of the working class must therefore aim at improving the economic conditions of the workers by the overthrow of the capitalist class and the capture of the governmental

[15] Dr. Lin Tung-hai, "The Labor Movement in China," in the *People's Tribune*, April 16, 1933. Shanghai, pp. 285-302.

machinery. And to accomplish these objects the use of force was deemed essential." [16]

The Third National Labor Conference took place at Canton in May, 1926, and attracted 502 delegates representing 699 unions with 1,241,000 workers. At that time the political leaders of the Revolution were anxious to have the coöperation of the workers and accordingly the Labor movement was encouraged and its aims declared to be dear to the hearts of the Kuo-min-tang. Thus the Manifesto issued by the Third Conference and the various resolutions passed therein not only laid emphasis on the importance of working-class solidarity but described the Chinese working class as the forerunner of the Revolution, and the workers as the vanguard of the Nationalist movement against Imperialism. The Manifesto called upon the workers to coöperate with the farmers. They were also called upon to support the National Government whole-heartedly by participating in the Northern Expedition—this with the object of eliminating the Northern militarists and in the hope of "securing for the workers freedom of assembly, of speech, and of the press, as well as the legal establishment of a minimum wage and shorter hours of labor." Of course at that juncture the Chinese Revolution was advancing in coöperation with the Communists, which is why the Conference recommended to the workers that they follow the leadership of the Comintern. This was stressed still more emphatically at the Fourth Labor Conference held at Hankow in June, 1927, and especially at the Pan-Pacific Trade-Union Congress, in session there at the same time, for it was attended by delegates not only from all over China but also from the Soviet Union, Japan, Korea, the United States, Great Britain, France and Dutch Indies.

With the advent of the Nanking régime the Labor movement of China was officially dead. "The purifying of the Kuo-min-

[16] Dr. Lin Tung-hai, *ibid.,* pp. 285-286.

tang from communistic influences resulted in the virtual suppression of the Labor Movement and of all union activities." [17]
It was not until 1929, after the promulgation of the Labor Union Law, that it made even a nominal reappearance, and even now all labor activities are strictly supervised by the Kuo-min-tang, if not actually suppressed. The workers under Nanking control have only the power to organize strikes, which are numerous and frequent. Even the official estimates published in the Kuo-min-tang press granted that over half a million workers participated in strikes during 1930, more than 700,000 in 1931 and more than one million in 1932.[18] The workers under Chiang Kai-shek are openly supporting the Communists. Many of them join the Red Trade Unions [19] and many of them express their sympathy with the Soviets by taking up collections among themselves for the material support of the "Reds." Little though they earn they are still willing to sacrifice something for the "cause." Women sew various articles for the "Red" soldiers; children in schools make collections of coppers, and a Society of Friends of the Red Army has been organized at Shanghai. After the bombardment of certain Soviet villages by the Nanking airplanes the Shanghai workers opened a campaign to collect money to buy and send an airplane to be called "The Shanghai Worker," to the Soviets; while other workers prefer direct participation and join the Red Armies in person.[20] As for the Red Trade Unions they are not as yet well organized and have no good leaders in the regions beyond the Soviet

[17] Dr. Lin Tung-hai, *ibid.*, p. 299.
[18] "The Labor Movement in China," an article in the *Problemi Kitaia*, No. 11, 1933, pp. 210-234, and also an article by P. Mif in the *Communistichesky Internazional*, April 1, 1933.
[19] According to Wellington Koo (*ibid.*, p. 775), in Shanghai alone there were in 1929 sixty thousand workers belonging to the Red Unions, and in his estimate about 15-20 per cent of the total, all over China, are affiliated with the Red Unions.
[20] On several occasions, too, the striking workers have received money from the Soviet areas. Such was the case in the trolley-car strike at Shanghai.

borders. In addition their work is seriously hindered by the "opposition," represented by the followers of Chen Tu-hsiu and the remnants of the Li Li-san group. At present the Red Trade Unions are concentrating their efforts on the unification of all these elements and on gaining sympathy among the workers, in order to organize Labor on a large scale in preparation for an open uprising. But the most effective influence on the working masses outside of the Soviet areas comes not from the Red Trade Unions, but from the rumors penetrating into the factories and shops about the better living conditions of their brethren in the Soviet districts. The Soviets have already done much in this respect; working hours have actually been cut down in all the Soviet-controlled and even some of the privately operated industries, to eight from fourteen to sixteen hours a day; wages are higher than before; social-insurance is in operation; hospitals are opening and public health work is in progress.

As for trade in the Sovietized areas, the policy is to leave individual merchants unmolested provided they comply with the new regulations. The open market and free exchange are not only tolerated but considered at this juncture as the most feasible methods of distribution. Along with private trade, of course, coöperative consumers' societies and coöperative manufacturing are being developed, but their number so far is not very large.

With the beginning of control exercised over the marketing and exchange of commodities, an appreciable difference between the prices of primary products in the Soviet districts and those in the rest of China was discernible, in the opinion of *China Forum.*[21]

The introduction of the system of progressive taxation,

[21] "Five Years of Kuomintang Reaction," a reprint from the *China Forum*, Shanghai, 1932, p. 134-5.

applied to the farm lands—single tax—by which the major burden of taxation is expected to rest on the well-to-do elements has naturally affected the traders too. The imposition of a progressive business tax means that the major burden is similarly expected to rest on the richer merchants rather than on the smaller traders. Small and middle traders are protected by the Soviet régime in the present phase of its development.

The same principle of leniency toward the existing institutions has been applied in the Sovietized areas to the banks, certain of which were allowed to continue their operations, always provided that they readjusted their policies to the régime and complied with the new laws. A number of Soviet Banks were opened also, and new banknotes were freely circulating even outside the Soviet areas, but finally Nanking issued orders prohibiting their use and, to some extent, they are no longer acceptable beyond the Soviet borders.[22]

Economic conditions in the Soviet districts are comparatively bad, partly because of the scarcity of certain commodities in these territories, partly owing to the blockade. Other factors include the lack of qualified industrial and financial leaders, and trained workers; and the constant struggle with the Chiang Kai-shek forces. But even so the lot of the masses in these districts seems better than in most of the areas under the Nanking Government. Such, at any rate, was the opinion expressed by certain foreign missionaries in 1932 and published in the *New York Times*.[23] "Foreign missionaries writing from the zones recently overrun by the Reds," declared this paper, "report that the peasants and common people are giving a hearty welcome to the returning Communists. They said that

[22] In their turn the Soviets, naturally, are not encouraging the circulation of the depreciating, multiform currency of the militarists in the Sovietized areas.

[23] January 31, 1932, quoted from *Soviet China*, by James and R. Doonping. New York, 1932, p. 22.

after comparing their status under previous Communist rule with the bad government and confiscatory taxation enforced upon them after the arrival of the Nanking troops last Summer, they enjoyed greater liberty and a greater degree of prosperity under the Reds than under Nanking." Since then, however, the Soviets have succeeded in extending their control over more territory and have worked for the improvement of the lot of the toiling masses for another two years. One may be pardoned for believing that if such was the situation in 1932 it must be still better at present.

"The important fact to register from the viewpoint of the liberated masses of the Soviet districts is not that they have not yet been able to make much positive progress," wrote another close observer,[24] "but that these millions have broken their chains, are raising their heads, conscious of a new freedom— conscious, indeed, for the first time of the very fact that they exist as human beings! With energies unloosed and the forces of repression lifted, they are making the smallest beginnings at the forging of a new life and a new world. Their success has so far been necessarily meagre—but the gulf that separates their condition of life from that of the toiling millions still under the yoke of the Reaction is the gulf between masses themselves holding the power to make or mar their destiny—and masses still held in tradition."

EDUCATION, HEALTH WORK

In spite of all the difficulties they are facing, and especially the lack of funds, the Soviets are striving, and not without success, to promote the cultural development of the masses. A number of elementary and other educational institutions, some of which are called Lenin-schools, are already functioning throughout the Sovietized areas. Special educational work is

[24] "Five Years of Kuomintang Reaction," Shanghai, 1932, p. 134.

also carried on in the Red Army, which in its turn is trying to contribute toward the enlightenment of the people. The Red Army is widely regarded as a constructive factor, and actually is doing much good for the population, as numerous letters from those areas reveal.

The Chinese theater also plays its part in the raising of the cultural level of the people, and its repertory now includes a number of new revolutionary plays. The press, controlled by the Soviets, is naturally doing its part. Some of the leading publications are: the *Lenin Weekly,* a magazine devoted to Marxism-Leninism; *Party Life,* mainly for members of the Communist Party; *The Soviet,* a popular periodical; *Hung-chi* or the *Red Banner,* the official organ of the Central Executive Committee of the Communist Party of China; and the *Red Fighter* and the *Life in the Red Army,* both for the Red soldiers. Outside of the Sovietized areas there are also periodicals and newspapers, such as the *Shanghai-Bao* or the *Shanghai News,* published clandestinely at that port.

The extent of the cultural work in the Sovietized areas can be properly understood only after grasping the fact that everything is done on a large scale. The masses participate in and control all such activities, though, undoubtedly under supervision of the Communists.

THE RED ARMIES

As we have seen in Chapter VIII, describing the anti-Communist Campaigns, the total force of the Red Armies of the Chinese Soviets was estimated at the opening of the year 1934 as 350,000 regulars and about 600,000 volunteers. In characterizing its personnel the *Memoranda* prepared for the Lytton Commission said: "Its nucleus consists of former Government soldiers or those who were associated with them. Those detachments with extremist tendencies rallied under the red flag in groups together with their Commanders after the rupture of the Kuo-min-tang and the Nationalist Government with the Communist Party. The number increased as individual deserters joined their ranks. The leaders might have definite revolutionary ideas, but the mass of the troops have only vague impressions rather than convictions. The majority of the soldiers under the command of Ho Lung and Chu Teh have on the whole good military discipline. With them are the former bandits, who have been attracted there by the bait of comparatively regular pay and of plunder after successful expeditions. Then there are the miserable, ruined peasants, victims of civil wars, or drought and floods. Lastly come those who are enrolled and recruited on the spot who, one can be certain, do not enter service out of any conviction. All these different elements join the same ranks and no wonder they are so heterogeneous. . . . The higher officers are perhaps better organized because a good number of them have received and continued to receive technical training in the different schools of the USSR. One may find among them non-Chinese elements (Koreans, Formosans, Annamites, Mongolians, Bouriats, etc.)." [25]

Quite a different story is told by the Communists. In the first stages of the revolutionary struggle, they say, there was, naturally a high percentage of professional soldiers in the ranks of the Red Armies. These included deserters from the government troops, as well as a large number of peasants who belonged either to the peasant societies or to the various secret societies, the membership of which always was quite mixed. The influx of deserters from the Nanking ranks continues, of course, to impair the Red ranks, but by now the major part of the latter consists of proletarians and poor peasants who are better selected and well disciplined. The Soviets are taking care to secure the best elements for their fighting force.

[25] Wellington Koo, *ibid.,* pp. 759-760.

At the end of 1933 there were four Red Armies and a number of smaller units. Though operating in various widely scattered regions, their actions were coördinated to a certain extent by the directives coming from the Central Soviet Government.

Side by side with the regular army are the Red Guards and other auxiliary organizations. The Red Guards are divided into the active and the territorial groups, both employed mainly in the rear to cover the communications of the army and to protect the population. Discipline is reported to be very strict and is based not on cruelty and subservience but on enlightenment and coöperation. For the latter purpose propaganda and educational work in general have a prominent place in the Soviet Army life.

As the result of their numerical growth, better equipment, accumulated experience and constant training, the Red Armies no longer limit their activities to guerrilla warfare, but are now engaging also in major encounters on the lines of general tactics.

The regular tactics of the Red Armies described in their manuals of military instructions, as quoted in Wellington Koo's *Memoranda* of 1932, consisted of the following features:

1. Attack the Government forces in the sovietized regions, or in the regions where there are thick forests or wild mountains, and lead them to an ambush.
2. Separate these troops in making them pursue you, then turn around and strike them at their flank or their rear.
3. Where the Government forces are concentrated, avoid them by dispersing; when they are in an inferior position, converge the attacks upon them or surround them.
4. Utilize the population of the sovietized districts to harass and frighten the Government forces (for example by planting red flags on the hills which surround them or by increasing the sound of the trumpets) or place the peasants in the vanguard and do not attack

with the main body of the Red Army until the enemy should be tired or be on the point of exhausting his munitions.

5. Do not attack the works of permanent defense, do not deliver yourselves up to arranged battles. Avoid fighting in the regions where the population is not yet sovietized.

6. Undermine the morale of the Government forces by the propaganda agents, farmers, workers and women.

Commenting on this Dr. Koo wrote: "The Communist armies conform themselves very precisely to these prescriptions so that it is rather difficult to join and destroy them. As soon as the Government troops arrive in any great number, the Communist detachments which do not have uniforms disperse, hide their arms and assume the appearance of innocent workers, who would combine again to attack the regular forces as soon as the latter, fooled by the quiet appearance of the country, are no longer on their guard. Furthermore, the Communist Armies operate only in the mountainous and woody regions which are difficult of access and deprived of means of communication. The Communist Armies go in for pitched battles only for possession of cities which they need, because it is from these cities that they raise a portion of their taxes and obtain their supplies. . . ." [26]

In the opinion of the Communists themselves the main strength of the Red Armies lies in the whole-hearted support received from the population, which is willing to feed and shelter the soldiers, to join them, if necessary, in the fight, to comfort and nurse the wounded, and to take care of the families of the soldiers when the latter are away from home. This loyalty of the population to the Red Armies also serves to demoralize the Government troops, who desert the ranks in increasing numbers as they learn of the way the population of the Soviet China is treating the Red soldiers.

[26] Wellington Koo, *ibid.*, pp. 761-762.

Even Dr. Koo's *Memoranda* asserted that 30% of the arms of the Reds has been supplied by Government troops joining the Communists. But after having read the story of the anti-Red Campaigns [27] one is inclined to consider this figure very modest. It must be much larger; and the Communists themselves have even nicknamed these recurrent campaigns the "new transports of arms."

[27] See Chapter VIII.

CHAPTER XII

PEASANT MOVEMENT OUTSIDE THE SOVIET AREAS

ESTIMATING the total area of China, including the border states, at about 4,278,000 square miles, and the total number of inhabitants at approximately 450,000,000, we arrive at an average density of population of only 105 persons per square mile. This does not seem bad at all, but unfortunately such figures are quite misleading. Of the enormous total area of over four million square miles China proper has only 1,532,-420, or about one-third; and if we exclude deserts and many high and rough mountainous regions, which are not arable, and certain regions with rainfall of less than 20 inches per year, we shall see an entirely different picture. Actually 83% of the entire population of China is found in about 17% of her territory, representing a density of more than 500 per square mile. This, incidentally, is an even higher rate than that of Japan, who continually points to her crowded living conditions as justification for her aggression and the occupation of Chinese territory.

The most thickly populated parts of China are the Middle and Lower Yangtze Valleys, where the average density is over 1,000; next comes the great plain of North China, where Hopeh, Shantung, Honan and Anhwei provinces are located, with an average of 650 per square mile. If all the cultivable land in China were divided equally there would only be three mou, or about half an acre, to each person.[1] But the land is not

[1] W. H. Wong, *The Distribution of Population and Land Utilization in China*, China Institute of Pacific Relations, Shanghai, 1933.

equally distributed and the acreage per person is appallingly inadequate especially in the Southern provinces. Dr. Chen Han-seng, estimates that 65% of the entire rural population of his country is in need of land.[2]

The overwhelming majority of the peasants of China are paupers, a great number are entirely landless, and have no choice but to work for the more "fortunate," and wealthy. Generally speaking, the majority of the peasants in the North are merely hired workers in the villages, while those in the South are mostly small tenants. In Hupeh, for instance, the landless and those with insufficient acreage were estimated by Dr. Chen at over 65%, and the majority of the landlords in that province do not cultivate their own land but are rather managers employing hired labor. In the Yangtze Delta, more-over, the landlords are little more than rent collectors; managing landlords being the exception. Furthermore, the monopoly of land-ownership in certain districts of that region has become so general that 3% of the population now possesses 80% of the land. Another phenomenon typical of the Yangtze Basin region is that the small and the middle landlords enjoy the predominancy in land ownership.[3]

In Kiangsu the overwhelming majority of the landlords do not manage their estates. Not more than 5% do. Yet, though they only form 5.7% of the total number of families, they possess over 47% of the land. In the mountainous region between the basins of the Hwai-Ho and Yangtze-Kiang, where the soil is inferior, the inequality of distribution of the land may be judged from the fact that over 65% of the total peasants are poor, and that this 65% holds only about one-fifth of the total soil. In Kwangtung the situation is similar. The poor families, constituting about 74% of the total, possesses

[2] Chen Han-seng, *The Present Agrarian Problem in China.* Shanghai, 1933.
[3] Dr. Chen, *ibid.,* p. 4.

less than one-fifth of the cultivated land, though the rich families, representing only 2% of the total number, have more than one-half of the total land.

The land-hunger of the poor peasants in China is aggravated by the parcellation system with its tendency to further divisions. This is "the surest barrier and obstacle against agricultural production, and against a rational treatment, conservation and improvement of the soil itself," writes Dr. Chen. In China the average yield even of rice is much lower than in other countries.[4]

At present, thinks Dr. Chen, the poor peasants in China have a faint hope of obtaining more land, for "under modern economic influence, the process of individualization of property in China has been going on for a century. State and community lands have been constantly usurped by big landowners, who practically, though illegally, enjoy a full monopoly of rent collection from these lands."[5] The system of community lands in China is also crumbling. "Temple land, which plays an important part in agrarian relations mostly in the Yangtze provinces, is being secretly mortgaged and sold by powerful monks, or publicly auctioned by local military authorities."[6]

It is true that land-taxes are not only rapidly rising but are increasing in excess of the advance in the rents. In Kiangsu, for example, the land-tax has increased by nearly 90% in the last ten years, and is very often collected for years in advance.[7] Thus many landlords are only too glad to sell their holdings, while others have flocked into cities, abandoning their land, and thus avoiding taxes. Heavy taxation, however, does not

[4] *E.g.*, in 1928-30 in China it was 18.9 quintals per hectare, though in Japan, 35.9; in the U. S. A., 22.7; in Italy, 46.8; and in Spain, 62.3.
[5] Dr. Chen, *ibid.*, p. 11.
[6] *Shun-Pao*, Shanghai, April 10, 1930, and *Chungking Shang-Wu-Ju-Pao*, February 7 and August 2, 1930.
[7] In certain districts of Szechwan the main land-tax was already collected for 20-40 years in advance.

mean the breaking up of landlordism itself, remarks Dr. Chen. "It simply hastens the downfall of those old landlords who, under modern circumstances have been rendered impotent to dodge the various land-taxes, and ultimately gives birth to new ones who are capable of evading or sustaining the same. Chinese taxes are very often progressive in name, but quite retrogressive in reality." [8] Powerful absentee landlords sometimes do not pay taxes at all, in which case their share of the tax burden falls on the shoulders of the resident families, most of whom are poor peasants.

At present, partly as the result of the Sovietization of many Southern counties where the tenant-farmer prevailed, partly as the result of the generally changing nature of politics and business, the number of landlords who are purely rent collectors is diminishing, while the number of those who command capital is increasing. These latter have been characterized by Henry See [9] as "quadrilateral beings: they are rent collectors, merchants, usurers, and administrative officers."

According to Dr. Chen, "the village administration in China is simply permeated by the omnipresent influence of the landlord. Tax, police, judicial, and educational systems are built upon the power of landlord. Poor peasants who fail to satisfy the landlord officials in tax and rent payments, are brutally imprisoned and tortured. The big landowners, landlords and the rich peasants, take advantage of the poverty of peasants, a poverty chiefly due to lack of land, and play with the twin balls of usury and trade capitals. They corner grain, manipulate prices, and extend loans of all sorts. As years go on, they double, treble, and manifoldly increase their original holdings of land property."

Because of the extremely small farms, poor peasants cannot

[8] Wong Yin-seng, *Requisitions and the Peasantry in North China* (in the Chinese). Shanghai, 1931.

[9] Henry See, *Esquisse d'une Histoire du Régime Agraire.* Paris, 1921.

secure the credit they need from the banks directly. Thus they have to apply to the usurers, and to pay from 36% to 60% per annum, and even more. Rich peasants in China dabble in usury and trade much as the landlords do. But owing to the land parcellation, heavy taxation, and the drastic drop in grain prices, they are rarely able to develop into capitalists nowadays.

If the heavy taxes oppress even the rich peasants and the landlords, they fall far more severely on the poor who are actually becoming pauperized. But even without the extra burden of taxation, what the tenants pay to the landlords in the shape of rent absorbs frequently not merely a part of their profit, to which they are entitled as possessors of their own instruments of productions, but also a part of their normal wages, which they would receive under different conditions for the same amount of labor. Rent in China usually amounts to 40% to 60% of harvest.[10]

Add to all this that the poor peasants in China are deprived of the necessary farming animals, implements and fertilizers, forcing them rapidly to surrender their tiny patches of land, and it is easy to see why they are so desperate, why they are ready to join any movement which promises better life, stricter justice, more land and more humane treatment.

"The boundless exploitation of the peasants by the landlords, the usurers, the piling taxation, arbitrarily imposed by the war lords, the effect of the world economic crisis, aggravated by the floods and the Japanese aggression, are the factors working for the growth of discontent in the countryside and prepare the ground for the Sovietization of new territories," writes Mr. P. Mif, in the *Communistichesky Internazional*.[11]

During the Summer of 1932 a wave of peasant uprisings,

[10] Dr. Chen, *ibid.,* p. 22.
[11] "News in Development of the Revolutionary Crisis in China," in the *Communistichesky Internazional,* April 1, 1933.

incited by hunger,[12] swept Kiangsu, Chekiang, Anhwei, Shensi
and other Central and North-Western provinces. These insurrections resulted in the creation of Soviets and formation of
Red Armies in a number of new areas. Early in 1932 the
XXIVth Red Corps was formed in the North-West, and in
October of the same year the XXVIth came into existence on
the border of Kansu and Shensi. In other words, the peasants
of the Northern and North-Western provinces began to join
the Soviet movement. The Communists of China claim that
they directed the armed uprising on the border of Hunan-
Kwangsi-Kweichou. They were the leading spirit in supporting
the "volunteers" who resisted the Japanese invaders in Manchuria.

One of the characteristics of the recent development of the
agrarian revolt, in the opinion of Eugene Kuo,[13] was the spread
of the uprisings from the remote villages of Kansu and Shensi
to the economically more advanced provinces of Kiangsu and
Chekiang. The first manifestations of these uprisings usually
are found in a refusal to pay taxes and rents. Then follow con-
fiscations of grain and other property of the wealthy. A second
important characteristic of the moment is that the peasant uprisings are involving larger and larger numbers. In some
instances several thousands of men, armed mostly with pitch-
forks, sickles, sticks, and so forth, and occasionally even with
firearms, have participated in demonstrations and raids. In
other words, the movement is becoming a mass movement.

The third characteristic, points out Mr. Kuo, is that the
period of petitions, requests and so forth is over, and has been

[12] It was estimated that in 1927 there were 9,000,000 people affected by
famine; in 1928, 27,000,000; in 1929, 57,000,000; in 1930, 75,000,000; in
1931, 90,000,000; and in 1932 more than 100,000,000. To this we can add
that in 1933 the harvest was only 60-70 per cent of the average good year.
[13] Eugene Kuo, "Peasants' Revolutionary Movement in the Kuo-min-tang
China, and the Tasks of the Communist Party," in the *Communistichesky Internazional,* No. 23, 1933.

succeeded by use of violence. The fourth is that this struggle, even in the North and North-West, is developing along the lines of Sovietization. A fifth point to be noticed is that in certain parts of the Northern and North-Western provinces the influence of Communists is already evident.

In spite of all this, however, the peasant movement in the North and North-West continues to develop very slowly and unevenly and still falls far short of affecting the entire territory. The situation here is different from that in the South; for it must be remembered first of all that in the South the majority of peasants were landless paupers and tenants over-burdened with rent and debts, while here in the North and North-West, they are still under the spell of ownership. In other words, some of them have their own land, little though it may be; and though both are economically ruined, those in the North will probably continue for a while to be hypnotized by the idea of ownership and to hope for better days.

The revolutionary work carried out in the South between 1924 and 1927 did not penetrate as far as the Northern provinces, which were then still under the reactionary Chang Tso-lin and men of his ilk; hence the population here has no revolutionary training, has no experience of their brethren in the South. The Communist Party has not succeeded so far in establishing itself solidly enough in those regions to prepare the peasants for open and organized revolt.

Up to the present most of the uprisings in the North and the North-West have been led by the numerous secret societies, and were poorly organized, if organized at all. Though ready enough to incite revolt these societies are rarely able to supply intelligent leadership, for most of them are composed of illiterate or semi-literate people; furthermore if their mysticism attracts membership, it can also be used to dupe the masses, and there have been numerous examples where landlords, "kulaks," and militarists have actually controlled such societies and used them for their own interests. That is why certain of the peasant uprisings were started with the purpose of restoring the monarchy, while others stressed the necessity of returning the Confucian doctrines to the schools, and still more advocated all sorts of reactionary reforms.

Well aware of all this, the Communist Party of China is anxious to gain the trust of the Northerners, to establish itself in their territory, to organize armed forces and to bring the masses together for a widespread and unified revolt. Its program for that purpose seems first of all to launch guerrilla warfare in the regions still controlled by the Kuo-min-tang, especially in the areas bordering on the Soviet districts,[14] where coöperation with the Red Armies is easier; and then to persuade peasants to refuse payment of taxes and obedience to the orders of the authorities, including those for the delivery of the supplies for the Government troops. To achieve this the Communists are depending to some extent on the secret societies because of their popularity among the masses,[15] but recognizing the difficulties offered by their mysticism, and abuse of the ignorant, the Communists are using these societies as temporary connecting links with the masses rather than as permanent allies. More direct coöperation is sought with the peasant unions, which are usually free of the elements of mysticism and other methods of exploiting ignorance.

Considering the industrial workers and city proletariat in general as the most promising revolutionary elements, the Communists are doing their best to enlist these classes in support of their program, and, of course, are seeking their active participation in the leadership of the peasants.

[14] The Chinese Soviets, of course.
[15] After 1927 most of the peasants' unions were suppressed; when they revived, many fell under the control of the Kuo-min-tang. This served only to increase the influence of the secret societies, the Red, Yellow, Black Spears, the Big and Small Swords, etc.

The best, though the most involuntary ally of the Communists is, however, the Nanking Government itself, with its agrarian reforms which cannot impress the peasants or make them good friends of the Kuo-min-tang. Restoration of old conditions in the areas reclaimed from the Communists, with the inevitable reëstablishment of the landlords on their old estates, cannot be welcomed even by those peasants who have been bamboozled into enlisting in those societies which demand the reconstitution of the monarchy, and are praying for the extension of landlord control. They all need land, and there hardly can be any doubt that they will all rally eventually to the side fighting for the same.

"There is no doubt," wrote Tsiang Ting-fu in the *People's Tribune,* the periodical published by the Left-Wing Kuo-min-tang, "that the peasants in the Communist-controlled areas have gained definite economic benefits . . . so if the Government aims at restoring the old conditions and sends back the old landowners to their old property, discussion would inevitably arise regarding right and wrong, profit and loss. There are only two alternatives before the Government, they must recognize and stabilize the peasant situation or restore the *status-quo-ante.* . . . This is the major problem in China today. It seems clear that the present situation must be recognized. Proof of rights of property in the Soviet-controlled areas have been effectively blotted out. An attempt to restore them would merely create chaos and confusion . . . it is known that when Communist districts have been recovered by the Government troops, the landlords have relied on the soldiers to take revenge on their behalf and to get back their land . . . often the landlords claimed other people's land as part of their old property, thus taking advantage of the uncertainty of the situation."

The only natural result was that more-embittered peasants, who were previously anti-Communist, were turning "Red," and willing to support the Communists at all costs. "The Government must find a way to convince the peasants that the Government is not fighting for the land-owning class against the peasant class," naïvely commented certain Chinese liberals, though they draw the correct conclusion that "the best way of doing this is to regularize the present division of land and recognize the *status-quo.*"

It is true that the proprietors in many parts of China would probably prefer to get rid of their holdings, since the taxation and the growing unrest make profitable exploitation of the land almost impossible, but they would expect "reasonable" compensation, and where is the money to pay them? The argument is advanced in certain circles that it would be very dangerous to recognize the *status-quo* because the inhabitants of non-Communist districts would want to profit by the situation. That, of course, can hardly be avoided; hence certain authorities urge Nanking to set up immediately in the provinces still free of Communists, organs for study of the land question, in order to put into effect the principle that "land belongs to those who work on it." They claim, with much justification, that unless the land problem is solved neither the Government nor the economic system of China can endure. The division of property right must take place sooner or later, and it is therefore, in their opinion, more statesmanlike to adopt and carry out a reasoned plan of agrarian reform, however drastic, than to persist in emphasizing the military aspect of the question with a consequent aimless shedding of innocent blood.

In 1930, as we know, a new land law was passed by Nanking, and instructions for the redistribution of land, notably in Western Fukien, were even published. But as indicated in Chapter XI, law as a whole failed to make adjustment satisfactory to the poor peasants. In other words, since the poor constitute the overwhelming majority of the population, the law failed to settle the major problem. The specific instructions for its application, as in the case of Western Fukien,

proved that Nanking paid no real attention to the poorer peasants, and was making no sincere effort to meet their just
demands. One clause in these instructions, one indeed, rendered them entirely inacceptable to the peasants, since the right
to receive land was granted to every citizen of the province,
regardless of his previous occupation or profession, including
even the absentees.

But instructions or no instructions, actually the landlords and
the gentry received back their old land in the rehabilitated
areas, and once back in power they demonstrated to the peasants
most convincingly the nature of their own interpretation of the
word "reform." Punitive expeditions, executions, cruel suppression of any attempt at protest, disbandment of the peasant
societies, were among the methods of friendly coöperation they
adopted toward those whom they had been accusing only a few
weeks earlier of cruelty and barbarism in dealing with the
mighty and rich.

Rumors of this, as of the life in the Sovietized districts, and
the successes of the Red Armies, are rapidly penetrating into
the Kuo-min-tang-controlled areas. The effect is exaggerated by
the surrounding secrecy, and coupled with their desire to believe
in something better than their own lot, is affecting these people
profoundly. Increasing numbers of the peasants, therefore,
are being attracted to Communism and are seeking for contacts
with the Communists. Some leaders of the secret societies,
whether or not through motives of jealousy and alarm, are
opposing this trend, but once and again they are forced by the
irresistible public curiosity, if not by logic, to withdraw either
their opposition or their claims to leadership. Hence the contacts grew more and more numerous, influence of the Communists waxes and preliminary steps to Sovietization are already
being made in many new places.[16]

[16] *Revoluzionny Vostok*, No. 2, 1933. The Chinese Crisis.

CHAPTER XIII

ATTITUDE OF THE OUTSIDE WORLD

As we have seen in the preceding chapters, the Chinese Soviets are found principally in the rural districts; the larger cities, and especially the great ports, remain under Kuo-min-tang control. We also have seen that the explanation of this is to be found first of all in the predominantly agrarian aspect of the nation-wide discontent on which the entire movement feeds; and, secondly, in the fact that the larger industrial centers, and especially ports, like Shanghai or Hankow, are under the guns of the Powers. This means that they are under constant menace of bombardment if and when Sovietization is attempted.

This geographical peculiarity of the Chinese Soviet movement prompted certain commentators to regard it merely as a sort of "Jacquerie" or peasants' revolt, in which the industrial proletariat had no part. Such commentators predicted its swift defeat. But a number of Soviet areas have now been in existence for five years or more, and their defeat has not yet come. Furthermore, we know that the assertion that the proletariat has nothing in common with the movement is not in accordance with the facts.

Among the commentators of this persuasion is such a prominent observer as the former Minister of Foreign Affairs of Belgium, Mr. Vanderwelde, who after a short visit to China in 1930 wrote in the now defunct German Socialist organ, *Vorwärts*, an article on "Communism in China." In this article he declared that the whole movement was no more than a series of local peasant uprisings, sometimes bordering on mere banditry, and that though the Communists were agitating among the population and attempting to lead the discontented, the whole affair was of no importance. He even expressed the opinion that Nanking counted upon stopping it immediately after defeating the rebellious generals of the North. However, it must be remembered that Mr. Vanderwelde, as the leader of the Second International, is not, generally speaking, in the best conceivable position to make an objective report on things Communistic, and in this particular pronouncement he was unfortunate to an unusual extent.

Another observer from a more radical group, M. N. Roy, asserted in a book on Revolution in China,[1] published in 1930, that the Chinese Soviets were not genuine Soviets, as the latter can be organized and led only by proletarians. The peasants of China are not fighting for Communism, he said; and on that point he was obviously correct. Elsewhere,[2] however, Mr. Roy also expressed the opinion that "the new China can be neither Capitalistic nor Confucian. There can be only a Communist China, created by the working class." In other words, he stressed the rôle of the industrial proletariat, a class unrepresented, in his opinion, to any considerable extent in the Chinese Soviet movement at the time his book was written. But, as we have seen, the industrial workers had actually not only participated in it but had virtually led the movement, though undoubtedly they are not numerous in this movement, since they are not numerous in China at large.

The same theory that the peasants are unable to create a Soviet system by themselves was voiced also by Leon Trotzky, whose disagreement with the "general line" of the Comintern on the Chinese problem was one of the causes of his downfall and final banishment from the USSR. Trotzky declared that the

[1] M. N. Roy, *Revolution und Kontrrevolution in China.* Berlin, 1930, pp. 465-466.
[2] *Ibid.,* p. 73.

important question was not whether China was economically ripe for Socialism, but whether she was politically ripe for the dictatorship of the proletariat? [3] "The peasantry cannot by itself create a Soviet system, neither can it create an army. Peasants, undoubtedly, had formed armed groups of 'partisans' in China as in Russia and elsewhere, and those 'partisans' fought gallantly and stubbornly. But they were closely bound up with definite limited areas and were unable to undertake strategic operations on a large scale. Only under the hegemony of the proletariat of large industrial centers is the creation of Red Armies possible; and then extension of Soviets into the rural districts will be feasible. It will be a long time before the workers of China and their Communist vanguard develop into really conscious leaders of Revolution. . . ." In some of this there was, of course, no disagreement with the orthodox Communist position. But Trotzky advocated, as the means of achieving the necessary fusion of the rural and the urban elements, the convocation of the Constituent Assembly,[4] and this was bitterly assailed by the Comintern as an attempt to slow down the revolutionary process.

Indignantly denying that the Chinese Soviet movement is a disorganized revolt of disunited communities, and flatly repudiating the statements that industrial workers are not participating in the movement, and that the Red Armies are purely peasant troops, the orthodox Communist authors writing on this subject [5] stress the fact that the entire movement was actually started by the industrial proletariat, first at Wuhan, then at Nanchang, Canton and other places. They also argue that the Red Armies evolved from government troops, which included a considerable percentage of the city-dwellers of proletarian

[3] L. Trotzky, *The Permanent Revolution*. Berlin, 1930, pp. 143-162.
[4] *Bulletin of the Opposition*, No. 15-16, September, 1930.
[5] *The Soviets in China*, 1933. Moscow, p. 29.

origin. They point to the fact that most of the Soviets, beginning with those of Haifong and Loofong, were started by Communists, and that Communists were and are the leaders of most of the present Soviets. The Red Armies, they say, are under Communist commanders. The revival of the Soviet movement in 1929-30 was decidedly linked with, if not actually stimulated by, the growing revolt in urban districts. In spite of the fact that these large cities, "protected" by Imperialist warships and gunboats, are not Sovietized, they harbor large numbers of Communists and are the centers of their work outside of the Soviet areas. The records of the Chinese Soviets indicate that the progress of the movement is linked with the increasing influence of the urban proletariat and the growth of the leadership offered by the latter to the rural masses.

But the opinions of commentators, friendly or otherwise, are of little moment compared with the attitude of the Great Powers toward the Soviet movement in China. That attitude has a direct, sometimes painful, and always vital bearing on the Communist cause. Generally speaking, it may be defined by the one word "hostility." Quite naturally, this hostility is leading to further interference in the internal affairs of China in connection with attempts to eradicate the "Red Menace."

The situation in China in general, of course, is quite complex. There is no powerful, central government to deal with. The Nanking régime, which alone has been recognized by the Powers and is consequently the only government with which the representatives of these Powers may officially negotiate, is far from being in control of the entire situation. There are still several more-or-less independent generals in control of their respective provinces. Indeed, Nanking can actually claim to dominate no more than five or six of the eighteen provinces which constitute China proper. As for Mongolia, Sinkiang,

Thibet, to say nothing of Manchuria, its control there is nil or almost nil.

A further complication is ever present in the almost irreconcilable interests of the various nations exploiting China. At the moment this conflict is further aggravated by the Manchurian "success" of Japan and the recently demonstrated "revolt" of the Country of the Rising Sun against the "Whites." This revolt, as we know, has been manifested in Japan's wholesale defiance of international treaties and agreements, including those which had established the principles of the "Open Door" and respect for China's territorial and political integrity. This "revolt" makes the coöperation of the Powers still more illusory.

Though united in their disapproval of, if not hatred for, Communism, and anxious to see its success in China checked and the entire movement eradicated, the ruling groups of the world are nevertheless unable to offer a united front against its expansion, if only because they cannot come to terms on the more tangible problem of dividing up the markets of China. Openly, or otherwise, they continue to quarrel among themselves.

Discussing the Far Eastern problem in general and the results of the foreign intervention in the internal affairs of Russia after her revolution in particular, Lenin remarked in 1920: "The Japanese said to the American: 'Of course, we can crush the Bolsheviks, but what are you going to give us for that? China? Well, we are going to take it anyhow. Why should we fight here with the Bolsheviks while you Americans remain ten thousand miles away, in our rear? No, sir, that is a poor scheme.' " In Lenin's estimate, Japan failed to defeat the then weak Soviet régime because she had, at the same time, to deal with China, and did not receive actual support from the United States and other Powers. Conscious of the menace of a united front of the Capitalist countries against the first Workers' Republic, Lenin nevertheless also maintained that the conflict of economic interests among different Powers was making their coöperation for the sake of an abstract idea not so simple, if feasible at all.

With this in mind, let us examine the respective attitudes of the Powers toward the Chinese Soviets and China in general.

England's attitude: The Chinese policy of England was revised in 1926 to effect better coöperation with Nanking. The British Government then issued a Memorandum declaring: "the idea that the economic and political development of China can only be secured under foreign tutelage should be abandoned by the Powers," and expressly disclaimed "any intention of foreign control upon an unwilling China." Unfortunately, soon after this announcement, London changed her mind and returned to old ways and means.

More recently Great Britain's policy of "coöperation" with Nanking has been accompanied by an extension of her own protectorate over Thibet, established in 1913-17, and by some unusual activities in Chinese Turkestan. Thibetan troops with English "encouragement," to say the least, were lately marching into Szechwan. English agents of various descriptions became deeply interested in Sinkiang, where a British subject was even expected to become King of an "Islamic" state.

The British Minister at Peiping, Sir Miles Lampson, paid a visit to Szechwan in 1933, in spite of all the inconveniences of a long journey far from railway lines. "It seemed scarcely possible that the lure alone of the Upper Yangtze's mighty gorges had been sufficient to draw His Majesty's envoy to distant West China," commented a Chinese reporter. The Japanese asserted that Sir Miles Lampson went to Szechwan to negotiate a boundary settlement between Thibet and Hsikang and to discuss with the local war lord, Liu-Hsiang, the possibility of a twenty million dollar loan for arms and munitions.

The Chinese commentator on this excursion expressed the opinion that the renewed interest of England in these parts of China, adjoining Thibet, which is under their complete control,[6] strangely coincided with the new aggression of Japan, and may have some bearing on the rather sympathetic attitude taken by London to the latest Manchurian adventure. To consolidate her hold on Thibet, England now seems to be seeking a degree of control over the adjacent provinces, such as Szechwan, with Hsikang and Chinghai,[7] on the East and Sinkiang on the North, *i.e.*, provinces also bordering on the Soviet areas of China and Soviet Russia.

The Mohammedan uprising in Sinkiang, in 1933, against the nominal authority of the Chinese, had all the earmarks of English participation. The rebels were armed with British rifles and, through the good offices of a retired British colonel, had apparently, obtained munitions from the British agencies in India.

If we remember how recently the Russians completed the so-called Turksib railway, which runs along and near the border of Sinkiang, we may see the cause of British anxiety. Indeed, that railway is probably destined to play a very serious rôle; for it is likely that it will increase the intercourse between the peoples living on both sides of the border. Hence England must be anxious not only over the prospect of losing trade carried on with Sinkiang through India, but also over the possibility

[6] In 1913 a treaty was signed by England with the Thibetan Da-Lai-Lama, by which Thibet became virtually a vassal state of Great Britain, similar to the native states of India. In 1917 England served on Peking "Twelve Demands" with regard to Thibet similar to the "21" of Japan in 1915.

[7] These two constitute the so-called Inner-Thibet.

of the awakening of these and other "backward peoples." The oppressed millions of Sinkiang, as well as those suffering from British Imperialism, in adjacent India on one side and in Afghanistan on the other, now have at their doors the example of an entirely new life. This example may well prove inconvenient to those who live by the exploitation of others, so long as those others remain backward.

Thus the drive of the Britishers toward Sinkiang seems linked with a fear of the growth of Soviet-Russian influence in that part of China, similar to the fear of the Sovietization of the Chinese provinces to the East of their own India and Thibet. So far the British "Drang nach Osten" meets only nominal resistance by Nanking; it must face, however, the disfavor of the French, who are jealous for Yunnan and, probably, for Szechwan, as well. When, for instance, the British proposed to build a railroad from Mandalay across Upper Burma to the Yunnan border, and wanted a concession to extend it further through Chinese territory to connect with the head of navigation on the Yangtze River, the French issued a warning, and the project was dropped.

In Sinkiang the British agents must furthermore compete with those of Nippon. The Japanese also employed a Mohammedan prince, the son of the deposed Sultan of Turkey, though without any success, to carry on their own intrigue in that part of the world; for it seemed important to them to prevent direct contact between the USSR and the Chinese Soviet areas. As a matter of fact, hardly any Russians from the Soviet Union are to be found in Sinkiang, though there are a few thousands of the "White Russians" employed by the local war lords as mercenary troops. These, however, are not considered undesirables either by the English or by the Japanese *Kulturträger*.

France's attitude: "France, like all the Imperialist Powers, follows an aggressive anti-Communist policy," wrote Paul

Vailiant-Couturier.[8] "On this point the united front is well-forged among all the capitalist powers who maintain 'influence' or 'interests' in China. This policy has two aspects. First there is the anti-soviet policy with regard to the USSR. Despite all the sweet-sounding diplomatic exchanges there remain the facts of France's support of Japanese aggression, France's friendly attitude toward Manchukuo, France's open support of Tsarist military organizations, and in Shanghai France's employment of Tsarist Russian military men and others in their police forces. . . . The second is the anti-soviet policy with regard to China which expresses itself in military and police aid to the Kuo-min-tang under the usual pretext of 'keeping the peace.' . . . Communism, as sharply contrasted with the capitulations and repeated betrayals of the so-called 'National Government,' represents now in the eyes of the imperialists the only real danger of China becoming independent and unified. Communism, it is feared, holds forth the only chance for putting an end to those 'disorders' in China which the imperialist partisans of 'law and order' have always so carefully fomented. . . . The maintenance of large land and sea forces in China are meant only to deal with this 'menace.' Certainly the protection of 300 French merchants and a handful of missionaries doing business which represents 1.3% of China's imports, could scarcely be held to justify the very considerable land and naval forces which are held in constant readiness. Not even the imperialists could get far with this argument."

Yunnan is the French sphere of influence in China—a sphere which originated during the "orgy of concessions" at the end of the Nineteenth Century. By 1898 France had already obtained the contract to build the Tonkin-Yunnanfu Railway, and actually constructed the latter.[9] She obtained also the right

[8] The editor of *L'Humanité*, in an article for the *China Forum*, September 18, 1933.
[9] Tonkin section built in 1901, the Yunnan section not till 1909. Cf. T. A. Bisson, *The Dismemberment of China*, April, 1934.

to build another railroad from Yunnan into Szechwan, thereby securing a certain tangible interest in that latter province also, though she did not actually build the road. It is an old story that by building railways the foreigners acquire economic control over respective parts of China, and such was the case with France. She is now the greatest practical beneficiary of the trade handled by the Tonkin-Yunnanfu Railway, the only line in that enormous area; and that trade amounts in good years to almost 100,000,000 Mexican dollars.[10]

As the French proverb says, *"L'appétit vient en mangeant,"* or "appetite grows while eating." So, after having established economic control over Yunnan, France attempted to extend her economic and political influence into Kwangsi and Kweichau. These two provinces, adjacent to the Sovietized areas of China, are naturally of specific interest in connection with the Communist movement. The French, however, would probably prefer to say that they are important as protectives against Red contagion threatening French Indo-China. The explanation, of course, resembles that offered by the British for their expansion into Szechwan and Sinkiang.

Japan's attitude: The noble efforts of the Japanese to eradicate Communism are already well known. Manchuria and Jehol have ceased to be even nominally under the control of Nanking. Certain parts of China proper, including the demilitarized zone in the North, have become to all practical purposes semi-Japanese protectorates, and this is true also of sections of Inner Mongolia. But these seem hardly to exhaust the "spoils" of Japan for her efforts to combat "dangerous thoughts." Her agents, sometimes with soldiers behind them, are busily engaged in the process of "awakening" the Mongols and other backward peoples. All this is done, of course, with the single

[10] *China Forum,* August 6, 1933, p. 6. See also the very interesting survey by Wilbur Burton, *The French Strangle-hold on Yunnan,* Shanghai, 1934.

aim of bringing peace and order; that is well understood by those who believe the Japanese officials who are traveling all over the world for the sole purpose of clarifying these problems, on which other people do not see eye to eye with the leaders of Nippon.

Japan wishes "to free" Outer Mongolia from the yoke of Soviet domination, their officials explain; and then, of course, to open the doors of trade for the benefit of all nations. The facts are strangely out of tune with this pretty lullaby. First of all Outer Mongolia is only allied with the Soviet Union; it is not under Russian occupation as Manchuria is occupied by the Japanese. Outer Mongolia is neither invaded by Russian soldiers, nor governed by Russian advisers, as Manchuria is by the Japanese—a point which should not be overlooked by the latter when they embark on their civilizing campaigns designed to save Mongolia.

The anti-Communist attitude of Japan is too well known; it is openly reiterated by the Japanese officials even more often than would seem reasonable. This overemphasis indicates the probable presence of other objectives, and one is justified in supposing that one such aim was to obtain a free hand in Manchuria. That was granted, but with what results!

The Japanese attitude toward the Sovietization of China is quite complicated. On one hand, being outwardly, at least, Monarchistic to the core, and posing as the arch-enemy of Socialism and Communism, Japan must naturally be interested in the eradication of the Soviet movement in China and sympathetic to Chiang Kai-shek's campaign. In reality, however, Japan is not only pouring water on the mill of Soviet China by an aggression which naturally increases the number of the discontented, but is also blocking the efforts of the Nanking régime to cope with the "Red Menace." There has even been a rumor that Japanese were behind the Red Armies on certain occasions.[11] This might have been explained by the desire of Japan to embarrass Chiang Kai-shek and to make Japanese coöperation in his struggle with the Communists more and more desirable to Nanking. In the end, possibly, that régime might be forced to accept any and all conditions imposed by Japan. Much of the Japanese propaganda is directed toward convincing the Chinese people that their salvation and the salvation of all Asia rests on the coöperation of China, Japan and Manchukuo. To this end the Japanese are seeking to promote various Pan-Asiatic schemes; and for a time the Japanese press was filled with inspired accounts of a transformation in Tokyo's policy toward China. This policy was described as being based upon the conclusion of a military-economic alliance by Japan, China and Manchukuo for the organization of Asia to the exclusion of any third power. In return for entering such a bloc the Chinese Government would be aided in the anti-Red campaign and the suppression of the revolutionary movement.

Attitude of the other Great Powers: There is at least one country whose nationals are already more actively engaged in the Chiang Kai-shek's fight with the Communists. This is Germany, whose officers (on the reserve list, of course), headed by General Seeckt, are taking part not only in drawing the plans for his campaigns, but also serving on his general staff.

The position of the United States can probably be summed up as that of a good friend of Nanking. Reliance, so far, has been placed on Chiang Kai-shek, to whom different favors, whether or not in the form of a cotton-and-wheat loan, airplanes, and other supplies have been rendered.[12] More or less similar is the position taken by Italy, especially in regard to the

[11] Certain students believe that was one of the Nanking propaganda charges designed to disrupt Communism in China.
[12] A considerable number of American pilots are now in Nanking's air-force.

sale of airplanes to China; and her determination not to permit the success of Communism, of course, remains.

On the other hand, the USSR's attitude toward the Soviet movement in China is undoubtedly one of sympathy and good will, but there seems not the slightest evidence of any direct coöperation between the two.

If there are indications of connection between Communism in China and elsewhere, they are mainly to be found in the form of leadership by the Comintern, which has its seat at Moscow. The Comintern, however, includes not only Russians and Chinese, but delegates from practically every country of the world. Such work, furthermore, as the study of the adaptability of Marxism-Leninism to the peculiar problems of China's Sovietization are carried on by the Research Institute on China, which is attached to the Communist Academy at Moscow. A number of Chinese youths have been and are being trained at the Institute for the Orientals in Moscow, and quite obviously a number of the Chinese Soviet leaders are graduates of that Institution. But so far as we know, there are no Russians attached either to the Central Soviet China Government, or to the Red Armies, as was the case at the time of Borodin, Blucher-Gallen, and others in 1924-27. Nor is it likely that any material help is coming to the Chinese Soviets from the USSR either.

Solution offered: One of the solutions of Nanking's woes, advanced especially by British experts and supported by a number of the Kuo-min-tang officials, is a concentration of effort on the development and consolidation of the Yangtze Basin. This area is advantageously located—at least as far as gunboats can be effective—and undoubtedly much of the British and other foreign interest is found in this area. In addition, it lies also just between the Sovietized, or Soviet-threatened, South, and the not yet infected North. Therefore the soundness of this proposal from the anti-Communist point of view cannot be denied. The question remains whether it is feasible. It must not be overlooked that there are various interests involved which are not easily to be reconciled.

When describing the four-year plan he had devised for China, the Nanking Minister of Industry, Mr. Chen Kung-po, accepted the idea of first developing a central area, as a starting point for his country's industrial reconstruction "rather than theorizing about a national reconstruction plan." [18] He found, "after mature consideration" that there is no more suitable place for such a purpose than the Yangtze Valley. The points in favor of this choice, he claimed, are many. In the first place, the seat of the Government is established on this river. Secondly, this area offers the best communication—the Yangtze alone is about 3,200 miles long—and with six of the most fertile provinces, it brings within reach the purchasing power of some two hundred million people. Thirdly, the foreign trade passing through Yangtze ports represents about 60% of China's commerce with the world.

But as the Minister properly remarked, "confidence is essential" for the materialization of such a scheme; and where he expects to find that confidence he did not reveal in his article. In this connection a few questions may well be asked and answered. First of all, is there really a sincere desire by the Powers, on the good will of whom Nanking relies, to sponsor or even to tolerate such industrial development of China? Hardly so! Are they really interested in the national reconstruction of China? Are they willing to see the consolidation of her industrial foundation? Unfortunately there are no signs to justify such optimism. The Yangtze Valley is under control of the foreigners; their interest is first of all in the security of trade; and they are more or less in an agreement that order along the Yangtze Valley would be of great benefit. They are

[18] Chen Kung-po, "A Four-Year Plan for China," in the *Observer*, August, 1933. Shanghai.

naturally anxious to prevent Sovietization of that area, and that is about all upon which these various interests can agree. After that begin the differences, the rivalries, and the intrigues, which are unusually abundant on the Chinese arena and unusually complex.

Economic nationalism is now in full swing. Naturally it is a handicap to any coöperation in trade, and particularly in trade and investments in such a country as the China of today, where foreign interests are cultivated in a most unwholesome atmosphere, familiar with slogans like "get rich quick" and *"après moi le deluge."* Generally speaking, neither foreign traders, nor foreign manufacturers in China can pretend that theirs are solid businesses run under normal conditions. They are working on the edge of a crater. They are far from being comfortably entrenched in their positions, and are hardly justified in looking for sympathetic treatment in case of a serious social upheaval in China.

In other words, we do not entertain any over-optimistic opinion about the ability of either Westerners or the Japanese to withstand the mounting tide of the Chinese indignation. And the stubborn resistance of the foreigners to the revival of China must prove, in the long run, not only futile but very costly to those who block the normal desire of the Chinese people to live more decently.

"The final outcome of the contest between the two systems," said Lenin, "is foretold by the fact that Russia, India, China, etc., constitute the overwhelming majority of the human race. This majority of the peoples are getting involved, on a more and more rapid tempo, into the struggle for their emancipation, and there can be no doubt about the final result of this world-wide struggle." [14]

[14] Quoted from the article "Lenin's Opinion on the Chinese Question," in the *Problemi Kitaia*, No. 11. 1933, p. 77.

CHAPTER XIV

SUMMARY AND CONCLUSIONS

Socio-economic background: From the foregoing brief study of economic, political, and social conditions in China, it should be possible to see why the Soviet movement in that country is rapidly gaining ground.

For long years the incessant strife, aggravated by abuses committed by the foreigners, has made peaceful existence in China almost impossible. The collapse of the agricultural system, rendered worse by the stubborn, though futile, resistance, offered by the landlords and gentry to any kind of radical reforms, brought about the pauperization of farmers. Unemployment, intensified by the world-wide economic crisis and the opposition of foreigners to the development of domestic industries in China, accompanied by the growing banditry recruited from the impoverished masses and the discontented soldiers, plus such natural calamities as the ever-recurring floods and famines, made China a most fertile field for Communist propaganda and subsequently insured the success of the Soviet movement in its first beginnings.

Pauperization of farmers: The pauperization of the enormously large rural population, constituting over 75% of the total, results, as we have seen, from a complexity of causes. Among these the inadequacy of landholdings by the overwhelming majority of the farmers, is probably the chief. About 50% or more of the peasants are landless, and about 25% have parcels insufficient to support a family. In addition, most of them are heavily in debt. Falling prices of agricultural

195

produce was another factor; in 1933 these prices were only 25% to 30% of what they were in 1929. With an average gross income of eight or ten dollars silver per mou per annum on good arable land, it is hardly possible to make a profit. After deducting the amounts paid for taxes, fertilizers, implements and labor (providing, of course, that the land is cultivated by the owners themselves), it is hard even to make ends meet. To this difficulty must be added merciless exploitation by landlords and gentry, who are ordinarily usurers as well. They charge an average of 50% of the crop as rent; the interest on money loaned runs as high as 60% and some times even 100%. The burden of excessive taxation, already beyond endurance, is piled still higher by the war lords and *tuchuns*, who often collect taxes for years in advance. Aside from the taxes assessed by the central, provincial and local governments, the taxpayer must pay an extra 25%-50% to the tax-collectors. All these, naturally, have combined to cause the disintegration of China's agricultural life. In such circumstances little can be done by the existing régimes to alleviate the sufferings of the Chinese farmers. Only a radical revolutionary change will suffice.

Retarded industrialization: The backward economic state of China is linked up first with the fact that her industry is still in infancy, and to a considerable extent owned by foreigners; and second—that her system of transport and communication also is in an embryonic stage, and is likewise controlled by the foreigners.

The handicraft industries, for example, are naturally unable to compete with imported machine-made foreign goods. Until very recently these were admitted practically duty-free, since the tariffs were limited by the treaties in such a way as to make the development of domestic industries practically impossible. Similarly, owing to the primitive methods of production and extraction, Chinese products, and even raw materials and semi-finished goods, are losing markets abroad. In other words, in spite of the shockingly low cost of labor in China, many of her products are unable to compete with machine-made goods offered by others. This decline of exports has latterly been hastened, of course, by the constant civil wars and the ensuing general chaos.

For a number of years now, China has been importing more than she has been exporting, and has had no "invisible exports" to meet the adverse balance. The importation of food-stuffs, steadily increasing, has already reached 300-400 million Mexican dollars a year. This has been due partly to diminishing yields as the farmers became too poor to buy fertilizers and to use better implements, partly to the fact that warfare has forced the peasants to cut down their sowing, and partly to the famines and floods.

Political factors: Among the political factors responsible for the present-day situation in China, and favoring the Soviet movement, we may list: (1) the absence of a powerful and popular central government, able to control and direct the country's life; (2) endless strife among the militarist factions, undermining agriculture and ruining industry; (3) the abuses by foreign Powers who not only exploit China economically, as if she were a colony, and interfere in her foreign and domestic affairs to such an extent that popular indignation is inevitable, but who are also cutting off from Chinese territory their own "spheres of interest," protectorates, etc. The outrageous way in which many foreign residents of such settlements as Shanghai and Tientsin treat the Chinese, also contributes to the bad feeling toward foreigners in general.

Social factors: The social factors, favoring Sovietization of China, include: (1) those remnants of the feudal system which lead to endless abuses and widen the abyss between the classes;

(2) the growing accumulation of wealth in fewer and fewer hands, which also deepens the antagonism between the classes; and the agrarian crisis, which also intensifies the strife between the poor, the middle class and the rich, rendering the class struggle in the Chinese village quite acute; (3) the abnormal position of women, whose rights are restricted and who are underpaid and otherwise abused, with a consequent reaction on the social outlook of China like that caused by (4) the employment of children, sometimes of very tender age, under horrible conditions in all sorts of unhealthy work, causing high mortality, crippling, and various dangers to the physical and moral standards of the younger generation; (5) the illiteracy of the masses who were practically deprived of any educational opportunities until recently, which makes the intercourse between the various sections of Chinese society still more difficult, and which adds to the general misunderstanding, mistrust and animosity.

The growth of industry, slow as it is, has tended to intensify the differentiation of classes in the new China; the gulf widens between the employers, who in this Machine Age possess the tools of production, and the employees who have the desire for a means of livelihood. A survey of the working hours, wages, and other conditions in Chinese industry reveals appalling conditions. Working hours run as high as 16 to 18 per day; working conditions, in most of the factories and shops, are very bad; wages are pathetically low, and absolutely inadequate for any sort of decent living.

Rising tide of industrialism: In such circumstances the economic structure of China cannot remain as it is. Today its very foundation is endangered by the rising tide of modern industrialism.

The particular phases through which China has been passing for the two decades since the Revolution of 1911 have brought an influx of new ideas to the former Celestial Empire. In part these new ideas may be traced to such outside influences as the World War and the Revolution in Russia, and to the profound changes taking place all over the world since that war with its economic aftermath, including the present economic crisis; and in part they were the offspring of the domestic events and conditions described above. In the Chinese mind there has been growing up a consciousness of the economic backwardness of the country as compared with other nations. This gradually has brought about the determination to see a change for the better. It quickly became plain, however, that no real betterment was possible without a complete and genuine overhauling of the entire economic structure on which the nation rests. Yet the new governments which followed the abdicated Monarchy continued to use the old methods of feudal times. The cupidity of the war lords ruined the country and made paupers out of the peasants.

Another lesson quickly learned by the "emancipated" Chinese was that the foreigners, with their Imperialistic tendencies, remained the principal stumblingblocks to China's healthy development. Imperialists were obstructing—though, probably, not always deliberately—the process of industrialization of China, as they did in their own colonies and other semi-colonial countries like China. They preferred to exploit China as a market and a source of cheap raw materials.

By now, apparently, the Chinese have learned that their salvation lies in their complete and genuine emancipation from those doubtful friends.

It is quite obvious that China no longer remains isolated from the rest of the world. As a matter of fact she is not isolated now; there are numerous contacts with Western civilization, including, of course, the industrial achievements of the Machine Age. But China still has before her the problem of readjusting her traditional philosophy under the pressure of more modern thought coming from the West. There can be little doubt that a more up-to-date interpretation of her own philosophies is imperative.

One such attempt at reinterpretation is offered by the modern Chinese philosopher, Dr. Hu Shih, who is well known in the United States, where he studied under Dr. John Dewey and other leaders of thought. Hu Shih has no particular respect for the ancients. He is a modern *par excellence,* insisting that China must turn toward Western civilization without delay. He advocates the renaissance of his country through development of an attention to science rather than metaphysics, and through industrialization. He believes, apparently, that Capitalism is the proper means to that end.[1] To the three main principles, (1) of national independence; (2) popular sovereignty or democracy, covering liberty, equality and fraternity, and (3) social organization providing decent life and equal opportunity to all, laid down by Dr. Sun Yat-sen, were added numbers of other new ideas. New hopes were aroused in the masses through the Fourteen Points of the late President Wilson—only to be followed by new and bitter disappointments from the Versailles Treaty and other injustices. Then appeared the revelations of the Russian "experiment," and soon after came the Russians themselves. For three years (1924-27) the Chinese masses received a liberal training in self-organization, the creation of the machinery of revolution, spurring latent energies, and arousing revolutionary enthusiasm; in bringing to fruition the ideas and ideals that Chinese themselves had cherished for years but had not as yet been able to realize owing to the lack of program and leadership.

The achievements of the Sovietization of China have been fully treated in Chapters VII to IX, and are now recalled only

[1] Hu Shih, *Outlines of History of Chinese Philosophy.*

for the purpose of recording present conditions, before we proceed to discuss their power of endurance.

"Whether one likes it or not," wrote Mr. Lowe in 1933,[2] "the most alluring feature of the Communists in South and Central China today is their policy of agrarian revolution. Because of these efforts in redistributing land, countless farmers have turned Red, even though they may not have the least comprehension of the intricate theories of Karl Marx. Such a radical transformation in land tenure is a most disturbing problem for the present Chinese régime to face. Unless the Kuo-min-tang, which has copiously advocated the doctrine of 'enabling the peasant to own the land he tills,' makes an equal attempt to improve the status of the Chinese peasantry and carry out certain long-overdue reforms, Communism will not (be) likely (to) fade away in the rural districts."

Is Communism possible in China? Is there a Communist movement in China? Can it be successful in that country? Will China turn Communist? When such questions are asked, it is best to be more specific and to indicate as precisely as possible in what sense the term "Communist" is used. It is one thing if applied to Marxism in general or to the theory and practice of social revolution further elaborated by Lenin and Stalin,[3] and another thing when this term is used more loosely just to cover attempts, successful or otherwise, to apply this theory to life under special conditions, at a given time, and in a particular country, such as Russia or Hungary, China or Outer Mongolia.

We need hardly reiterate that a distinct Communist movement is actually in progress in China. But even when we recognize that there is a Communist movement in that country, and

---

[2] Lowe Chuan-Hua, *Facing Labor Issue in China*, Shanghai, 1933, p. 156.
[3] Class struggle for emancipation; and a classless society as the goal, where every one is expected to contribute according to his capacity, and must be provided for according to his needs.

that this movement is to a certain extent successful, we must still discover whether the peculiarities of Chinese history, philosophy, economic structure and usages can offer serious obstacles to its survival.

To assert that China will turn at once Communist in the orthodox meaning of that word, is going rather far. In view of the multitude of unknown factors, present and future, any attempted answer to such a question in terms of time would be purely speculative. A number of Chinese authors have, indeed, asserted that Communism is not possible in China. But we can at least examine their grounds for this statement, and form an opinion on the validity of their arguments.

Dr. Wellington Koo's scepticism: In listing the reasons why, in his opinion, Communism cannot succeed in his country, the official spokesman of Nanking, Dr. Wellington Koo, has declared the Chinese are essentially positivists whose common sense abhors Communism.

"Communism has a certain mystical halo around it," writes Dr. Koo. "It is a belief and for some of its followers a religion. But the Chinese, brought up in positivist and pragmatic philosophy of Confucius, are not mystical at all. The human element always ultimately triumphs over the speculative element. Mysticism is an innate spiritual disposition. It cannot be created in a milieu unfavorable for it." [4]

One may question this statement of Dr. Wellington Koo. Most of the numerous secret societies of China have been affiliated, one way or another, with Taoism; and Taoism was decidedly mystical, appealing to the emotions. Confucianism, certainly, was rational; but it was a moral code, teaching order and wisdom; its function was somewhat different from that of Taoism. The latter exerted probably a greater spell over the

---

[4] Wellington Koo, *Memorandum on Communism* for the Lytton Commission, p. 781.

Chinese masses than the former, which was better adapted to the educated and, incidentally, to the well-to-do.

One of the eminent contemporary philosophers of China, Kang You-wei, whose sympathies are not with the moderns, endeavored to interpret Confucianism in accordance with our own time and to seek in it some new meanings. According to him, Confucius held as social ideals Democracy, International Federation, and Communism.[5] In Kang's interpretation the ideal community of Confucius will be realized in three stages. The third stage, The Age of Great Peace, will see the disappearance of the state from World Society, with universal equality and the extinction of private property.

Another scholar, Professor Chen Tu-hsiu,[6] who is a Marxist, considers Confucius's philosophy merely in relation to the age in which its founder lived. According to Chen, "since the doctrine produces the society and conversely the society produces the doctrine, there can be no doctrine that is eternal."[7] In his opinion the philosophy of Confucius was endowed with every characteristic of feudalism.

Kang's interpretation is here introduced only to show the presence of certain ideas of the "early Communism" in the Chinese philosophies, even that of Confucius, on which Dr. Wellington Koo based, apparently erroneously, his assertion that the Chinese are averse to this doctrine. Other Chinese advocates of primitive Communistic ideas have existed, including scholars and such practical statesman as Wang An-shih, who, as we have seen, was Prime Minister under the Emperor Shen Tsung of the Sung dynasty.

"Chinese philosophies were originally what should be called

---

[5] Kyoson Tsuchida, *Contemporary Thoughts of Japan and China.* Knopf, New York, 1931, pp. 194-199.
[6] One of the originators of the Chinese Communist Party, who latterly became the leader of the Right-Wing Opposition.
[7] K. Tsuchida, *ibid.,* p. 198.

social philosophies," wrote K. Tsuchida, the Japanese historian of the Chinese philosophy. "China was for a long time under severe restraint, and has but recently changed to the life of a new Republic, thus producing all sorts of modern social movements. The majority of the people, of course, are still in their long sleep, but small bands of progressives are engaging in extraordinary new social movements." [8]

Among the latter, Socialism was naturally prominent; and in the opinion of the same author, the most eminent among Socialists in China was the late Dr. Sun Yat-sen, who "in the closing years of his life seemed to be more inclined toward Bolshevism." As far as we know, however, Dr. Sun never called himself a Socialist, though his famous Three Principles were indeed very close to Socialism.[9] As for his inclination toward Communism the best testimony is found in the letter he wrote on his deathbed to the leaders of Moscow, to whom he expressed himself as follows:

"I charge the Kuo-min-tang to continue the work of the revolutionary movement so that China, reduced by Imperialists to the position of a semi-colonial country, may become free. With this object I have instructed the party to be in constant contact with you. I firmly believe in the continuance of the support which you have hitherto accorded to my country. Taking leave of you, dear comrades, I want to express the hope that the day will soon come when the USSR will welcome a friend and an ally in a mighty free China, and that in the great struggle for the liberation of the oppressed peoples of the world these allies will go forward to victory hand in hand." [10]

---

[8] K. Tsuchida, *ibid.,* pp. 223-224.

[9] The rather naïve attempt to prove that Dr. Sun Yat-sen was averse to Socialism because he had read the criticism of Marxism by Dr. M. William (which hardly can be considered as an authoritative treatise on that subject) and even made a number of quotations from it, would hardly deserve to be noticed were it not rather too enthusiastically quoted by those who are anxious to show that Dr. Sun Yat-sen was opposed to the theories they dislike so passionately themselves.

[10] J. W. Hall, *Eminent Asians,* 1930, pp. 88-89.

The other reason for his countrymen's aversion to Communism listed by Dr. Wellington Koo is that "the Chinese is very individualistic in his opinions. It is necessary to appeal to his reason in order to make him change them. He is not inclined to follow the ways of others by simple discipline, but that and the subordination of the faculty of individual criticism to the dictation of the Party are precisely the essential characteristic of Communism." [11]

Here again we may ask Dr. Wellington Koo if it is not true that in China the individual counts for little. Is it not true that for many centuries the family, with its unlimited power and hierarchical structure, was the basis of the Chinese social system? It is easier to agree that the Chinese dislikes the discipline of governments; that he is opposed to regimentation. But it is hardly proper to say with Dr. Wellington Koo that the subordination of the faculty of individual criticism to dictation by the Party is an essential characteristic of Communism. If we are not mistaken, this is so only in the transition period, and is no permanent part of the ideal scheme for society. [12]

The next point on Dr. Wellington Koo's list is that "the Chinese family opposes Communist individualism . . . this idea is alien to the Chinese who regard family duties as being of greater importance . . . tradition and the respect for the ancestors are important Chinese social characteristics . . . it is the family which for the Chinese is at bottom of the social structure. . . ."

It is certainly true that family ties have been powerful influences in Chinese life. They are still important to a certain extent, but in a decidedly decreasing degree.

The final point made by Dr. Wellington Koo that "the Chinese are attached to individual property," probably does not

[11] Wellington Koo, *ibid.,* p. 782.
[12] Besides dictation and discipline, when they are in accord with the economic necessity, coincide with real freedom—for then they increase control of nature and so serve the individual to his own advantage.

take into consideration those Chinese who have no individual property, who are paupers. As these are the majority, that consideration hardly seems valid. Furthermore, it might well be asked of Dr. Wellington Koo if it is not true that the idea of communal organization and the equalization of property, particularly land, has long been familiar to Chinese thinkers and reformers?

A historian of the early phases of the Chinese Revolution, Tang Leang-li, declared [13] that the family system of China permitted the co-existence of the well-to-do with the landless members of the same family, since the latter had to be supported by the former.[14] He asserted that their ideas and ideals were identical. But a few lines further the same author declared that the landless quite often became "hoboes," and many of them joined gangs of bandits. Thus it seems reasonable to suppose that the landless were interested, to some extent, in redistribution of land. If so, how could they have identical ideas—political, social and economic—with their more fortunate, well-to-do relatives? This the historian fails to explain.

The "pro"s are stronger than the "contra"s. Another Dr. Koo, Dr. T. Z. Koo, who is also well known abroad, founded his doubts of the success of Communism in China on the following assumptions: [15]

"(1) The social ethical code of China exalts virtues such as filial piety, respect for age and learning, and chastity and obedience in women, and emphasizes tolerance and benevolence in the mutual relations between man and man, and property for all classes.". . ."The strongest bulwark against Communism

[13] Tang Leang-li, *The Inner History of the Chinese Revolution.* London, 1930.
[14] When Chinese society was purely feudal this was correct, but since China started on her road of Capitalism it has been changed, as everywhere else.
[15] In an article to the *World Tomorrow*, July, 1933, reprinted in the *China Weekly Review*, August 19, 1933, p. 495.

in China," asserts Dr. T. Z. Koo, "is not political and military suppression, but that sense of decency and propriety so strongly ingrained in us through twenty centuries of ethical training." [16]

"(2) The Communist Party of China has been in existence as an organized movement since 1920. In organization and program it is, perhaps, the most compact and efficient political party in existence. But it is essentially a mass movement, and as such requires a new leadership as well as following. These elements are absent in the general situation in China. The Communist Party is dealing with an undisciplined mass through an untrained leadership. Such a combination of handicaps is enough to cripple even a popular political movement, and the Communist movement in China has already outlived its days of popularity (1923-27). [17]

"(3) The close connection of the Chinese Communist Party with the Third International is another factor against its success in this country. Its program for China is hatched in Moscow. When national feeling is so strong in China, as it is at this moment, any political party which takes orders from an extra-national source is bound to be working under a serious handicap. [18]

"(4) Ever since 1927 the Communist Party was torn by a series of violent internal dissensions. These have seriously affected the strength of the Party and they show no signs of abatement. . . . Whether the Communist Party will ever recover from this serious blow is quite open to doubt. I think

[16] We already commented on this point as not convincing, for there is a distinct change in all the phases of China's life, her prevailing thoughts, interpretation of ethics, etc.

[17] Mr. Lowe, whom we quoted above, is of the opinion, however, that such an assertion is more comforting than true. "Not only are the Soviets in China well organized," he writes, "one can find a considerable number of men of unusual calibre, noble motives and world-wide experience" among their leaders.

[18] Certain control by the Comintern, naturally, exists, but the Comintern is not foreign. China is represented therein as are other countries.

the Communist movement will degenerate for some time into the status of 'Liu-Kou' or roving bandits." [19]

The entire list of the unfavorable factors, on which Dr. T. Z. Koo based his optimistic conclusion, is quoted in order to show how unconvincing they are, especially in the light of all that has enabled us to write the preceding chapters. It is also desirable to place this list side by side with Dr. T. Z. Koo's own additional list of factors favorable to success of the Communist movement.

"The first of these," writes Dr. T. Z. Koo, "is to be found in the economic life of China. As a nation predominantly agricultural, we are face to face today with the growing disintegration of our rural economic system, which is steadily reducing a large portion of our rural population to a life of hopeless penury. This in turn is driving many rural workers in the cities to conditions of congestion and unrest. Such a situation throws both the village and town open to the Communists. If our Government cannot find a way out of this rural economic problem in the near future, then, to many people, Communism will seem to be the only alternative. In my opinion this is the strongest factor in the general situation which favors the growth of Communism in China.

"A second factor favoring this growth is the rule of the War Lords. Since the Revolution of 1911 military leaders have lived off the land and misgoverned it by usurping the authority of the civil arm of the government. This misgovernment has taken largely the form of over-taxation and inadequate protection of life and property against banditry. Again, unless something is done to this situation, Communism will seem to many to be the lesser evil of the two.

---

[19] The dissensions existed, but at the present are of no particular importance, as far as disruption of the work is concerned. To talk about "recovery of the Party" under such circumstances is hardly proper.

"A third factor favorable to Communism is that in our intellectual life we have long been familiar with the idea of communal organization and the equalization of property, particularly land . . . it is, therefore, not surprising that Communistic ideas have had a ready entrée into student circles in China today.

"A fourth factor in favor of the growth of Communism in China lies in the international situation, particularly in the aggressive pressure from Japan. . . ."

From a comparison of the "Pro"s and "Contra"s it would seem that there is little to substantiate the conclusion that Communism cannot be applied at all in China, or has no chance to survive there. On the contrary, if we weigh the relative merits of the "Pro"s and "Contra"s of the authorities quoted above, we must conclude that there are no reasons whatsoever why Communism cannot survive in China. Nor need we ask if it can be introduced there, for we have seen convincingly enough that it is there already, though, probably at the present stage it is only embryonic and in a modified form, adapted to the peculiarities of China.

Development of the revolutionary crisis: There can be little doubt that further extensification and intensification of the revolutionary crisis in China is inevitable, and it is quite likely that the process will follow the lines of Sovietization. And Sovietization, apparently, is the road to Communist society, for the slogan "Soviets without Communists" seems absurd.

Partial set-backs must, of course, be expected. Severe defeats may even be inflicted by the counter-revolutionary forces of China, so well supplied with the foreign-made modern instruments of warfare, if not by Japanese or other foreigners participating directly in the suppression of the Red Menace. Local retreats of the forces of Revolution are to be expected also; the errors of leaders will be followed in many cases by disappointment among the masses and a temporary withdrawal of their support from certain political leaders, and even abandonment of certain slogans. But in general one is inclined to predict a mounting tide of the revolutionary waves. The Chinese masses are awakened and revolutionary action seems the only solution for their problems. The first step for the extensification of the Soviet movement seems to involve penetration of those provinces where Kuo-min-tang or other war lords are still in control. In consideration of the growing discontent and the sympathetic reception that Communist propaganda enjoys in these regions, it seems at least feasible.

The circumstances under which the Chinese Revolution is going on, favor rapid movement and accordingly swift progress. The present world-wide economic crisis is one of the phenomena which must facilitate the revolutionary process. Another is the success of the Russian Revolution, offering an enduring example of attainment. Indeed, Communist writers believe that China need not pass through the Capitalist stage at all, but may enter the socialist stage directly.

Comintern's Resolution on China: The Resolution on China passed in July, 1930, by the Comintern declared:

"The revolutionary democratic dictatorship of the proletariat and peasantry of China will differ considerably from the democratic dictatorship which was planned by the Bolsheviks in 1905 on consideration of the specific conditions which existed at the time of that revolution. First of all this difference is linked with the international position of the Chinese Revolution, and the existence of the USSR, *i.e.,* the country of dictatorship of the proletariat which is successfully proceeding with socialist construction. On the other hand, the situation, as it is developing in China, justifies the expectation that Communists will be in a majority in the Government. Thus the proletariat will be enabled to achieve not only ideological leadership, but also hegemony over the peasants. Moreover, it should be taken into account that the Chinese Revolution has to carry on a bitter struggle not only with feudalism and the militarists, but also with the foreign and Chinese capitalists. The democratic dictatorship in China will face the necessity of gradual confiscation of enterprises belonging to the foreigners, and so to make considerable steps of socialist character.

"This pressure of the socialist elements will constitute tne specific characteristic of the revolutionary democratic dictatorship of proletariat and peasantry in China. The Chinese Revolution in its advance from Capitalism to Socialism will have a larger number of consecutive transitory stages than the October Revolution had, but it will be able to shorten considerably the time required for its outgrowth into the social revolution; *i.e.,* will accomplish that advance, from the bourgeois-democratic to the socialist stage, more swiftly than it was expected under conditions prevailing at the time of the Revolution of 1905. . . ."

The "non-capitalist" development: In other words, "If successful, the bourgeois-democratic revolution of China will open the opportunity for socialist development." The words are those of a Communist commentator, Mr. P. Mif, who goes on to say that "its first, bourgeois-democratic, stage is preparing the prerequisites for the dictatorship of proletariat and the social revolution." [20]

Long ago Marx and Engels expressed the opinion that China might advance socio-economically at a more rapid tempo, because she does not need necessarily to go through the whole process of capitalistic development. Lenin elaborated this idea later on and maintained that to skip the Capitalist stage in China was quite feasible. In his opinion the way was through the application of the Soviet system, under the leadership of

[20] P. Mif, *The Chinese Revolution.* Moscow, 1932, p. 313.

the growing proletariat of China, and with the support of the USSR.

The work performed by the Russian Communists in China between 1923 and 1927 was by no means in vain. The seeds sown in these years came to flower in 1930. The enormous mass of labor and peasantry, which owned nothing, heard the call of Sun Yat-sen to rise in revolution against Imperialism and against the militarists with their well-to-do followers. The slogan of the revolution resounded, calling for the right of all classes to participate in the determination of living conditions; and Chinese—not Russian—Communists organized the masses and showed the way to the achievement of these aims.

"Any and every political crisis," wrote Lenin, "is useful, because it brings to the light what was hidden, reveals the actual forces involved in politics; it exposes lies and deceptive phrases and fictions; it demonstrates comprehensively the facts, and forces on the people the understanding of what is the reality." [21]

Accumulation of the revolutionary momentum: The new alignment of classes is already taking place in China. In this process the problems of the Revolution are being better defined, and the Soviet movement is developing concurrently. Increasingly the masses are attaining consciousness of their own strength. The revolutionary energy is coming to the surface among these discontented and desperate masses, and is being organized by the Communist Party, as the leader of revolution.

Its very first task, of course, is to be found in the agrarian revolutionary changes. Here the Communist Party and the industrial proletariat must coöperate with the peasants. This coöperation must bring about the unification of these main sources of revolt. When united they will form a mighty stream, against which no barriers can stand, whether they be set up by

[21] Lenin, v. XVII (the Russian edition), p. 350, as quoted in the *Problemi Kitaia,* No. 11, 1933, p. 35.

the bourgeoisie of China or by foreign Imperialists in the attempt to prevent the Chinese renaissance. Gradually, too, the agrarian revolution directed against the remnants of feudalism and landlordism, will develop into a national revolt against the foreign abuses.

"The successful 'today' of the Chinese Revolution," wrote A. Safaroff,[22] "is preparing its 'morrow.' The present struggle for land, though meeting the resistance of the guns of the Imperialists, is preparing the road for the future non-capitalist development of the country, which is only beginning to throw off the chains of the colonial slavery. This stage may be long, for the task of awakening the hundreds of millons of people who live under inhumanly hard conditions, is a task requiring enormous stores of revolutionary energy. Naturally it depends on today how, and how soon, the morrow will come. But, whatever the particular difficulties and temporary set-backs in the process of this revolutionary ascent and the development of the Chinese Revolution as a whole, one thing is quite certain that it is marching on. . . .

"The international system of the Imperialist Powers is decaying. The temporary 'stabilization of Capitalism' is disappearing at a high and accelerating tempo. The Imperialist domination over the colonials, the prevalence of the international system of world-wide grab and robbery, make the national revolutionary wars inevitable. Such wars against Imperialism require enormous concentration of forces. To overtake and crush the superior military technique, and the superior military strength of the Imperialists, enormous numbers of humans must be brought into the struggle under the hegemony of the proletariat and under the leadership of the Bolsheviks.

"All classes of colonials must pass an examination in the anti-Imperialist struggle. The Chinese bourgeoisie, which

[22] In *Problemi Kitaia*, Nos. 4 and 5, 1930, pp. 31-32.

seemed to the opportunists highly promising in that respect, ignominously failed at that historic test. Already for almost five years it has been chopping off the heads of thousands and thousands annually, and is doing this with a deadly methodicism. Only in that respect is it demonstrating perseverance and stability. . . . But, the cause of the Chinese Revolution is winning, and must win, for it is the cause of hundreds of millions of people, who cannot be anything but victorious."

Foreign intervention: Because the Chinese Revolution is already developing at such a tempo there is certain danger that the Powers may attempt to interfere in order to stop it; and this, according to certain students, may result in the partition of China. Personally we doubt that a unified front of the Imperialists for that end can be easily formed. The Powers may continue their policy of lopping off parts of China, to the constant refrain that the USSR is the "menace and aggressor"; but it is to be doubted if they will undertake a united effort to crush the Chinese Soviets. Nor are they likely to prevent the Soviets from following their own course, to aid in the reconstruction of China or to help her financially.

"Considering the conditions of present-day China, it seems quite unlikely that she can receive any large-scale financial assistance from the Powers. Without such assistance she can hardly hope to put her house effectively in order. It must be rather razed to the ground and built anew. . . . The Revolution is incomplete. It will persist and continue to develop, regardless of resistance from outside or within." So we wrote in 1931.[23] To these lines we must now add that since Tokyo's declaration of April, 1934, advising the Western Powers to keep hands off China, their coöperation becomes proportionately unlikely.

[23] V. A. Yakhontoff, *Russia and the Soviet Union in the Far East.* Coward McCann, New York, p. 230.

The Outlook: Undoubtedly foreign help to Nanking and to other enemies of Soviet China has prolonged the struggle. But, judging by what the Chinese Soviets have accomplished in spite of it, one may suppose that were this support withdrawn, most, if not all, of China would "turn Communist," probably within a very short time.

APPENDICES

CONSTITUTION OF THE CHINESE SOVIET REPUBLIC [1]

The first All-China Soviet Congress hereby proclaims before the toiling masses of China and of the whole world this Constitution of the Chinese Soviet Republic which recites the principal purposes to be accomplished throughout all China.

The accomplishment of these purposes has already begun in the existing Soviet districts. But the First All-China Soviet Congress recognizes that this Constitution can be given full virtue and effect only after the rule of imperialism and the Kuomintang shall have been finally overthrown and the Soviet Republic shall have established its power throughout all China. Then alone will the Constitution as hereby drawn up find more concrete application and become in all its detailed provisions the Constitution of the Chinese Soviet Republic.

The First All-China Soviet Congress calls upon all Chinese workers, peasants and toilers to proceed to put this Constitution into operation throughout all China, under the guidance of the provisional government of the Soviet Republic, and to fight for the realization of the following principal aims:

1. It shall be the purpose of the Constitution of the Chinese Soviet Republic to guarantee the democratic dictatorship of the proletariat and peasantry in the Soviet districts and to secure the triumph of the dictatorship throughout the whole of China. It shall be our task to finally establish this dictatorship throughout China. It shall be the aim of this dictatorship to destroy all feudal survivals, to annihilate the might of the war lords of China, to unite China, systematically, to limit the development of capitalism, to build up the economy of the state, to develop the class-consciousness and organization of the proletariat, to rally to its banner the broad masses of the village poor in order to effect the transition to the dictatorship of the proletariat.

2. The Chinese Soviet Government is building up a state of the democratic dictatorship of the workers and peasants. All power

[1] Courtesy of the "International Publishers."

shall be vested in the Soviets of Workers, Peasants and Red Army men and in the entire toiling population. Under the Soviet Government the workers, peasants, Red Army men and the entire toiling population shall have the right to elect their own deputies to give effect to their power. Only capitalists, landlords, the gentry, militarists, reactionary officials, *tukhao,* monks—all exploiting and counter-revolutionary elements—shall be deprived of the right to elect deputies to participate in the government and to enjoy political freedom.

3. In the Chinese Soviet Republic Supreme Power shall be vested in the All-China Congress of Soviets of Workers', Peasants', and Red Army Deputies. In the interval between Congresses the supreme organ of power shall be the provisional All-China Central Executive Committee of the Soviets; the Central Executive Committee shall appoint a Council of People's Commissars, which shall conduct all governmental affairs, pass laws, issue orders, etc.

4. All workers, peasants, Red Army men and all toilers and their families, without distinction of sex, religion or nationality (Chinese, Manchurians, Mongolians, Mahometans, Tibetans, Mao, Li as well as all Koreans, Formosians, Annamites, etc., living in China) shall while on Soviet territory, be equal before the law and shall be citizens of the Soviet Republic. In order that the workers, peasants, soldiers and toiling masses may actually hold the reins of power, the following regulations concerning Soviet elections shall be established:

All the above-mentioned Soviet citizens who shall have attained to the age of sixteen shall be entitled to vote and to be voted for in the elections to the Soviets. They shall elect deputies to all congresses of Workers' Peasants' and Red Army Deputies (Soviets); they shall discuss and decide all national and local questions. The workers shall elect their deputies in the factories; the peasants, artisans and urban poor shall elect deputies according to their several places of residence. Delegates to the soviets shall be elected for a definite term; they shall participate in the work of one of the organizations or commissions attached to the town or village Soviets and shall periodically submit reports to their electors concerning their activities. The electors shall have the right at all times to recall their deputies and demand new elections. Since the proletariat alone can lead the broad masses to Socialism, the Chinese Soviet Government grants special advantages to the proletariat in the elections to the Soviets by allowing it a greater number of deputies.

5. It shall be the purpose of the Soviet Government radically to improve the standard of living of the working class, to pass labour

legislation, to introduce the eight-hour working day, to fix a minimum wage and to institute social insurance and state assistance to the unemployed as well as to grant the workers the right to control industry.

6. In setting itself the task of abolishing feudalism and radically improving the standard of living of the peasants the Soviet Government in China shall pass a land law, shall order the confiscation of the land of the landlords and its distribution among the poor and middle peasants, with a view towards the ultimate nationalization of the land.

7. It shall be the purpose of the Soviet Government in China to defend the interests of the workers and peasants and restrict the development of capitalism, with a view to liberating the toiling masses from capitalist exploitation and leading them to the socialist order of society. The Soviet Government in China shall free the toiling masses from all burdensome taxation and contributions introduced by previous counter-revolutionary governments and shall put into effect a single progressive tax. It shall adopt every conceivable measure to suppress all attempts at wrecking and sabotage on the part of either native or foreign capitalists; it shall pursue an economic policy which shall be directed towards defending the interests of the worker and peasant masses, which shall be understood by these masses and which shall lead to socialism.

8. The Soviet Government in China shall set itself the goal of freeing China from the yoke of imperialism. It shall declare the complete independence of the Chinese people, shall refuse to recognize any political or economic privileges for the imperialists in China and shall abolish all unequal agreements and foreign loans made by the counter-revolutionary Chinese governments. No foreign imperialist troops, whether land, sea or air, shall be stationed on any territory of the Chinese Soviets. All concessions or territories leased by the imperialists in China shall be unconditionally returned to China. All customs houses, railways, steamship companies, mining enterprises, factories, workshops, etc., in the hands of the imperialists shall be confiscated and nationalised. It shall be lawful for foreign capitalists to renew their leases for their various enterprises and to continue the operation of the same, provided these capitalists shall fully comply with the laws of the Soviet Government.

9. The Soviet Government in China does its utmost to bring about the culmination of the workers' and peasants' revolution in its final victory throughout the whole of China. It declares that it is incumbent upon every toiler to participate in the revolutionary class struggle. The gradual introduction of universal military service and

the change from voluntary to compulsory military service shall be worked out specially. The right to bear arms in defence of the revolution shall be granted only to workers, peasants and the toiling masses; all counter-revolutionary and exploiting elements must be completely disarmed.

10. The Soviet Government in China guarantees to the workers, peasants and toilers freedom of speech and the press as well as the right to assembly; it is to be opposed to bourgeois and landlord democracy, but is in favour of the democracy of the workers and peasant masses. It annihilates the economic and political might of the bourgeoisie and the landlords, in order to remove all obstacles on the road to freedom for the workers and peasants. The workers, peasants and toiling masses alone shall enjoy the use of printing shops, meeting halls and similar establishments as a material basis for the realization of these rights and liberties. Furthermore, all propaganda and other similar activities by reactionaries shall be suppressed and all exploiters be deprived of all political liberties.

11. It is the purpose of the Soviet Government in China to guarantee the emancipation of women; it recognizes the freedom of marriage and puts into operation various measures in the defence of women to enable women gradually to attain to the material basis required for their emancipation from the slavery of domestic work, and to give them the possibility of participating in the social, economic, political and cultural life of the country.

12. The Soviet Government in China shall guarantee to all workers, peasants and the toiling masses the right to education. The Soviet Government will, as far as possible, begin at once to introduce free universal education. The Soviet Government defends the interests of youth and gives youth every opportunity of participating in the political and cultural life of the country with a view to developing new social forces.

13. The Soviet Government in China guarantees true religious freedom to the workers, peasants and the toiling population. Adhering to the principle of the complete separation of church and state, the Soviet Government neither favours nor grants any financial assistance to any religion whatsoever. All Soviet citizens shall enjoy the right to engage in anti-religious propaganda. No religious institution of the imperialists shall be allowed to exist unless it shall comply with Soviet law.

14. The Soviet Government in China recognizes the right of self-determination of the national minorities in China, their right to complete separation from China and to the formation of an independent state for each national minority. All Mongolians, Tibetans,

Miao, Yao, Koreans and others living on the territory of China, shall enjoy the full right to self-determination, i.e., they may either join the Chinese Soviet state or secede from it and form their own state as they may prefer. The Soviet Government in China will do its utmost to assist the national minorities in liberating themselves from the yoke of the imperialists, the Kuomintang militarists, the princes, lamas and others, and in achieving complete freedom and autonomy. The Soviet Government must encourage the development of national culture and of the respective national languages of these peoples.

15. The Chinese Soviet Government offers asylum to Chinese and foreign revolutionaries persecuted for their revolutionary activities; it guides and assists them in restoring their vigour so that they may fight with increased strength for the victory of the revolution.

16. All foreign toilers living in districts under the jurisdiction of the Soviet Government shall enjoy the equal protection of all rights granted to toilers under the Soviet law.

17. The Soviet Government in China declares its readiness to form a revolutionary united front with the world proletariat and all oppressed nations, and proclaims the Soviet Union, the land of proletarian dictatorship to be its loyal ally.

LAND LAW [1]

The peasant struggle launched under the leadership of the proletariat continues to develop and each day rises to new heights. Despite the violent resistance of the imperialists and militarists, the Soviet movement grows and expands. In one area after another the Chinese peasantry, armed and organized in the ranks of the Red Army, casts off the century-old yoke of the feudal barons and landlords, the *tukhao* and the gentry; it confiscates and redistributes the land of these exploiters; it demolishes the feudal order of society, destroys the power of the Kuomintang and builds up the workers' and peasants' Soviet Government—a government which will consistently and finally solve the problems of the anti-imperialist and agrarian revolution.

The First Congress of Soviets of Workers', Peasants' and Red Army Deputies of China ratifies the confiscation of the lands of the landlords and of other big landowners. In order to establish uniform regulations for the confiscation and distribution of land, the First Congress, in defence of the interests of the basic peasant masses and in order to safeguard the further development of the revolution,

[1] Courtesy of the "International Publishers."

has passed the following agrarian law which will best secure the solution of the agrarian question.

Article 1: All the lands of the feudal lords and the landlords, the militarists and the *tukhao,* gentry and other big private landowners, shall be subject to confiscation without any compensation whatever, irrespective of whether they themselves work their lands or rent them out on lease. The Soviets must distribute the confiscated lands among the poor and middle peasants. The former owners of confiscated lands shall not be entitled to receive any land allotment. Agricultural labourers, coolies and toiling peasants shall enjoy equal rights to land allotments, irrespective of sex. Independent workers living in the villages who shall have lost their previous work shall likewise be entitled to a portion of the land, subject to the consent of the peasant masses. Aged persons, orphans and widows, who shall not be in a position to work and who shall have no relatives on whom to be dependent, must be given social relief by the Soviet Government, or it shall be necessary to see to it that their land allotment shall be attended to.

Article 2: The Red Army is the front rank fighter in the defence of the Soviet Government and the overthrow of the rule of imperialism. Therefore each Red Army man must be given a plot of land, and the Soviet Government must see to it that his land is tilled, whether his home shall be in a district where the Soviet Government shall be in power or whether a counter-revolutionary government still exists there.

Article 3: It is a peculiar feature of the Chinese *tukhao* that he is at one and the same time a landowner and a usurer; therefore his land shall be also subject to confiscation. If any *tukhao* after his land has been confiscated, does not participate in any counter-revolutionary action and shall agree to work his land by the use of his own labour power, he may be assigned land, but not of the best quality, dependent in size upon the amount of labour of which he is capable.

Article 4: All the property and lands of all counter-revolutionary organizations and of the military organizations of the white army, as well as of the active participants in counter-revolution, shall be confiscated. However, exceptions to this rule shall be permissible in the case of poor and middle peasants who shall have been drawn into the struggle against the Soviets because of their ignorance and concerning whom this fact shall have been recognized by the local Soviet. But their leaders shall without fail be dealt with according to the provision of the present law.

Article 5: The First Congress recognizes the principle that an equitable distribution of all land is the most consistent method of destroying all feudal agrarian relations and the shackles of the private ownership of land by the landlords. However, the local Soviet Governments shall on no account carry out this measure by force, by an order issued by higher authorities, but shall explain this principle to the peasantry from every angle. This measure may be put into operation only with the direct support and at the desire of the basic masses of the peasantry. Thus, if the majority of the middle peasants so desire, they may be excluded from the operation of the principle of equalitarian distribution.

Article 6: All lands belonging to religious institutions, to temples and all other public lands shall without fail be delivered into the possession of the peasants by the Soviet Government. However, in disposing of these lands, it shall be essential to obtain the voluntary support of the peasants, so that their religious feelings may not be offended.

Article 7: The well-to-do peasantry seek to have the land distributed according to the means of production. The First Congress considers this to be a counter-revolutionary effort on the part of the *tukhao* to hinder the development of the agrarian revolution and to further their own ends; determined resistance must be offered to all such attempted extortions. The local Soviets, in conformity with the local conditions of every village, shall choose the method of land division most advantageous to the poor and middle peasants: according to a standard of labour or consumption,[2] i.e., division on a mixed principle; or division of the land among the middle and poor peasants as well as agricultural labourers in equal portions according to the number of consumers, and among the *tukhao* according to the labour power supplied. That is in localities where equalitarian distribution shall take place according to the number of consumers, every *tukhao* capable of working shall receive as much land as shall be allotted to one consumer. In dividing up the land, not only the area of the land assigned but also the quality of its soil, especially its productivity, shall also be taken into consideration. Furthermore, in dividing up the land it shall be essential to introduce all possible land reforms in order to create the necessary conditions for destroying feudal survivals like scattered land holdings or highways running across fields.

[2] *I.e.*, shall allot such a plot as a man is capable of working with his own hands, or as is required to feed himself and his family.—ED.

LABOUR CODE [1]

(Adopted by the First All-China Congress of Soviets)

1. General Regulations

Article 1. This Labour Code shall apply to all persons working for wages in industrial enterprises, workshops, or in any other productive undertaking, or in any institution (including government, co-operative and private institutions).

Article 2. This Labour Code shall not apply to the enlisted men or the commanders serving in the land, sea or air forces of the Chinese Soviet Republic.

Article 3. Every collective agreement—agreement of hire or other labour contract, already in operation or to go into operation in the future, shall be declared invalid if it shall include any conditions of labour less advantageous to the workers than those fixed by the present Labour Code.

Artice 4: Besides the general decrees embodied in this Labour Code, special decrees shall be issued by the Central Executive Committee, the Council of People's Commissars and the Central Commissariat of Labour concerning the conditions of labour of the agricultural labourers, forestry workers, seasonal workers, workers employed on communications, coolies, domestic workers, cooks and other persons working under special labour conditions.

Article 5. The Central Commissariat of Labour shall in addition prescribe definite weight limits which may be carried by coolies (including transport workers, porters, boatmen, wheelbarrow-men, palanquin-bearers and dock workers). The Central Commissariat of Labour shall also publish detailed regulations concerning the right of independent toilers, when working for wages, to enjoy the provisions of the present Labour Code.

2. Regulations Governing the Hiring of Workers

Article 6. Workers shall be hired in accordance with the terms of collective agreements and through the medium of the trade unions and labour exchanges. It shall be strictly prohibited for workers to be hired through the medium of contractors, employment agents, compradores or any form of private employment office for the hiring of workers, foremen, etc.

Article 7. All labour exchanges shall be organized and controlled

[1] Courtesy of the "International Publishers."

by the Commissariat of Labour. All private labour exchanges and offices acting as agencies for the hiring of labour shall be strictly prohibited.

Article 8. It shall be unlawful to exact any payment from any worker, or to deduct any amount from his wages, in lieu of commission for having procured work for him, and any violation of this prohibition shall be severely punished.

Article 9. Any person seeking work shall register at one of the labour exchanges to be organized by the Central Commissariat of Labour or by a local labour branch, and shall be entered on the list of the labour exchange.

3. *Collective Agreements and Labour Contracts*

Article 10. A collective agreement is a contract entered into collectively between a trade union, as the representative of all the industrial workers and office employees of a given enterprise, on the one hand, and the employer on the other hand. The collective agreement shall determine the conditions of labour of those working for wages in any enterprise or institution, in the family, or in private employ; the agreement shall also state the terms on which the employer will contract to employ any person hereafter.

Article 11. The conditions of the collective agreement shall be valid as regards all persons working in the given enterprise whether such persons shall be trade union members or not.

Article 12. Collective agreements registered in the Commissariat of Labour shall become effective on the day on which they shall be signed, or on the day stipulated in the agreement.

Article 13. A labour contract (or agreement) is an agreement between one or several workers and their employer; any condition in a labour agreement which shall be worse than the corresponding provision contained in the Labour Code or in any labour decision in effect or in the collective agreement shall be invalid. No collective or labour agreement shall be concluded for any period of time exceeding one year. The trade union shall have the right to demand the annulment of the agreement before the term fixed in the agreement for its expiration.

4. *Working Hours*

Article 14. According to the present Labour Code the normal working day of any person working for wages shall not exceed eight hours.

Article 15. The working day of adolescents between sixteen and eighteen years of age shall not exceed six hours, and for children between the ages of fourteen and sixteen years it shall not exceed four hours.

Article 16. In branches of industry where work is dangerous or injurious to health (for example in underground mining, in working with lead, zinc or other harmful substances) the working day for industrial workers shall be reduced to six hours or less. A list of industries injurious to health stating the corresponding reduction in the working day for the respective industries, shall be drawn up and published by the Central Commissariat of Labour.

Article 17. Workers engaged on night work shall be entitled to have their working time reduced by one hour as compared with the corresponding normal working day of the day workers: (thus, where the normal working day is eight hours, it shall be reduced to seven; where the normal working day is six hours, it shall be reduced to five, etc.).

Note. Any work between 9 o'clock in the evening and 6 o'clock the following morning shall be considered night work.

Article 18. No overtime work in excess of the working hours fixed by the Labour Code shall be allowed in any branch of industry or in any seasonal work except in special cases, when special permission shall first be obtained from the labour inspection bodies and trade unions in question.

5. *Rest Time*

Article 19. Every worker shall be given a regular, unbroken, weekly rest for a period of not less than 42 hours.

Article 20. Any person who shall have worked for a period of more than six months at any one enterprise shall be entitled to an annual vacation of at least two weeks, with full pay. Workers engaged in injurious industries shall be entitled to an annual vacation of four weeks with full pay.

Article 21. It is unlawful to work on any of the following anniversaries or holidays: January 1—New Year's Day, January 21—Lenin Memorial Day, the anniversary of the death of the leader of the world revolution; February 7—anniversary of the shooting of the Peking-Hankow railway workers by the militarists; March 18—Anniversary of the Paris Commune; May 1—International Labour Day; May 30—Anniversary of the Shanghai events in 1925; November 7—Anniversary of the proletarian revolution in the Soviet Union and the formation of the Chinese Soviet Republic; December 11—Anniversary of the Canton uprising.

Note.—Local labour organizations in agreement with the local trade union councils may establish special holidays or rest days to meet the special conditions which prevail in any locality. Wages must be paid for all holidays and rest days.

Article 22. On days immediately preceding rest days or holidays, the working day shall not exceed six hours.

Article 23. The working day established by the present Labour Code shall include an interval of half an hour or an hour for meals, with no deduction in wages for this interval.

Article 24. Leaves of absence given to industrial workers and office employees because of illness or pregnancy shall not affect the length of the annual vacation stipulated in Article 20.

6. *Wages*

Article 25. No worker shall receive a lower wage than the absolute minimum wage fixed by the Commissariat of Labour. The minimum wage for the workers of various branches of industry shall be re-examined by the Commissariat of Labour not less than once every three months.

Article 26. In actual practice the rates of wages at all enterprises (state, co-operative and private) shall be fixed by the workers (trade union representatives) and the respective owners or managers in their collective agreements.

Article 27. For all overtime work permitted by the bodies of the workers' inspection and the trade unions, double the normal wage rates shall be paid.

Article 28. For all work performed on rest days or holidays and permitted by the bodies of the workers' inspection and the trade unions, double the normal wage rates shall be paid.

Article 29. Working women and adolescents, producing the same amount of work as adult working-men similarly employed shall receive the same wage rates as the latter. Children and adolescents shall enjoy reduced working hours but they shall be paid a full day's wages according to the wage rate in effect in the given branch of industry.

Article 30. Night work shall be paid at rates higher than the normal rates, *viz.,* as follows: a person doing eight hours' night work shall be paid at a rate one-seventh higher than the normal rate, and persons doing six hours' night work (on dangerous work) shall be paid at a rate one-fifth higher than the normal rate. Any person doing piecework at night time shall be paid an additional one-seventh of his average wage if he shall have an eight-hour working day, and an additional one-fifth of his average wage if he shall have a six-hour working day.

Article 31. All wages to which a worker may be entitled shall be paid in cash (not in kind) regularly each week or twice a month (never less than two a month). Moreover, any failure to pay wages promptly shall be strictly prohibited. All wages must be paid direct to each worker personally.

Article 32. Wages for the regular annual vacation shall be paid to the industrial workers and office employees in advance, before the commencement of their vacations.

Article 33. Piecework rates shall be fixed by collective agreements between the workers (acting through their trade union representatives) and their employer. Piecework rates must be based on the average work performed per day and the average daily wage (calculated according to the time required in the given branch of industry to produce the given article).

7. *Woman Labour, Adolescent Labour and Child Labour*

Article 34. In addition to the general rights granted to women, adolescents and children by the provisions of the Labour Code which specifically safeguard the labour of women, adolescents and children, the following special regulations shall be established:

Article 35. No women, adolescents or children shall be allowed to work in branches of industry where the work is especially heavy or injurious to health. A list of the industries in which women, adolescents and children shall be prohibited from working shall be drawn up and published by the Central Commissariat of Labour. (This list shall include underground work in mines, work in rubber, lead, copper, mercury and pewter plants or in foundries, etc.; forest work in places too high or too low, etc.)

Article 36. Women shall be prohibited from doing work which requires the carrying of weights exceeding forty pounds; if the carrying of heavy weights shall constitute a necessary part of the work in any particular industry, the working day for women shall not exceed two-thirds of the normal day.

Article 37. All night work shall be strictly prohibited for male or female workers under the age of eighteen, for pregnant women, and for nursing mothers.

Article 38. All women engaged in physical labour shall be granted leaves of absence before and after childbirth to the extent of eight weeks in all, during which time they shall be paid the wages in full. Women employed in offices, or engaged in mental work in institutions (for example: women managers, secretaries, etc.) shall be given a total of six weeks' leave of absence before and after childbirth, during which time their wages shall be paid in full. After an abortion or miscarriage, working women shall be granted two weeks' leave of absence with full pay.

Note.—The wages due for the period of such leaves of absence before and after childbirth and in cases of abortion shall be paid by the enterprise. Where social insurance is in force, it shall be paid by the insurance office.

Article 39. No woman worker may be dismissed from work during the five months preceding childbirth and the nine months following thereafter. Nor may such women workers be assigned work in a different enterprise without their consent.

Article 40. Working women who are nursing their children shall be granted a half-hour interval every three hours to feed their children, which intervals shall be over and above the interval established in Article 23, and for which no deduction in wages shall be made. Moreover, a room shall be set aside at each enterprise for feeding the children and a children's room shall be provided with attendants specially secured on the responsibility of the enterprise.

Article 41. It shall be strictly prohibited to employ children under the age of 14. Children between the ages of 14 and 16 may be employed only after the competent labour inspection bodies have granted permission.

Article 42. Each undertaking shall keep a complete and detailed list of all adolescents employed therein, indicating their respective ages, working hours and wages.

Article 43. Special courses enabling adolescents and young workers between the ages of 14 and 18 to raise their qualification, and also for general educational purposes, must be organized in all factories and shops; the cost of such courses shall be borne by the enterprise.

The old system of apprenticeship and of "training workers" shall be strictly prohibited. All forms of contracts concluded with apprentices which establish worse conditions for them than those provided for in the decrees comprising the present Labour Code concerning working hours, wages, treatment of workers, etc., shall be declared null and void.

8. *Labour Protection*

Article 44. No enterprise or institution shall start work or change its location unless a proper labour inspection body shall first have inspected the working premises and granted permission to work there.

Article 45. All machinery shall be supplied with the necessary safety-guards; new machines may not be put into operation unless they shall first have been examined by the proper labour inspection body and the necessary safety-guards been set up.

Article 46. Special workers' outfits shall be supplied to the workers at all enterprises. The type of outfit and the length of time for which it shall be worn before new outfit shall be issued shall be specially regulated by the Central Commissariat of Labour.

Article 47. In enterprises where the conditions of work and the labour process itself are particularly injurious to the health of the workers or shall endanger their lives (abnormal temperatures, poisonous gases, etc.), the administration shall provide special safety apparel and other preventative appliances such as eye-glasses, masks, respirators, soap, special foodstuffs; butter, milk, etc., and in enterprises where workers come into contact with poisons, the corresponding antitoxins must be on hand. It shall not be the duty of the workers themselves to attend to these measures. Moreover, it shall be necessary for all workers to undergo periodical medical examinations.

Article 48. It shall be strictly prohibited to deduct fines or other penalties from wages. Similarly, deductions for breakages or bad work shall likewise be prohibited. It shall further be strictly prohibited to require cash deposits or cash guarantees of any kind from any worker after he shall have been taken on to work, irrespective of the length of time for which they are to be made.

Article 49. All deductions from workers' wages for stoppages at work for which the owner shall be responsible (breakage of machinery, lack of raw materials, refusal of the owner to carry out the regulations of the Soviet Government, etc.) shall be prohibited.

Article 50. All deductions from the wages of workers who shall have been absent from work in order to participate in elections to Soviets, or to attend Soviet congresses, or trade union congresses or conferences, who shall have been absent by reason of work done in factory committees, or by reason of a summons to attend court as witnesses, experts or lay judges shall be prohibited, regardless of the period of time during which they shall have been so absent.

Article 51. A worker or office employee, who shall be called to military service in the Red Army and who in consequence shall lose his employment, shall be paid three months' average wages in advance.

Article 52. The employer shall be obliged to supply the worker with the instruments of labour, and no deduction in wages shall be made for the use of these instruments. Where a worker shall use his own instruments, the owner shall compensate the worker to the extent of their original cost. This shall be provided in detail in the collective agreements.

Article 53. Communal dwelling-houses shall be built for the workers at the expense of the enterprise and shall be put at the disposal of the workers and their families free of charge. Enterprises which shall not have built communal dwelling-houses shall pay the workers a sum of money monthly as rent allowance.

Article 54. In the event that the employer shall rescind the labour agreement, without authority to do so, he shall pay two weeks' average wages as relief while new work is being sought.[2]

Article 55. In case an industrial worker or office employee shall be temporarily disabled, the employer shall be obliged to keep his position open for him and shall pay him his previous average wage.

Article 56. Labour inspectors shall have the power to close any enterprise in which it shall appear, upon verifying the extent to which the provisions of the labour laws have been complied with, that the health and lives of the workers are in direct danger. The functions and tasks of the labour inspectors shall be published by the Commissariat of Labour as a supplement.

Article 57. Any ailment acquired by any worker during the process of work shall by virtue of the present Labour Code be deemed an industrial accident and full compensation shall be paid therefore.

9. *The All-China Federation of Labour and Its Local Organizations*

Article 58. The All-China Federation of Labour shall unite the industrial workers and office employees of all enterprises and institutions throughout the country. All trade unions, including their local organizations, shall be organized according to the Rules passed by the All-China Congress of the Chinese Federation of Labour. No body of workers organized in any other way than on the basis of these Rules shall receive the status of a trade union, or enjoy the rights granted by law to trade unions.

Article 59. The Soviets guarantee freedom of action to the trade unions. The unions shall have the right to declare strikes and to lead them; they shall also have the right to negotiate and conclude collective agreements on behalf of the workers. Provincial and industrial trade union councils shall have the right to conclude collective agreements on behalf of all workers in a given branch of industry or all workers of a given locality.

[2] With the aim of undermining the economic position in Soviet districts, owners used to close down their enterprises and thus compel industrial workers and office employees to quit work "of their own accord." In order to combat this practice the present article of the Law was added.—ED.

Article 60. All collective and labour agreements shall be executed under the control of the factory or shop committees which shall be the basic organs of the trade unions in the enterprises. The latter shall also see that the Labour Code and all decisions on labour questions are complied with.

Article 61. The main functions of the trade union shall be to represent the workers individually and collectively, to defend the interests of all persons working for wages, to strive to raise the economic and cultural level of the workers and to give every possible active encouragement to the consolidation, development and defence of the Soviet movement and the Soviet Government.

Article 62. The trade union shall directly participate in the management of all state and co-operative enterprises; in private enterprises the trade unions shall set up special bodies to control industry.

Article 63. The Soviet Government shall render material assistance to the trade unions and shall grant them reduced rates for postal, telegraphic and telephone service, electric lighting, water supply and other communal services; also for the use of railways or steamships.

Article 64. The employer shall pay 2 per cent. of the total amount paid out in wages to defray the maintenance expenses of the trade union; he shall also pay 1 per cent. which shall be applied to the cultural requirements of the workers.

Article 65. When an employer shall desire to discharge a worker, he shall be obliged to secure the consent of the trade union. The trade union, factory, or shop committees, as the case may be, shall by virtue of being the workers' representatives, be members of the conflicts commissions to be established for settling conflicts which may arise between the workers and the capitalists.

Article 66. At each enterprise the factory committee shall institute a labour protection commission to consist of from three to seven of the most active workers. The functions of these commissions shall be as follows:

(*a*) To see that the articles concerning labour protection contained in the Labour Code as well as all provisions of the collective agreement shall be carried out;

(*b*) to see that the orders and directions of the labour inspectors are carried out.

Article 67. The trade unions shall have the power to propose decisions concerning labour to the Soviet Government and to recommend and elect labour inspectors. The members of the factory committee shall have the right, on presenting their factory committee certificates, to enter and leave without let or hindrance any part of the factory premises and to inspect the same.

10. *Social Insurance*

Article 68. Social insurance shall extend to all wage workers, irrespective of whether they shall be employed in state, co-operative or private enterprises and regardless of the length of the working day or the form of additional payment.

Article 69. Employers shall be obliged to pay in addition to the workers' wages, a sum amounting to from 10 to 15 per cent. of the total wages, which shall constitute the social insurance fund.

Note.—On no account may the social insurance fund be appropriated for purposes having no relation to social insurance.

Article 70. Social insurance benefits shall be given in the following form:

(*a*) *Free Medical Aid.*—The expenses incurred in all cases of sickness shall be paid by Social Insurance. All ailments of a general nature, all diseases contracted while at work, and injuries received through accident and all occupational diseases shall be included herein. The members of the families of those working shall also be entitled to free medical aid.

(*b*) Relief granted in connection with *temporary disablement;* this shall include wages paid during sickness, injury, pregnancy, childbirth and the care of sick members of the family. *Sick benefits* shall be paid from the first day of sickness in an amount equal to the total wages of the patient but not exceeding a definitely stipulated maximum; disablement benefits may also be paid to invalids who have become disabled in consequence of an occupational disease, in such amount as shall be fixed for invalidity.

(*c*) *Unemployment Relief*

1. Trade union members shall be entitled to unemployment relief after one year's work; and after two years' work for persons who are not trade union members;

2. Unemployed persons shall be entitled to unemployment relief only if they shall be registered at a labour exchange, or local branch of their trade union, or if they shall produce documents proving that they were wage workers and attesting their trade union membership where the same is claimed;

3. The length of the term during which unemployment relief shall be paid may be limited according to local conditions and the state of the social insurance fund.

Note.—Unemployment benefits shall likewise be paid to adolescents, regardless of the nature of their work and the length of time for which they shall have worked.

(*d*) *Disablement and Old Age Benefits.* Any worker who, in consequence of general causes, accident or occupational disease, shall have become partially or completely disabled, or who shall be incapable of working in consequence of old age, shall receive cash benefits as soon as his application shall be approved by the special commission appointed to investigate the same and ascertain the degree of his disablement as well as the size of his family.

(*e*) *Childbirth Relief*. Any working woman shall for a period of ten months be entitled to additional relief for the purchase of articles required for her child. This additional relief shall not exceed a total of two months' wages.

(*f*) *Funeral Relief*. In the event of the death of a worker, or of a member of his family, the insurance office shall grant him a relief payment to cover funeral expenses;

(*g*) *Poor Relief*. The family of a worker who before his death was the sole support of the said family, shall, after his death be entitled to special relief, the amount and duration of which payment shall be ascertained by a special commission, dependent upon the number of persons in the family. This relief shall be granted to all persons who have been wage workers for over six months.

Note.—Until the insurance funds shall be organized, all the relief granted under the present article must be paid by the employer.

Article 71. The employer shall have no right to interfere in the management of the insurance office of the expenditure of the social insurance fund. While it shall be the duty of the employer to pay his social insurance contribution, the social insurance commission, which shall be appointed by representatives of the trade unions, confirmed by the government and controlled by the Commissariat of Labour shall be in charge of receiving all monies of the insurance fund, and of the application of the same.

11. *Bodies for the Adjustment of Labour Conflicts and the Determination of Labour Code Violations*

Article 72. The violation of any of the provisions of the Labour Code and all disputes between workers and capitalists shall be heard and either adjudicated by mandatory order of the labour session of the People's Court, or shall be adjusted by amicable decision of the conflicts commission consisting of representatives of the workers and capitalists; and the arbitration commission of the Commissariat of Labour. Detailed rules to govern conflict commissions, and arbitration commissions will be published subsequently by the People's Commissariat of Labour.

Article 73. All cases of violations of the Labour Code, of decisions on labour questions and of collective agreements shall be heard by the Labour Session of the Court irrespective of the kind of penalty that attaches under the criminal law.

12. *Amendments*

Article 74. Doubtful and disputed points in the interpretation of the present Labour Code shall be adjudicated by the Central Commissariat of Labour; and in those Soviet districts which shall not be contiguous to the Central Soviet region, such points shall be clarified by the labour departments of the corresponding provincial Soviets.

Article 75. In any Soviet districts which shall not be contiguous to the Central Soviet Region, the supreme governmental authorities shall be empowered to establish rules and regulations otherwise in the exclusive jurisdiction of the Central Commissariat of Labour with the same force and effect as if they had been established by the Central Commissariat of Labour.

Decision of the Central Executive Committee of the Chinese Soviet Republic Concerning the Carrying Out of the Code of Labour

The Central Executive Committee has passed the following decision concerning the carrying out of the code of labour:

1. The Code of Labour passed by the First All-China Congress of Soviets of Workers', Peasants' and Soldiers' Deputies shall be put into operation.

2. The Code of Labour shall go into effect on January 1, 1932.

3. From the moment the Code of Labour shall go into effect, all labour legislation and all decisions on labour questions previously passed or handed down by governmental bodies shall be null and void.

4. On the basis of the Code of Labour the Council of People's Commissars and the Central Commissariat of Labour shall be entitled to publish special regulations and orders developing the Code of Labour.

5. Changes and amendments to the Code of Labour shall be published as Decrees of the Central Executive Committee.

6. The Labour Code shall be valid throughout the whole territory of the Chinese Soviet Republic.

7. The violation of any decision of the Labour Code or of any regulation on labour which may be published in the future shall be punishable as a criminal offence.

MAO TSE-DUN,
    President of the Central Executive Committee.
SAN IN,
CHANG GO-TAO,
    Vice-Presidents.
December 20, 1931.

CIRCULAR TELEGRAM OF THE PROVISIONAL CENTRAL GOVERNMENT OF THE SOVIET REPUBLIC OF CHINA DECLARING WAR AGAINST JAPAN [1]

Since the military occupation of Manchuria on September 18, 1931, Japanese imperialism has unceasingly used its naval, military, and air forces against the people of China, invading Shanghai and other towns, threatening ports along the seacoast and the Yangtse river, killing by bombardment the people of China and burning their dwellings. This plunder and destruction cost unestimable losses in the North—East and Shanghai—Woosung areas. This destruction and slaughter is still being continued, is being extended.

The counter-revolutionary Kuomintang government and the militarists of all cliques following their general practice of capitulation to imperialism, surrendered Manchuria, Shanghai, and Woosung one after another to Japanese imperialism, leaving unchecked the slaughter of the Chinese people. At present, the Kuomintang, under the pretext of negotiating for peace, is selling the whole of China. It is exerting the utmost effort to hasten the imperialist partition of China. To demonstrate its loyalty to imperialism, the Kuomintang with all the means at its disposal suppresses the nation-wide anti-Japanese and anti-imperialist revolutionary movement, all anti-Japanese organizations, breaks all anti-Japanese strikes of the workers, shoots down the anti-Japanese masses, compels soldiers of the 19th Route Army and the People's Volunteers (who are voluntarily carrying on a war of resistance to Japanese invasion at Shanghai and Woosung) to retreat. The so-called "prolonged resistance," the so-called "negotiate peace while offering resistance" of the Kuomintang Government and of the militarists of all other cliques are in reality nothing but phrases concocted to fool the masses.

The Soviet Districts are free of the yoke of imperialism. Yet the Kuomintang Government and its militarists not only willingly handed over Manchuria, Shanghai, and the whole of China to imperialism, but also carried on with all its military strength an attack against the Chinese Red Army, which is the only force really fighting the national revolutionary war. By this attack the Kuomintang is attempting to destroy the Soviet power. All the demagogy of the Kuomintang is calculated to cover up the acts of betrayal of China and of their guilt in the degradation of the Chinese people. Actually, the Kuomintang is the tool of imperialism. It is an obstacle to the advance of the national revolutionary war.

[1] As published by the *Friends of the Chinese People*, New York, 1934.

The Provisional Central Government of the Soviet Republic of China has formally declared war on Japan. It leads the Workers' and Peasants' Red Army and the oppressed toiling masses of China to engage in the national revolutionary war to drive Japanese imperialism out of China, to oppose the imperialist partition of China, to obtain for the Chinese nation real emancipation and independence.

The Provisional Central Government of the Soviet Republic of China declares before the workers, peasants, soldiers and the oppressed toiling masses of all China: in order to carry on the national revolutionary war, to engage really in war against Japanese imperialism, we must first of all overthrow the Kuomintang counter-revolutionary régime that helps imperialism, suppresses the national revolutionary movement, and prevents the national revolutionary war. Only in this way can we directly and unhindered fight against Japanese imperialism; only in this way can we develop the national revolutionary war throughout the country. The Central Soviet Government solemnly states: had not the Kuomintang thrown its entire military strength in attack against the Soviet Districts and the Red Army, the toiling masses and the Red soldiers of the Soviet Districts would have joined together with the heroic anti-Japanese soldiers and Volunteers in direct combat with the Japanese invaders. Therefore, without overthrow of Kuomintang rule, there can be no real national revolutionary war. The Central Soviet Government is now leading the All-China Workers' and Peasants' Red Army and the toiling masses of the Soviet Districts in an intensified revolutionary war for the conquest of important cities and centres to destroy the rule of the Kuomintang. *This, the real way of carrying on the national revolutionary war, is a preliminary step toward direct war with Japanese imperialism.*

We call upon the workers, peasants, soldiers, students, and all the toiling masses of the White Districts to initiate the organization of Anti-Japanese volunteers, to capture the arms of the Kuomintang militarists, to arm yourselves for direct war on Japan, and to establish in every locality revolutionary military committees to give unified command to these actions.

Soldiers in the White Army! rise in insurrection! Down with the reactionary officers! Conduct self-initiated war against Japan and organize into a Red Army!

We must realize that only the Soviet Government is really able to lead the whole country in the national-revolutionary war, to fight directly against Japan, and against the imperialists' partition of China. We must realize also that only the Workers' and Peasants' Red Army is the armed force of the masses genuinely carrying on the national revolutionary war. It must be pointed out that only with the alliance of the proletariat of the capitalist countries, of the oppressed masses in the colonial countries, of the Soviet Union in support and solidarity with the Chinese masses can we more successfully fight against the forces of world imperialism. Therefore, the Provisional Central Government of the Soviet Republic of China calls upon the workers, peasants, soldiers, and the broad toiling masses of the country: Under the red banner of the Soviets, all rally and participate intensively and extend the revolutionary war! In the White Districts, take up arms to overthrow the counter-revolutionary Kuomintang régime! For the establishment of the Soviet power of the masses of all China; for the formation of workers' and peasants' Red Armies! Unite with the proletariat of the world, the colonial oppressed masses, and the Soviet Union in order to realize by means of a national revolutionary war the ousting of Japanese imperialism from China, the prevention of the imperialist partition of China, and the real and complete independence and emancipation of the Chinese people!

April 26, 1932, Suikin, Kiangsi.

DECLARATION OF THE PROVISIONAL CENTRAL GOVERNMENT OF THE SOVIET REPUBLIC OF CHINA AND THE REVOLUTIONARY MILITARY COUNCIL OF THE WORKERS' AND PEASANTS' RED ARMIES.[1]

To the People of China!

On this First of May we send our revolutionary greetings to all toilers of China; to the workers and peasants and the city-poor groaning under the bloody rule of the imperialists and the Kuomintang; to the soldiers compelled against their will to fight against the workers and peasants of China; to the revolutionary students and youth participating in the anti-imperialist struggles; to thousands of political prisoners jailed and tortured in the prisons of the Kuomintang.

The further advance of Japanese imperialism, the ever-increasing danger of complete dismemberment of China, the deepening of the all-national crisis induces us to appeal again to all those who struggle in the interest of China and its toiling masses.

The present situation is characterized by the fact that Japanese imperialism advances unhampered into the Peiping-Tientsin area. At

[1] *China Forum*, May 4, 1933, Shanghai.

the same time British imperialism is advancing into Sinkiang and through its Tibetan and other puppets is preparing the seizure of West China. In the secret negotiations conducted between the Japanese Government and the Kuomintang, Chiang Kai-shek has made another deal with the imperialist robbers. Tang Yu-jen, Secretary of the Central Political Council of the Kuomintang, secretly negotiated for the Nanking Government and Chiang Kai-shek, the cowardly butcher of the workers and peasants of China, the man who asked the Japanese Militarists in 1929 to remain in Shantung, the man who in 1932 stabbed the defenders of Shanghai in the back has deserted the Northern front and has reinstated the traitor Tang Yu-lin who opened the passes of Jehol to the Japanese militarists. Chiang Kai-shek did not go to the North to fight the Japanese militarists, but to take over the inheritance of his friend, the chief and traitor Chang Hsueh-liang. Nor do the Southwest Governments and the Fukien militarists oppose the Japanese and other imperialists. Their recent propaganda about "going to the North and resisting Japan" is a lie to deceive the masses. In reality their object is to extend their own territory and to attack the Soviet Districts and the Red Army.

Why did Chiang Kai-shek return to Kiangsi? Why did he desert the Army in the North, leaving it without equipment, barehanded, to face the Japanese military machine? Why does the Kuomintang and its Governments concentrate huge armies, all aeroplanes and technical equipment against the workers and peasants in Kiangsi and other Soviet Districts? Because they are conspiring with the Japanese and other imperialists to sell China like a piece of personal property; because they hope that Japanese and other imperialism will accept them as puppet-rulers of a few provinces. Because they want to butcher the Chinese people in order to maintain the rule of imperialism, of the landlords, bankers, and big capitalists.

In order to hide its capitulation and treason the Kuomintang gives out lying statements that Japanese imperialism is assisting the Red Armies with money and supplies, that the Government of the Soviet Republic of China conducts negotiations with the Japanese militarists. Such mean and shameful rumors have been smashed to pieces for a long time by many facts.

We, the Provisional Government of the Soviet Republic of China and the Workers' and Peasants' Red Armies of China are the only mass rule and armed forces opposing all imperialist invasions. In the frequent wars of the past it has been proved that the Soviets and the Red Armies will never capitulate before Japanese or other imperialism. Of course, we are inseparably bound together with the workers and peasants of Japan who heroically struggle against the Japanese militarists and who are robbed, suppressed, tortured and killed by a rapacious ruling class. The Japanese militarists and imperialists are our common enemy.

We are fighting for the interests of the toiling masses of all China, for the independence, unity, and integrity of China. The need of the hour is to fight against Japanese and other imperialism; those who oppose this fight must be swept away.

We believe that the struggle of the workers, peasants, and soldiers of China, the heroic defense of our Red Armies will prevent imperialism, Chiang Kai-shek, and the corrupt Kuomintang from succeeding in their plans to dismember China.

During the last three months the workers and peasants of Kiangsi and their Red Armies have defeated nine divisions of the enemy. More than 30,000 prisoners and rifles, besides huge stores of other equipment have been captured in a number of battles. Nine thousand Kuomintang soldiers have voluntarily joined the Red Army in Kiangsi. In Honan, Hupeh, Hunan, Szechuan our forces are growing. So deep is the disintegration of the enemy forces that the captured Staff of the 52nd and 59th Divisions of Kiangsi have issued a declaration denouncing the Kuomintang and Chiang Kai-shek, repenting their past crimes against the workers and peasants of China, and asking the soldiers and officers to stop fighting against the Soviet Districts and to turn against the Kuomintang traitors of the fatherland.

At the moment when the Red Armies are winning great victories, when the Kuomintang soldiers are wavering, when the masses in the whole of China are enraged against the treason of the Kuomintang Governments, such nation-traitors as Chiang Kai-shek, Wang Ching-wei and others try to prevent the broad masses of soldiers from joining the revolution by using such propaganda as "Communist suppression is resistance against Japan" and "before the extermination of the Communists no one is allowed to speak about resistance against Japan." These phrases are only surrender to the imperialists. But such deception and threats will not be successful but will more than ever expose the crimes of these traitors.

It is on the basis of our victories that we repeat again our offer of January, 1933, which smashes the slander of the Kuomintang that the Red Armies and the workers and peasants of the Soviet Districts prevent an active and effective resistance against Japanese imperialism. We recognize that if our proposals are accepted, it will be immediately possible to resist the invasions of the Japanese and all other imperialists. Therefore we repeat again our proposals to the whole Chinese people:

The Red Army is ready to enter into fighting operative agreements with any army or military detachment in the fight against Japanese invasion under the following conditions:

1. *Cessation of the advance against the Soviet Districts;*

2. *Granting of Democratic rights to the people of China (free speech, free press, rights of assembly, demonstration, organization, release of political prisoners, etc.);*

3. *Arming of the people, the creation of armed volunteer detachments to struggle for the defense, independence, and unity of China.*

Every worker, peasant, and soldier will understand that without these conditions no successful struggle is possible against imperialism. The policy of the Kuomintang is bankrupt; it leads to the dismemberment and division of China, to the further enslavement of its people, to the further increase of misery, starvation, and slaughter.

We appeal to all toilers and soldiers to work for the acceptance of our national revolutionary policy among the broad masses, amongst the military units and the volunteers. We appeal to the toiling masses and soldiers to help us to defend China and the rights of its people.

For the Provisional Government of the Soviet Republic of China.
MAO TSE-TUNG, *President.*
HAN-SIN,
CHANG KUO-TAO, *Vice Presidents.*
For the revolutionary Military Council of the Workers' and Peasants' Red Armies:
CHU TEH, *Chairman and Commander-in-Chief.*
April 15th, 1933.

LAWS RELATING TO THE URGENT SUPPRESSION OF CRIMES AGAINST THE REPUBLIC [1]

(Promulgated by the National Government on January 31st, 1931, and enforced on March 1st of the same year)

Article 1. Whoever, planning to threaten the Republic, by committing one of the following acts, shall be punished by death:

1. Disturbing peace and order,

2. entering into secret relationship with a foreign country in order to disturb peace and order,

[1] Wellington Koo. *Memoranda,* presented to the Lytton Commission, pp. 786-788.

3. associating with rebels in order to disturb peace and order,
4. instigating a military person to commit a non-disciplinary act, or to cause him to fail in the performance of his duty or to associate with rebels.

Article 2. Whoever, planning to threaten the Republic by committing one of the following acts, shall be punished with death or life imprisonment.

1. Instigating another person to disturb peace and order or to associate with rebels,
2. conducting a campaign of propaganda against the State by writing, sketching or speech-making.

Article 3. Whoever, committing one of the following acts, shall be punished by life imprisonment or imprisonment of more than ten years:

1. Committing a non-disciplinary act, failing in the performance of his duty or associating with rebels on the instigation of the criminal indicated in No. 4 of Article 1,
2. disturbing peace and order or associating with rebels on the instigation of the criminal indicated in No. 1 of Article 2,
3. conducting propaganda on the instigation of the criminal indicated in No. 2 of Article 2.

Whoever having committed one of the crimes specified in the preceding paragraphs on immediately and voluntarily reporting, shall receive an attenuation or exoneration of the penalty.

Article 4. Whoever, having knowledge that a certain individual is a rebel, shelters him without giving notification to the competent authorities, shall be punished by an imprisonment of more than five years.

Whoever, having committed the crime specified in the preceding paragraph, immediately and voluntarily reports, shall receive an attenuation or exoneration of the penalty.

Article 5. Whoever, planning to threaten the Republic by committing one of the following acts, shall be punished with death, or life imprisonment or imprisonment of more than ten years:

1. Obtaining or transporting military supplies for the rebels,
2. revealing or transmitting to the rebels military and political secrets,
3. destroying means of communication.

Article 6. Whoever, planning to threaten the Republic by organizing associations or unions or spreading doctrines incompatible with the "Three Principles of the People" shall be punished by an imprisonment of from at least five years to at most fifteen years.

Article 7. Whoever, committing one of the crimes specified by the present law in a region under a state of siege shall be tried by the highest military organ in that region: If he commits the crime within the limits of the suppression of banditry, he shall be tried by a provisional court composed of the magistrate of the district and two judicial officials.

The provisional court shall be established in the district and the magistrate shall be designated as the president of the court.

Article 8. In case a crime is tried by a military organ in conformity with the present law, that organ shall submit a statement of the trial to the competent superior military organ and the sentence shall be executed only after the approval of the latter; the case shall also be reported to the provincial government for reference.

The competent superior military organ or the superior court if it doubts the judgment passed by the organ which is its subordinate, can give to that organ an order for re-examination, or designate a special delegate to be present at the reconsideration of the judgment.

Article 9. The military organ or police which arrests a person suspected of having committed one of the infractions specified by the present law, shall report the matter immediately to the interested competent authorities.

Article 10. To all that does not fall within the limits of the present law, the provisions of the Penal Code are applicable.

Article 11. The duration of the application of the present law and the date of its enforcement shall be fixed by ordinance.

The provisional law suppressing the anti-revolutionary plots shall be repealed from the date of the enforcement of the present law.

EXTRACTS FROM THE PROGRAMME OF POLITICAL AND
ECONOMIC REHABILITATION IN CONNECTION
WITH THE CAMPAIGN AGAINST THE COMMUNISTS [1]

Pacification of the People
After the reoccupation of a district within the regions where a campaign against the communists has been conducted, the magistrate concerned would, on the one hand, issue proclamations inviting refugees to return to their homes without delay. Those refugees who are devoid of the means of returning to their native places may petition the magistrate of the district where they happen to be with regard to the true state of their affairs so that they may be assisted

[1] Wellington Koo, *ibid.*, pp. 793-804.

by him at his discretion in their homeward journey. On the other hand, the magistrate of the reoccupied district selects several persons of good reputation from amongst those inhabitants who have remained in their native city or village who are charged with the duty of ascertaining independently the location and the number of refugees, and to advise the clansmen, neighbours of those who are related to the refugees to arrange for their speedy return. The district magistrate also communicates to the people the measures adopted by the Government for reassembling the refugees.

With regard to the enforcement of this measure, there has been promulgated the procedure to be followed by the Party Political Council of the Headquarters of the Commander-in-Chief of the Land, Sea and Air Forces governing the reassembling of refugees.

Inhabitants who had really been coerced into submission by the communists may file, with the magistrate concerned, and subject to his approval, bonds of sincere penitence to be attested to or guaranteed by their fathers, elder brothers, chiefs of clans or upright and reputable gentry or elders of their respective ward. Those who are really penitent and return home on their own accord, and who have not received any important appointments from the communists or have not committed any serious crimes, may furnish bonds of sincere penitence to be guaranteed by their respective fathers, elder brothers, and five neighbours, such bonds to be submitted to the magistrate of the district concerned for his approval.

With regard to the enforcement of this measure, there have been passed regulations of the Party Political Council of the Headquarters of the Commander-in-Chief of the Land, Sea and Air Forces relating to the reconcilement of people coerced into submission or penitent in the regions where the campaigns against the communists are being conducted.

Inhabitants of districts within the regions for communist suppression, in the event of discovering communists lurking in the locality or any underhand dealings with them, must secretly report the fact to the competent authorities to be dealt with according to law. Those who have brought false accusations out of spite (of malice forethought) are subject to the same penalty for the offences charged. The judge who sits in trial of persons suspected of associating with the rebels, must be particularly careful during the time of examination and must not involve others. If relatives of inhabitants in the various districts have drifted into the sovietized regions and are rendering services to the communists or holding bogus offices under them, the authorities concerned, upon discovering the relatives who remain as residents in the localities to be innocent of any conspiracy, treat them as peaceful citizens and do not involve them into any joint criminal liability.

With regard to the enforcement of this measure, there have been promulgated regulations of the Party Political Council of the Headquarters of the Commander-in-Chief of the Land, Sea and Air Forces with respect to the prohibition of false accusation and joint liability for crimes in the different districts within the regions for the suppression of communists.

Establishment of Rural Rehabilitation Committees

Rural Rehabilitation Committees are established to take charge of districts and villages where lands have been distributed by the communists. The chief duty of such committees is the distribution of farming rights and the adjustment of proprietary rights on agricultural lands. Prior to such adjustments being definitely made, the agricultural lands in a district are placed under the control of the Rural Rehabilitation Committee of that locality for the purpose of distributing them for farming so as to meet the emergency of the case and to avoid non-cultivation. Such a committee is known as Rural Rehabilitation Committee of a certain village or of a certain town. Its organization and function is as follows:

(1) Organization.—The committees are of three kinds; namely the district committee, the ward committee and the village or mart committee. In a district committee, the magistrate is the chairman, with chiefs of divisions of his office and representatives from the different wards as its members. In a ward committee, the chief of the ward is its chairman with a representative from each of the villages in the ward as members. In a village committee, the chief of the *Pao* (1,000 families) is its chairman, with four inhabitants of the village who have lawful business as its members, such members to be elected by householders and chiefs of *chia* (100 families). Regulations governing its organization in detail will be promulgated separately. In dealing with its affairs, the Rural Rehabilitation Committee is guided by the rulings of the village or mart committee. Things which cannot be decided by the village or mart committee are passed upon by the ward committee, and those matters which cannot be settled by the ward committee are finally disposed of by the district committee.

(2) Functions.—The functions of such committees are of four kinds. The following is a brief account of the function in connection with the disposal of farming rights of land, leaving the others out of consideration:

The committee in its management of the lands under its control apportions the farming rights according to the number of persons to be supported. An adult can undertake to cultivate so much land as its products are sufficient for his support, the area for which shall be decided by the committee of a locality in accordance with its fertility or otherwise. A minor shall be allowed to cultivate one-half of this amount. The rent payable for each mou of land, that is to say, the share of its product to be contributed by the farmer to its owner is decided by the committee in accordance with the local custom. The rent realizable to the land, the ownership of which has not been definitely settled, is appropriated by the committee for use in the reconstruction of the village or other public utility.

If the family to which farming land has been given to cultivate should consist of only the old and the weak and the women folks without any able-bodied male to undertake the cultivation, the family itself can employ farm-hands to do the farming or the committee can do so on its behalf and attend to all the work for it.

Farmers who have had land distributed to them during the period of communist occupation, excepting those who, having undertaken important work for the red bandits, shall be tried and punished separately, uniformly enjoy the right of undertaking to farm according to the number of mouths to be supported. Products through cultivation of the land, harvested prior to the formation of the rehabilitation committee, excluding the portion which the farmer is entitled to keep, is disposed of as land rent according to the procedure stated above.

If owing to the decrease of population in a village or owing to the inhabitants having taken refuge elsewhere and having not all returned, there should be surplus lands left after apportioning for cultivation according to the number of persons, they may be cultivated by farm-hands employed by the committee or by farmers from another village. These lands may be redistributed from time to time upon the successive return of the refugee inhabitants. Lands under the control of the Rural Rehabilitation Committee of a certain village or mart, irrespective of their being cultivated by the proprietors themselves or by tenant-farmers, or distributed for cultivation at the time of communist occupation, are, after the formation of the committee, reported to it, with full particulars of the number of mou under cultivation, the location, the number of persons in the cultivators' household, whether aged, young or able-bodied. In the same locality inhabitants, who have not at the time any definite land for cultivation, should also report on the number of aged, young and able-bodied persons in their respective households.

The Rural Rehabilitation Committee, though, in the distribution of lands for cultivation, it is guided by the principle of apportionment according to the number of mouths to be fed, also acts upon the following rules to decide upon the order of precedence in awarding such farming lands.

With the exception of those who are willing to exchange with each other lands for cultivation, the following order of precedence is observed.

(1) The original cultivator before the land was distributed by the red bandits shall have first choice in the apportioning of farming lands.

(2) The original owner whose title has been definitely established and who is willing to cultivate his own land shall have the priority of claim.

(3) Where neither the proprietor-farmer is definitely ascertained nor is the original cultivator to be found, the one who has cultivated the land after being redistributed by the communists shall be accorded the order of precedence.

(4) Where the proprietor-farmer, the original cultivator and the farmer who has undertaken to cultivate after the land having been distributed by the communists, are all difficult to ascertain, the land shall be assigned anew for cultivation by the committee.

(5) If pieces of land cultivated by the original cultivators, proprietor-farmers, or those who have undertaken to cultivate after the distribution by the communists should exceed the standard of area measured by the number of persons in their respective families, the excessive portion shall be redistributed by the committee to those who have no land to cultivate, or those whose lands are not sufficient.

(6) In assigning lands for cultivation the committee should take into consideration the distance between the habitation of the prospective cultivator and the land to be cultivated.

Regulations Dealing with Land Tax, Land Rent, and Farmers' Debts

The following principles have been adopted for the settlement of disputes arising out of the question of land tax, land rent or farmers' indebtedness:

(1) Land Tax.—Land tax may either be totally remitted, reduced or reprieved under the following circumstances: Taxes in arrear before the 19th year of the Republic (1930) shall be totally remitted. Taxes in arrear after the 20th year of the Republic (1931) leviable in districts where land-distribution had been made by the communists shall be remitted for two years; but in districts where, though land-distribution had not been made by the communists, extensive devastation has been committed by them, resulting in the fields being

laid waste, the taxes shall be remitted for one year. In districts which have been devastated by the communists to a least extent, whether the tax should either be given a reduction of half the original amount or a reprieve of half a year is decided upon on reports being made by the magistrate of the district concerned.

(2) Land rent.—Rents in arrear before the 19th year of the Republic (1930) shall be remitted. Rents due during the year shall be remitted if the land is not under cultivation, and shall be proportionately reduced if the land is being cultivated, the rate of reduction to be agreed upon between the land-owner and the tenant-farmer, or to be decided for them by the co-operative societies of the various villages. The owners of land of more than one hundred mou shall contribute three-tenths of the rent accruing to them individually for the purpose of defraying the expenses in the formation of co-operative societies of the various villages, or to serve as foundation funds of such institutions.

(3) Debts of farmers.—Debts of farmers in districts where land distribution had been made by the communists shall all be granted a moratorium of two years, and the unpaid interest of the past shall be reduced or remitted. The highest rate of interest during the moratorium shall not exceed 12 per cent, and the interest above that rate shall be invalid.

PROCLAMATION ISSUED BY GENERAL CHIANG KAI-SHEK, INVITING THE RED-SOLDIERS TO DESERT THEIR RANKS.[1]

Published in the *Shen-Bao*, July 17th, 1932

(1) Every one deserting the Red Armies and joining the ranks of the Kuo-min-tang Army shall receive a reward. If he comes with his rifle he is entitled to 20 dollars; if with a Mauser to 30 dollars; with a machine-gun to 300 dollars. Those coming without any arms shall receive 5 dollars.

(2) Every one who joins the Kuo-min-tang Army after having killed a Colonel of a Red Regiment shall receive a reward of 500 dollars. For the assassination of a Division Commander or a Brigadier one gets 5000. For killing a Chief of a Battalion the reward is 300 dollars. For a Commissar of an Army Corps, 3000.

(3) Every one who joins the Kuo-min-tang Army and brings with him as a prisoner a Company or Battalion Commander of the Red

[1] Translated from the Russian, as given in the *Soviets in China*, pp. 467-8.

Army shall receive 500 dollars. For a Regiment Colonel or Brigadier the reward is 1000 dollars. For a Division or Corps Commander, 2000. For the Army leaders or various Commissars, 10,000. For the Army Commander or for the Commander-in-Chief, 30,000.

(4) We welcome particularly those who join the Kuo-min-tang Army bringing their arms. We welcome the Communists who repent, we welcome those who give us information on Communists. We protect the peaceful population, we send our greetings to the masses oppressed by the Communists and render a relief to the hungry population of the sovietized areas. On the other hand, we forbid the spreading of false rumors and accusations out of spite and vengeance. Every one who comes with sincere penitence is welcome. We strictly oppose mistreatment and abuse of the peaceful population. Those who help us in our struggle with the Communists will be rewarded.

REPORT OF THE PRESIDENT OF THE CENTRAL EXECUTIVE COMMITTEE OF THE CHINESE SOVIET REPUBLIC, MAO TSE-TUNG,[1]

Before the 2nd National Soviet Congress

Before the 2nd National Soviet Congress at Juikin, Red Capital of China, which opened on January 22, 1934, Comrade Mao Tse-tung, on behalf of the Soviet Republic of China, of the Central Executive Committee and of the People's Council, made a report on: the development of revolution during the past two years of both China and the world; the outcome and experience of the Soviet movement in China since the inauguration of the Soviet Central Government; the growth and consolidation of the Red Army and the increase of the Soviet territory; the intensification of the agrarian revolution; the improvement of the living conditions of the working masses; the emancipation of women; the rise of the cultural level. In addition to these, Comrade Mao also laid stress on the urgency of the Soviet victory in one or several provinces and in the whole territory of China. The report given below is an extract from the Jan. 26th edition of "Red China," organ of the Central Government of the Soviet Republic of China, which has a circulation of more than 40,000.

[1] As it appeared in the *Chinese Workers' Correspondence*, Shanghai, Vol. 4, No. 11, March 31, 1934, without any corrections or changes. The above organization is an official news agency of the Chinese Communist Party. (Courtesy of Miss Agnes Smedley.)

1.—*The present situation and development of Soviet Movement.*

Two years have elapsed since the 1st National Soviet Congress convened. Facts and events of the past two years tell us that the imperialist Kuomintang rule has further declined in the process of its debacle while the Soviet movement proceeded and developed vigorously towards its victory!

Now we have arrived at the era when the Chinese Revolution has become further acute and the whole world is passing its transitory period leading to a new turn of war and revolution. The opposition of the socialist world to the capitalist world has become much sharper. On the one hand, the socialist construction in the Soviet Union and the peace policy of the Soviet Government have achieved sweeping success all conducive to the consolidation of the position of the Soviet Union, in sharp contradiction to the capitalist world where the ever-sharpening of the economic crisis has led the imperialist powers to seek a workable solution in the attack on the Soviet Union and China. Preparations for the intervention against the Soviet Union have never ceased for a single minute while the imperialist division of China and the intervention against the Chinese revolution are in full swing.

But the world proletariat revolution and the revolution of the oppressed nations are extending in every direction precisely under the influence of the successful socialist construction in the Soviet Union and in face of the menace of the imperialist crisis and war. A part of the world revolution, the Chinese revolution is growing out of the sharpening of the national crisis, the collapse of national economy, the success of the Soviet movement at an accelerated pace, resulting in pushing the Chinese revolution to the foreground in the world revolution.

The dominating factors of the present Chinese situation are: Wide civil war; death-and-life struggle between revolution and counter-revolution; sharp contrast between the worker-peasant Soviet power and the Kuomintang power of landlords and bourgeoisie. On the one hand, the Soviet power is summoning, organizing, and leading the country-wide masses to fight in national revolutionary war to overthrow the rule of landlords and bourgeoisie throughout the country; to oust imperialism from China; to liberate the millions of the masses from oppression and exploitation by imperialists and Kuomintang; to save the country from colonization and to build up Soviet China of complete freedom, independence and territorial integrity.

The growing acute contrast between the two powers cannot but promote the death-and-life struggle between them to assume more and more violent proportions. It had now come to the decisive historical stage of the struggle. The Kuomintang is launching its 5th offensive against us. The historical task of the Soviet power is: to summon, to organize and to lead all revolutionary masses both in the Soviet districts and in other parts of the country to fight in this decisive war; to mobilize broad worker-peasant masses to join the Red Army; to improve the political, cultural and technical levels of the Red Army; to enlarge the local armed forces and partisans; to agitate for broad partisan wars; to strengthen the concentrated and unified leadership of the Soviet over all Soviet districts and Red Armies; to strengthen the working speed and quality of the Soviet work in every field; to strengthen the financial and economical work of the Soviet so as to guarantee the material demands of the revolutionary war; to develop the class struggle of the working masses; to organize the revolutionary initiative of the working masses into the struggle of smashing the 5th offensive of the enemy; to develop the agrarian revolution of the peasants; to mobilize the broad masses to fight for the acquisition and protection of land; to call all working and peasant masses of the Soviet districts and throughout China to fight with all efforts and at all cost in the revolutionary war. This is the way to smash the 5th offensive of imperialists and the Kuomintang, to save China from being colonized and to attain the Soviet victory in one or several provinces and in the whole territory of China!

2—The Anti-Imperialist Movement

The greatest events in the past two years in China since the inauguration of the Provisional Soviet Central Government were imperialist attacks and the 4th and 5th offensives waged upon revolution by counter-revolution. The occupation of Manchuria, Mongolia and North China by Japanese robbers and the intensified control of Tibet, Sikong, Yunnan, the Yangtze Valley by British, French and American imperialists are all directed by the Imperialists to wreck the Chinese Soviet power and to completely enslave the Chinese nation as a preliminary step toward the war against the USSR. The Kuomintang of landlords and bourgeoisie still sticks to its long followed policy of capitulation while, on the contrary, the anti-imperialist movement of the country wide revolutionary masses, with the unprecedented national crisis before them, has developed with extreme violence.

At the present moment two powers of opposite directions are laid before the country wide revolutionary masses: the Kuomintang which surrenders completely to imperialism and with all means suppresses the anti-imperialistic masses; the Soviet which is determinately anti-imperialistic and does it best to support and lead the anti-imperialist movement.

In the past two years the Provisional Soviet Central Government has repeatedly circulated statements denouncing the predatory wars waged by the Japanese imperialists and the traitorous capitulation of the Kuomintang. On April 14, 1932, the Provisional Central Government formally declared war on Japan and issued mobilization orders for war against her. The Provisional Central Government and the Revolutionary Military Council have more than once announced their readiness to conclude agreement with any armed unit of the Kuomintang for joint anti-Japanese and anti-imperialist military movement under the following conditions: (1) Immediate stop of offensive against the Soviet districts; (2) Guarantee of civil rights for the masses; (3) Arming of the masses and creation of anti-Japanese volunteers. The Tankoo Agreement concluded between the Kuomintang and Japan on May 30, 1933, and the Sino-Japanese direct negotiations since then are policies and actions against the national interests but repeatedly repudiated by the Provisional Central Government in its statements made public of late. The Soviet has supported the anti-Japanese struggle in any and every part of the country. To speak alone of the anti-Japanese strike of the textile workers in West Shanghai, 1932, the Soviet aided them with $16,000.

In the Soviet territories, imperialist privileges have been abolished and imperialist influence wiped out. Imperialist pastors and fathers were ousted by the masses; estates of the people seized by imperialist missionaries were returned; missionary schools were turned into Soviet schools. In short, the Soviet districts in China alone are liberated from the imperialist yoke.

These facts point to one thing; the Soviet is the sole anti-imperialist government. The Soviet Government wants to make known to the country wide masses: the greatest responsibility of the Soviet and the whole masses is to win victory over imperialists by means of direct war. The fulfillment of this work depends upon the development of the mass anti-imperialist struggle. First of all, the lackey of Imperialism, the Kuomintang, should be smashed because it is the greatest obstacle on the way before the anti-imperialist Soviet and masses.

3.—*The Imperialist-Kuomintang Offensive Repulsed*

Because the Chinese Soviet districts are the revolutionary base for the Chinese anti-imperialist movement, because the Chinese Red Army is the main pillar of the Chinese anti-imperialist forces, and because the Soviet movement and the revolutionary war are proceeding violently, the Kuomintang with the direct help of the imperialists and with all force at its disposal, waged four offensives and is now waging the 5th one against the Soviet and Red Armies in an attempt to put down the Chinese revolution and to fulfill its task of cleaning the ground for imperialism. But every offensive of imperialism and the Kuomintang ended in glaring failure. The victories of the Soviet and Red Armies have further confirmed the belief of the country-wide masses that the Soviet and Red Armies alone are fighting for the national independence and freedom, and that they are the sole forces for the salvation of China.

The 4th offensive of the enemy began right after the Kuomintang had surrendered Manchuria to the Japanese and concluded the Shanghai Truce Agreement of May 5th, 1932. The traitorous Kuomintang did not mobilize a single soldier to fight the Japanese aggression. On the contrary, despite the fact that the Soviet and Red Armies have more than once proposed to conclude an anti-Japanese military agreement with any anti-Japanese troops, the Kuomintang, led by Chiang Kai-shek, chief of all traitors, concentrated hundreds of thousands of troops to attack the Hupeh-Honan-Anhui and Hunan-Hupeh West Soviet districts and forced the Red Armies to withdraw from the cordon they formed around the district of Wu-Han. On our side, because of some tactical mistakes, coupled with our reluctance to have a district clash with a force of the enemy which was overwhelmingly stronger than ours, the 4th Red Army Corps was obliged to withdraw from the Hupeh-Honan-Anhui Soviet district and began the famous expedition to Szechuen where a new and big Soviet base embracing Tungkiang, Bachun, Nankiang, Hsunhan and Suiting has been created. During the expedition, the 4th Red Army Corps had widely disseminated seeds of the Soviet in the comparatively revolutionary backward zones of the Northwest where broad revolutionary struggles of the masses have been brought up to develop. In not more than one year, the 4th Red Army Corps has sovietized more than ten hsien and called forth the leaning of the Szechuen toiling masses and soldiers of the White troops toward the Soviet revolution. Meantime the 2nd Red Army Corps which evacuated from the Hung Lake zone not only has suffered no serious loss but also gained new success in the Szechuen-Hupeh-Hunan frontier regions in its operation in coordination with the 4th Red Army Corps. Even in the Hung Lake zone Red partisans are still active. In the Hupeh-Honan-Anhui Soviet district, we did not lose much of our base. On the contrary, we are now very successful there in the strife to consolidate our position and to develop partisan wars in the surrounding neighborhood.

As to the Central Soviet district (Kiangsi), it is the location of the Central Soviet Government headquarters of the country wide Soviet movement and the chief target of the offensive of the enemy. Around this district and its neighboring Soviet zones the enemy has concentrated most of its forces—the so-called "Central Government" troops, the units under the command of militarists Chiang Kwang-lai, Tsai Ting-kai, together with those under the command of Kwangtung, Kwangsi, and Hunan warlords. Through one year's hard struggles, we have gained unprecedented success. The biggest victory was that we gained in the spring of 1933 when the Red Armies of the Central Soviet district alone destroyed 23 regiments, 6 batallions and 2 companies of the enemy and smashed 3 divisions, 12 regiments, 3 batallions and 2 companies and captured twenty thousand rifles and one thousand machine guns and autorifles. Particularly in the battles of Tungpi and Hangpi, we annihilated a complete column of the crack troops of the enemy. These battles ended the 4th offensive of Nanking with a complete failure to the enemy.

The failure of the 4th offensive of the enemy had brought along qualitative and quantitative growth of the Red Army. The commanders and fighters of the Red Army have become more determined politically and more skillful in military technics, showing long strides of progress as compared with the time before the 4th offensive. Moreover, the Soviet territory has been enlarged. Besides the new Soviet district in Szechuen, we have now Fukien-Kiangsi province, another new Soviet district in the east part of Kiangsi, which increased the population of Soviet China by almost one million. Our old Soviet districts are further consolidated. This has been shown by the improvement of the Soviet work, by the rise of the militancy of the worker-peasant masses by the development of class struggle both in cities and villages, and by the suppression of the remnants of counter-revolution in the Soviet districts. This sum-total of the success of the Soviets revolution has also its influence in the Kuomintang-ruled districts where the struggling spirit of the oppressed worker-peasant masses has been further promoted, the soldiery and commanders of the White troops have shown their further wavering, and Chiang Kai-shek himself was even obliged to proclaim his desperate order of "Death punishment to all who do not fight the 'bandits' but demand to fight the Japanese."

Since the failure of the 4th offensive, the only manifestation of the Kuomintang has been to further shamelessly surrender to imperialism. From the imperialists the Kuomintang has received new loans and consignments of military supplies. Directly led by the imperialists and with foreign advisers helping it reorganize its forces (training of new recruits, air forces, and the Blue Jacket officials), the Kuomintang has been enabled once more to proceed with its 5th offensive against the Soviet and Red Army. The struggle of the C. E. C. of the Party, namely, "to make it impossible for imperialist crisis to seek its way out, or in other words, to struggle for the independence and freedom of Soviet China." Indeed, the struggle against the 5th offensive is to determine whether China goes down to complete independence, freedom, and territorial integrity.

We have acquired all fundamental conditions to win our struggle against our enemy since our victory over the 4th offensive. We have to point out that enemy has far more difficulties than we: the wavering of the soldiery of the white troops; the hatred against the rulers of the worker-peasant masses together with the broad petty-bourgeoisie in the enemy-ruled districts; the disintegration of the militarists; the clashes and conflicts among the imperialists who are supporters of the Kuomintang; the financial and economical bankruptcy of the Kuomintang. These are all objective conditions that show the possibility of victory for the revolution.

4.—*Fundamental Policies of the Soviet*

We get to know its environment, now and past, together with the tasks the environment calls forth, before we explain the fundamental policies of the Soviet. The Soviet has grown up from partisan wars and from many isolated and small districts beyond the boundaries of which is the world of the enemy. The enemy has been quite busy with the destruction and oppression of the Soviet. Yet the Soviet has been victorious. It is able to defeat the enemy and has grown up through its repeated victories over the enemy. This is the environment of the Soviet. In many respects, the environment of the Soviet at present is different from that of the past. It has a wider territory, broader masses and stronger Red Army. It has concentrated many of its scattered forces (although the work has not been complete). It has been organized into a state, the Soviet Republic of China which has now its central and local organizations. The Central organ, the Provisional Central Government, is the necleus of concentrated power depending upon the broad masses and their armed force—the Red Army. This Government is the power of workers and peasants themselves. It is the revolutionary workers peasant democratic dictatorship which is ever enlarging its influence throughout the country by virtue of the growing confidence of the broad masses in it. Evidently, the Soviet now no longer has the same environment confronting it as in the partisan war stage. Yet it still has to face constant warfare which is becoming wider and more violent. The reason is that the opposition between it and the landlord-bourgeois Kuomintang is growing daily acute and the time has come when the two contending parties have to fight a decisive battle. In short, before it there is at present a big scale offensive of imperialists and the Kuomintang and that is its environment nowadays.

This very environment determines the tasks of the Soviets. It must do its best to mobilize, organize and arm the masses, concentrate all of its strength for the development of the revolutionary war and fight out the other dictatorship together with the imperialist rule that has acted as the supporter and director of that other dictatorship. The aim of knocking down imperialism and the Kuomintang is to unify China, to bring the bourgeois democratic revolution to realization and to make it possible to turn the said revolution later to a higher stage of socialist revolution. This is the task of the Soviet.

From this we may understand what the various Soviet policies and tasks are. They are: to consolidate the victoriously established worker-peasant dictatorship; to develop this dictatorship to the whole country; to mobilize; organize and arm the Soviet and country-wide masses to fight in the determined revolutionary war to overthrow the imperialist Kuomintang rule and to consolidate and develop the worker-peasant dictatorship; to prepare the present bourgeois democratic revolution for its turn toward the socialist proletarian dictatorship in the future. All these form the starting point of the Soviet policies.

a. *The Armed Masses and the Red Army.*

Let us first speak of the armed masses and Red Army of the Soviet. To fight against the offensive of the enemy and to wage the revolutionary war the first task of the Soviet is to arm the masses and to organize strong and iron Red Army, local forces and partisans, and provisions, supplies, and transportations for the war. The Soviet has been successful in its work along this line during the past two years, particularly during the 4th offensive and the present determined struggle against the fifth one.

The formation of the Central Revolutionary Military Council has unified the leadership over the national Red troops and made the Red forces in every Soviet district and on any front to be able to fight and to operate in good coordination under the unified tactics. This is an important turn to convert the scattered activities of partisan troops into activities of regular and big scale Red Armies. The Revolutionary Military Council in the past two years has victoriously led the country-wide Red armies, particularly those of the Central Soviet district, in the smashing of the 4th offensive and in the initial successes of the struggle against the 5th offensive. The Red army is now several times bigger than it was two years ago. This work owes its success to the militancy of the broad worker peasant masses to join the Red army, to the improvement of the mobilization methods, and to the determined execution of the special treatment for the red fighters by the Soviet. During May, 1933, in the Central Soviet district alone, the Red army was increased by twenty thousand new fighters from the various hsien. This smashed the various opportunistic points of view that the masses are not willing to join the Red army or that enlargement of the Red army cannot be achieved in new Soviet districts. There are many models of the work to enlarge the Red army. For instance, in Changkanhsian, Kiangsi, 80 per cent of the men between 16 and 45 and in Shangwanshihsian, Fukien, 88 per cent of them are now serving in the Red army. In these villages with the overwhelming majority of the adults going to bravely fight in the revolutionary war, the daily affairs of farming production are not only not affected, but also improved and enlarged! Why is that so? The village labour power has been readjusted and reorganized better, and the difficult problems confronting the families of the Red fighters have been solved through the efforts exerted by the Labour Cooperatives and Farming Volunteers.

The strengthening of the Red army has proceeded along with its enlargement. Now the Red army is proceeding to assume the form of ironsides as regular revolutionary armed forces. The causes are: (1) Growth of the percentage of worker-peasant toiling masses in it; (2) More worker cadres and universal practice of political commissioner system; (3) The progress of political training strengthened the determination of the Red fighters to fight for the final victory of the Soviet, raised the class-conscious discipline and increased the relation between the Red army and the masses; (4) General rise of military technics; (5) Better organization increased the organized strength. These have promoted the fighting strength of the Red army and made it the formidable force of the Soviet.

Red Defence and Young vanguards are ready made reservists for the Red army on the fighting front, forces of defence for the Soviet districts and the bridge that is leading the present voluntary military system to the conscription system of tomorrow.

Partisan units are creators of new Soviet districts and inseparable detachments of the main force—the Red army. In the past two years more of them are developed in the various Soviet districts with their political and military training considerably improved. They have in the past offensives of the enemy showed marvelous success in their work for the defence of the Soviet districts and in their operation to take the troops of the enemy by surprise and to disturb their rear. Many of their performances were even thought by the enemy as miracles. Their activities have offered the greatest difficulties to the enemy in attempting to invade the Soviet districts. This has been particularly shown in the Central and Kiangsi-Chekiang Soviet districts.

To satisfy the Red army with supplies and provisions, to organize the military transportation between the front and the rear and to organize sanitary organs and hospitals for the Red fighters are all tasks of decisive importance to the revolutionary war. Since we have not yet captured many central cities and since the economic blockade of the enemy against us is very strict, there are numerous difficulties confronting us in our work along this line. However, in the past two years the militancy of the broad masses in the Soviet district has guaranteed continued supplies, provisions and transportation for the Red army. There is also one of our big successes.

The fundamental task of the Soviet is revolutionary war and to mobilize all mass strength to fight in the war. Around this fundamental task the Soviet has many urgent tasks. It has to practice wide democracy; to determinately suppress the counter-revolution under its jurisdiction; to promote class-struggle of the workers; to promote agrarian revolution of the peasants; to promote the militance of the worker peasant masses under the principle of workers leading the worker peasant alliance; to administer the correct financial and economic policies so as to guarantee the material needs of the revolutionary war; to wage the cultural revolution so as to arm the heads of the worker-peasant masses. All these, together with other policies, are but directed to one goal: to overthrow the imperialist-Kuomintang rule through revolutionary war, to consolidate and develop the worker-peasant democratic dictatorship and to be prepared to proceed to the stage of proletarian dictatorship.

b. *Soviet democracy.*

The Soviet of the worker-peasant democratic dictatorship is the government of the masses themselves, directly depending upon them, maintaining the closest relation with them and, therefore, able to operate its maximum strength. It has already been the organizer and leader of the revolutionary war and the mass life. Its enormous strength is incomparable to any form of state in the history. It needs a strong power to cope with its class enemy. But to the worker-peasant masses it exercises no strong power but wide democracy. The wide democracy of the Soviet is, first of all, manifested in its election. The Soviet gives the right to vote to all oppressed and exploited masses regardless of sex. This right to the worker-peasant masses is unprecedented in human history. The experience of the past two years tells us that the Soviet has been very successful in its election. The particulars of the Soviet elections are as follows: (1) The names of the electors are written on a big red paper and an election meeting with no exploiters participating in it takes the place of the general mass meeting of the past. (2) The proportions of social composition are as follows: one from every fifteen workers and their family members; one from fifty peasants and poor people; all the city and village Soviet councils are formed this way. The method guarantees the leading position of the workers in the worker-peasant alliance. (3) According to the Election Act proclaimed by the Central Soviet Executive Committee in September, 1933, the election units for the peasants are villages, while workers have another rule. This makes the election universal among the peasants, while the workers can also elect their best representatives to work in the Soviet Council. (4) During the two elections in 1932 and the election in the autumn of 1933, in many places more than 80 per cent of the electorate joined it. In some places, the sick people and those on defense duty did not join. (5) In the autumn of 1932, the nominee system was introduced in the election. The electorate could consider beforehand who would be their best representatives. (6) In many city or village Soviet councils women form a percentage of above 25 per cent. In the Soviets of Shangtsaishihhsian and Shiatsaishih-hsian, of Shanhan, in Fukien, the percentages of women are 60 and 66 per cent respectively. Broad woman masses are now participating in the affairs of state administration. (7) Before the election takes place the electors have the chance to hear reports about the past work of the City or Village Soviet in a preparatory meeting. They are led to give criticisms of the past work. This was more universally practiced during the fall election of last year. All these have helped the masses in getting familiar with the Soviet election, primary step of state administration, and have guaranteed the consolidation of the Soviet power.

Next, the Soviet democracy is also manifested in the City and

Hsiang councils which form the foundation of the organization of the Soviet. Two years progress gives us now better organization of the councils. The characteristics are as follows: (1) The delegates are scattered evenly to live among the people so that they will have the closest relation with them (usually one delegate leads and lives with 30 to 70 people). This makes the council not separated from its masses. (2) The delegates are grouped in from 3 to 7 with their fellow-members in the neighborhood having a head who serves as the immediate connector between them and the presidium of the council. The group has the regular task of summoning meetings of the people under them by order of the presidium to solve problems of minor importance. All groups in one village have a general head who is responsible for the whole village. This makes the connection between the presidium and the delegates very close and guarantees strong leadership over the work of each village. (3) There are various permanent or temporary committees under the City or Hsiang Councils such as Cultural, Irrigation, Sanitary, Food, Red Army Families Defence, etc., which absorb the active elements among the masses to work. In this way, the Soviet work is made into the form of a net and the broad masses can directly participate in it. (4) Election of City or Hsiang Soviet takes place once in six months and that of province or hsien Soviets once in a year. This makes it easy for the opinions of the masses to reach the Soviet. (5) Any delegate who commits serious errors may lose his seat through the suggestion of ten or more electors, seconded by more than one-half of the whole electorate or through the resolution of the council meeting.

The City and Hsiang Soviets are the foundation for the government organs of the Soviets above them; they are all formed by the Soviet congresses and their executives. Government workers are also appointed by election. If any one is found to be incompetent, he may be recalled by public opinion. The solution of all problems is based on public opinion. So the Soviet is really the government of broad masses.

The Soviet democracy is also shown by the fact that all revolutionary masses are given the right of free speech, free association, free assembly, free publication and free strike. The Soviet gives them all facilities such as meeting places, paper, printing shop, and other material needs. Moreover, to consolidate the worker-peasant democratic dictatorship, the Soviet always welcomes the supervision and criticism of the broad masses. Every revolutionary citizen has the right to disclose the error or shortcoming of any Soviet functionary in his work. Finally, the Soviet democracy is also found in the division of administrative districts. All the administrative districts from province down to hsiang are now smaller than before. This makes the Soviets of various grades to know exhaustively the demands of the masses and makes the opinions of the masses to be quickly reflected in the Soviets.

c. *Soviet attitude toward landlord-bourgeois.*

The Soviet is not democratic to the exploiters—landlord and bourgeoisie who have been knocked down by the revolutionary masses. The Soviet maintain a different attitude toward them. Although overthrown, they still have a deep foundation and their remnants have not yet been wiped out. They have a superior knowledge and technics. They are always thinking of the restoration of their power. Particularly in the course of the civil war, they are always seeking to support the attacking enemies through anti-revolutionary activities. Hence, the Soviet has to curb and oppress them from all sides.

First of all, the Soviet rules the exploiting elements out of the political power. In the Soviet Constitution, they are all deprived of the rights of election and military service. The Soviet has been ceaselessly engaged in bitter struggles against the alien elements in the Soviet organs. The past experience tells us that this task has been very important work of the Soviet. Secondly, all landlords and bourgeoisie are deprived of the freedom of speech, publication, assembly, and association.

Thirdly, anti-revolutionary activities are under the suppression of the revolutionary forces and revolutionary courts. The Soviet courts directly depend upon the mass armed forces, the activities of the State Political Defence Bureau, and the class-struggle of the broad masses. All these have offered strict suppression to the anti-revolutionary activities in the Soviet districts. The well known cases were the suppression by the Soviet courts of the activities of A-B Corps in the Central and Hunan-Kiangsi Soviets, of the Social-Democrats in Fukien, of the Re-organizationists in Hupeh-Hunan west, Hupeh-Hunan-Anhui, Fukien-Chekiang-Kiangsi, and Fukien-Kiangsi Soviet districts and of the Trozkist-Chen Groupings in Hunan-Hupeh-Kiangsi Soviet district. Through these suppressions, the State Political Defense Bureaus and the Soviet courts have acquired abundant experience and corrected many errors in the past that were committed through the diversion from the correct class line. The mass character of the Soviet Court, namely, the suppression of anti-revolutionary activities by the Soviet courts in coordination with the mass struggle against anti-revolutionary intrigues, has been making long strides of progress. The practice of the Traveling Court is a proof of this.

The Soviet has formally proclaimed prohibition of corporal punishment. In the Soviet prisons, except for those prisoners who are sentenced to death punishment, all other prisoners are put under reformatory education; that is to say, the Soviet policy for prisoners is to train them in the communistic spirit and with labour discipline. In sharp contradiction to this situation is the practice in full bloom of medieval tortures in the Kuomintang courts and prisons. To put down anti-revolutionary intrigues, to keep the Soviet territory in revolutionary order and to abolish all feudalistic and barbarous remnants in the field of jurisdiction constitute the aim of the Soviet court. The improvement of the Soviet in this direction is of historical significance.

In summary, the Soviet has by far the widest revolutionary democracy for the broad masses and out of it rises its enormous power—a power which is built upon the determined faith and self-conscious needs of the millions of the worker-peasant masses. Having this power in operation, the Soviet shapes itself into a dictatorship and organizes the revolutionary war and the revolutionary court which wage violent attacks upon the class enemy from all directions. This brings about the enormous function of the Soviet court in the Soviet territory.

d. *The Soviet labour policy.*

The Soviet, based on the class character of its political power and on its enormous task of arming the toiling masses to fight out imperialists and the Kuomintang through a revolutionary war, must initiate class struggles of workers, defend their every day interests, develop their revolutionary initiative, organize this initiative in the enormous revolutionary war and turn the workers into active leaders for the revolutionary war and pillars for the consolidation and development of Soviet power.

Interests of the workers are completely protected under the Soviet labour policy. The labour situation under it as compared with that in the past while under the Kuomintang rule, or with that of the districts now still ruled by the Kuomintang, forms a sharp contrast which is comparable only to the difference between heaven and hell. Before the Soviet districts came to exist, that is to say, when the Kuomintang were the rulers, the workers were slaves of employers. The long working hours, the meagre wages, the brutal treatment, and the absence of any legal means whatsoever for protecting the interests of workers are what will remain permanently in the memory of every worker. All these disadvantages for the workers still exist in the Kuomintang-ruled districts and are aggravated. Lately, the real wages of workers in the white districts have been cut by more than fifty per cent. Cut of production, mass-dismissal, and lockout, have been the common methods of capitalists to launch attacks upon their employees. It logically follows that broad unemployment has been formed. To speak of industrial workers alone the unemployed now exceeds 60 per cent. In the Kuomintang-ruled districts, strike is a criminal act in the eyes of the rulers. In March, 1933, the Kuomintang authorities at Hankow even proclaimed death punishment for strikers. Whenever there is a conflict between labour and capital, the Kuomintang never fails to stand on the side of the capitalist to suppress the workers.

In the Soviet districts these things have been completely wiped out. Under Soviet power, workers are masters themselves and are leading the broad peasantry in the enormous task of consolidating and developing the Soviet. Hence the basic principle of the Soviet labour policy is to protect the interests of the workers and to consolidate and develop the Soviet power. The Labour Act proclaimed in December, 1931, was based on this principle. It was revised and reproclaimed in March, 1933, better applicable to towns, villages, big enterprises and small ones.

The eight-hour system is now universally observed in the Soviet districts. There is also a wide practice of labor agreement and collective agreement. In many urban and rural districts, there are Labour-Inspection offices which send out inspectors to examine whether the Soviet Labour Act is violated by employers or not. There is the Labour Court for cases in which the employer is accused of violating the Soviet Laws. To guard against control of labor by employers and to work for the interests of the unemployed, the Soviet has the absolute control of employment. All employers must go to the Soviet for hiring workers. Unemployment relief measures are in broader practice. Generally speaking, unemployed workers can now get concrete relief. Village workers have their own farming land. The social insurance system is administered by a Social Insurance Bureau established in the Soviet towns. These are what the workers cannot get at all in the Kuomintang-ruled districts, but what the Soviet considers as its big responsibility to fulfill.

Because of the determined execution by the Soviet of its labor policy, the living conditions of the workers in the Soviet districts are greatly improved. First of all is the wages. The real wages of the workers of the Soviet districts has been generally increased as compared with the pre-revolutionary period. The following table is a comparison of wages of the workers in Tingchow before and after the revolution which may be taken as an example: (Remarks: P-r means pre-revolutionary period; A-r means after the revolution; d- means difference.)

	Maximum			Minimum			Aver.
	P-r	A-r.	d.	P-r	A-r	d.	A-r
Fruit workers	$10 monthly	$32	$22	$ 2	$22	$20	$30
Paper workers	$10 "	35	25	3	31	28	33
Oil workers	6 "	18	12	3	12	9	15
Medicine workers	6 "	18	12	2	26	24	28
Tobacco workers	7 "	36	29	3.5	30	26.5	28
Printers	15 "	36	21	5	28	23	34
Metal workers	6 "	18	12	14			16
Dyeing workers	5.5 "	20	14.5	2	18	16	19
Oil-paper workers	5 "	21	16	2	17	15	19
Wine workers	6 "	20	14	3	18	15	
Weaving workers	10 "	35	25	2	31	29	32
Carpenters	0.6 daily	0.8	0.2				
Boatmen	14 each travel from Tingchow to Shanghan				$46	$32	

From this table we can easily see the great difference in the wages of the workers in Tingchow before and after the revolution. The smallest increase is 32 per cent (carpenters) and the biggest is 1,450 per cent (weaving workers).[1] What a contrast it is as compared with the decreasing wages in the Kuomintang era! In other districts where the employers supply meals to the workers, the wage level is slightly lower. The wages of a carpenter and mason of Jukin is now 45 cents a day as compared with 25 cents a day in the pre-revolutionary period. The increase is 80 per cent.

Wages in the village are also increased. The following table is the comparison of daily wage scales in cents which prevailed in different periods in Tienchen district of Kanhsien:

	Handicraftsmen	Paper workers	Farming hands	Coolies
Maximum				
Pre-rev.	30	40	28	45
Before May 1, 1931	30	40	30	67.5
Now	35	45	32	96
Difference	5	5	4	51
Average				
Pre-rev.	22	22	10	26
Before May 1, 1931	25	24	15	39
Now	30	30	20	50
Difference	8	8	10	24
Minimum				
Pre-rev.	10	14	3	10
Before May 1, 1931	15	21	6	. .
Now	20	25	10	20
Difference	10	11	7	10

[1] Discrepancies like this are numerous in the text from which this is copied. (V. Y.)

This is the story of only one village. A similar situation is found in other villages. As to the wage scale prevalent in the state enterprises, there has been a general increase of from 20 per cent to 40 per cent in the past two years.

Generally speaking, the wages of the workers are paid on time. Because of the superintendence of the Soviet, very few employers delay their wage payments to workers. Some stubborn capitalists did try to do so, but were brought under control by the Labour Court.

Concerning the legal working hour, the 8 hour system has been introduced to all Soviet cities and towns in the past two years and in the villages there are but rare cases in which employees work more than eight hours a day. Employees between the age of 16 and 18 have shorter hours than do adults.

Protection for women and infants.—Equal work, equal pay, rest before and after confinement, prohibition of infant workers below fourteen years of age, and so on, are in general practice.

As to apprentices, the apprenticeship period is shortened, treatment improved and feudalistic oppression abolished. The living conditions of apprentices have been considerably made better. The wages of apprentices are increased. For instance, in Kiangsi apprentices receive allowance to the amount of from fifteen to thirty-six dollars annually.

Sanitary conditions and food supplies for the workers in general, and for the employees of the state enterprises in particular have been greatly improved. In the cities, the workers' food is rated at least six dollars a month. In the villages, the farming employees eat the same food as served to their employers.

The Soviet workers are organized in their strong class trade union which is the pillar of the Soviet power, burg for the workers themselves and school in which the broad working masses learn communism. With its interests protected by the Soviets, the membership of the trade union is ever on the increase. According to the statistics of the All China Trade Union Federation the trade union membership in the Central Soviet District, together with its neighbouring Soviet zones, amount to 229,000. The distribution is as follows: Central Soviet District 110,000 persons; Hsiang-Kan (Hunan-Kiangsi) 23,000; Hsiang-O-Kan (Hunan-Hupeh-Kiangsi) 40,000; Min-Che-Kan (Fukien-Chekiang-Kiangsi) 25,000; Min-Kan (Fukien-Kiangsi) 6,000; North Fukien, 5,000. According to statistics compiled by the Central Soviet District there are 3,676 non-trade union workers in the said district which means not more than five per cent of the whole working body. In other words, 95 per cent of the workers in the Central Soviet District are members in the Trade

Unions. In the district of Hsinkuo this percentage reaches as high as 98 per cent. Can this be dreamed of in the Kuomintang-ruled districts? Except for U.S.S.R., can this be dreamed of in any of the imperialist countries?

In short, in the course of only two years, the Soviet Labour Act has been generally observed in all towns and all villages. In the two years, the capitalists and the kulaks attempted to resist the Act. But the active struggles of the working masses, together with the close superintendence of the Soviet, have frustrated them. In dealing with independent producers and middle peasants who should have violated the Labour Act in their relation with farming hands or other employees, the method of convincing them with frank explanations has been used. All these account for the general improvement of the living conditions of workers, the development of their militancy in the revolution and their vital task in the revolutionary war and the Soviet reconstruction.

According to reports from Kun-lu Wantai, Lun-kan, Hsin-kuo, Shien-li, Sikiang, Yu-tu, Chinwu, Shanghan, Nin-hua, Changting, and Hsinchien, out of the 70,580 trade union members in these twelve Hsiens, 19,960 are now serving either in the Red troops or in the local partisan units forming 28 per cent of the whole membership, and also 6,752 in various Soviet organs forming 10 per cent. The two make a total of 38 per cent. The remainder amounts to 43,860 persons. It was they who cancelled the 2nd Government Bonds to the amount of $43,855 and bought recently the Government Reconstruction Bonds to the amount of $197,803. This means that every trade union member bought the bonds to the amount of $4.5 on the average. Among them, 12,435 are members of the C. P. or the Y. C. L., the percentage being 28 per cent.

From these statistics, one learns how ardently the working masses are joining the Red army, support the revolutionary war and favor the C. P. But these are nothing but the outcome of the work of the Soviet for their interests and to promote their militancy. Some one said that workers gained nothing since the revolution, neither has their militancy been promoted. This is completely a vile slander!

The Agrarian Revolution

The Chinese Soviet and Red army have grown up from the development of agrarian revolution, which liberates the broad peasantry from the brutal oppression and exploitation by landlords and the Kuomintang militarists. The principle of the land policy of the Soviet is to completely wipe out the feudalistic and semi-feudalistic oppression and exploitation. In any village of the Kuomintang district, past or now, there are horrible land rents (60 per cent to 80 per cent), horrible usury (30 per cent to 100 per cent), and horrible, onerous taxes (there are above 1,700 different kinds of taxes throughout the country). Consequently, the land is concentrated in the hands of landlords and kulaks. The overwhelming majority of the peasantry lost their land and are obliged to live in extreme misery. The relentless exploitation has exhausted them of their means to combat catastrophe. The whole country is, therefore, exposed to constant inundation or drought. The catastrophe striken area in 1931 amounted to 809 hsiens covering a population of 44,000,000. The exploitation has also exhausted the peasantry of their production power. Much land has been turned infertile or left uncultivated. Yet with their meager products, they have to face the dumping of the imperialist agricultural productions. All these lead the Chinese rural economy to the state of complete bankruptcy from which outbreaks the violent agrarian revolution.

The power of the agrarian revolution in the Soviet districts has wiped out all feudalistic remnants. The millions of the peasantry awakening from their long dark age confiscated land from all landlords and fertile land from the Kulaks, abolished usury and onerous taxation, knocked down all that are against the revolution and built up their own government. For the first time, the Chinese peasant masses break their way out of the hell and make masters themselves. This is the fundamental situation that differs the rural district under the Soviet from those under the Kuomintang.

The First National Soviet Congress proclaimed the Land Act which has since served as the correct guidance for the proper solution of the land problems in this country. There have been numerous arguments over the analysis of classes in the villages owing to the acute class struggle. Based on the experience of the agrarian revolution, the People's Council has passed a resolution on the various problems of the struggle for land. Undoubtedly, this will promote the further development of the village struggle. As to the methods of partition in connection with the distance, fertility, infertility, forests, waters, etc., it is now of urgent need to work out a definite resolution out of the experience of all places so as to make it the guidance for the partition of land in the new Soviet districts.

The inspection movement mobilized by the Central Government is directed to thoroughly wipe out the feudalistic remnants and to make sure that the real benefits resulting from the agrarian revolution have gone to the farming employees and poor and middle peasants. According to the statistics of July, August, and September, 1933, through this movement in the Central Soviet District that further called forth the revolutionary militancy of the peasant masses, landlords to the number of 6,988 families and the Kulaks to the number of 6,638 families were disclosed with land to the size of 17,539 Tan revoked and money forfeits from the landlords and fines from the Kulaks, to the sum of $606,916 seized. The Farming Employee Trade Union and the Poor Peasant Corps have now formed the pillars of the Soviet in the villages! This is only the result of three months' work which tells that the Soviet has to pay yet closer attention to the class struggle in the villages. The result also shows that the land inspection movement is an effective means to further develop the village struggle and to annihilate the feudalistic remnants in the rural districts. The class line of the agrarian revolution is to depend upon the farming employees and poor peasants, to ally the middle peasants, to exploit the Kulaks and to annihilate the landlords. The correct practice of this line is the key to the success of the agrarian revolution and foundation for all other policies of the Soviet in the villages. Hence the Soviet should deal seriously with those erroneous tendencies that attempt to infringe upon the middle peasants or to annihilate the Kulaks. At the same time, she should also not let go any error of making compromise with the landlords and Kulaks. That is the way to lead the agrarian revolution in the correct direction. In the past two years we have gained much experience in our mass work in the agrarian revolution. The summarized particulars are as follows:

(1) Full mobilization of agricultural workers, poor and middle peasants for struggle against landlords and Kulaks is necessary in the partition and inspection movements. The partition and inspection works should be done with concurrence of the masses. The determination of class should be passed by mass meeting. To conduct these works solely through the activities of a few Soviet functionaries is liable to cause danger of lowering the struggling spirit of the masses.

(2) When belongings other than land of the landlords and surplus drag animals and farming implements of the Kulaks are confiscated, the greater part of them must be shared by the poor masses. It is bad to have them only shared by a few for it will lower the struggling spirit of the masses on the one hand and favor the opposition of the exploiters on the other.

(3) The partition of land should be completed in the shortest possible period. Unless it is demanded by a considerable mass of the peasants re-partition is not a good policy, for otherwise the militancy of the peasant masses to promote agricultural production may be destroyed and the exploiters may take advantage of it to hinder the development of the struggle.

(4) The aim of the inspection movement is to disclose the exploiters, but not to disturb the exploited. So the inspection should not be made from house to house and from one piece of land to another. It should be done through the mobilization of broad masses.

(5) Those anti-revolutionary elements who work to hinder the partition and inspection movements should be seriously dealt with. They should be severely punished by mass judgment or through mass concurrence to serve imprisonment or even to face death penalty. This is necessary for otherwise the agrarian revolution will be handicapped.

(6) Class struggle should be promoted while clashes between families and localities should be avoided. The landlords and Kulaks are always thinking of displacing class struggle with family or local struggle.

(7) The development of the agrarian revolution depends upon the class-consciousness and organizational strength of the basic masses in the villages. The Soviet functionaries must have, therefore, broad and deep propaganda in the villages and work to strengthen the organizations of farming employees and poor peasants.

The aim of the agrarian revolution is not only to solve the land problem of the peasants but also to promote them to increase the productivity of their land. Because of the adequate leadership of the Soviet, and the initiative of the peasant masses themselves, the agricultural production has been restored in most places and in some places it is even increased.

On this foundation, the living conditions of the peasantry have been much improved.

In the past, for months in the year, the peasants lived on tree bark or grain husks. This situation no longer prevails and there is no more starvation in the Soviet districts. The life of the peasantry is better and better year by year. They are no longer in rags. They eat meat more constantly, which was a luxury to them in former times.

Which kind of government and which kind of life is liked by the peasants? We have this question for the peasants in the Kuomintang-ruled districts to answer.

Financial Policy of the Soviets

The financial policy of the Soviets assured ample supplies demanded by the revolutionary war as well as all the money needed by revolutionary work. With a comparatively small territory characterized by economic backwardness and pursuing a policy of taxation beneficial to the masses, the Soviets have got along fairly well in sharp contrast to the KMT who, controlling a vast territory and increasing its exploitation from day to day, is now facing financial bankruptcy. In accordance with the principle of class and revolution the Soviets raise its revenue from the following sources: (1) confiscation or requisition from all feudal exploiters, (2) taxation, (3) development of national economy.

Under the 1st heading landlords and kulaks both in the KMT and Soviet districts are required to raise funds for the Soviets, which, as shown by the past experience, form the largest item in the revenue of the Soviet government. This is in direct contradiction to the KMT, who always places the financial burdens on the shoulders of the toiling masses. The Soviet progressive taxation consists of two categories, namely, the commercial and agricultural taxes, both imposed on the exploiters. The commercial tax is again divided into two classes viz., the customs duty and business tax. The former is designed to control importation with a tariff ranging from entire exemption to 100 per cent duty, free from any intervention from any foreign power. It means that only the Soviets can realize customs autonomy in China. After payment of the customs duty all goods can flow freely within the Soviet territory without having to pay any more taxes, in contrast to the goods passing through the KMT territory which are still subject to various taxes similar to Likin.

The business tax is again progressive. It takes more from the larger enterprises with higher profit but less from the smaller enterprises with lower profit. Undertakings with less than $100 capital, cooperatives, farmers selling their own surpluses, are all exempted.

The agricultural tax is likewise progressive. It is heavier for the larger families who have obtained more land but lighter for those who have got less land. The poor peasants and middle peasants pay less but the kulaks pay more. Farm hands and families of the red armies are all exempted. This tax may be reduced or exempted in case of a disaster.

On the other hand, the KMT lays the principal burden on the peasantry and the small proprietors. It collects the surtax on the regular ones at a much heavier rate. According to the Ta Kung Pao, of Tientsin, March 21, 1933, the KMT collects as many as 1,756 taxes, and the Szechwan militarists have collected the land tax up to 1987. In Shensi the KMT has increased the tax by 25 times.

The development of national economy as a source of the Soviet finances forms an important part of the financial policy of the Soviets. It has begun to make progress in Mien-che-kang and Kiangsi. The financial and economical organs ought to do more in this direction. Here it may be pointed out that the state banks must issue notes to meet the needs for the development of national economy, considering financial needs as only secondary.

The use of money shall be governed by the principle of economy. Corruption and waste are the greatest crimes. Great achievements have been registered in the struggle against these crimes. "Save every penny for the revolutionary war" is the guiding principle of the Soviet accounting system.

With the expansion of the red army, with the development of the revolutionary war, the Soviets are of course facing financial difficulties which will, however, create conditions for their own solution. The Soviet finances will improve when conquering more territory from the KMT, developing national economy on a larger scale, etc., with the financial burdens placed on the exploiters.

Economic Policy of the Soviets

Confronted with an impoverished people, the KMT, however, spread lies against the Soviets, saying that the Soviet government is bankrupt. The KMT is bent on the destruction of the Soviets not only by guns and cannon but by economic measures, the most ruthless of which is "blockade." With the broad masses and the red army behind it, the Soviets have been able to smash the KMT drives one after another. And it has, too, succeeded to a certain extent in economic reconstruction within its territory, a step which has been taken to break the blockade of the enemy.

Engaged in a battle against imperialism and KMT, at the same time located in a region economically backward encircled by the economic blockade of the enemy, the Soviets must proceed, whenever possible, with the economic reconstruction, concentrate its forces on war supplies, improve the life of the masses, consolidate the alliance between the workers and peasants in the economic field, assure the leadership of the proletariat over the peasantry, create the premises for the development of socialist construction in future.

The central tasks involved in economic reconstruction of the Soviets are development of agricultural production, of industrial production of foreign trade, of cooperatives.

Agriculture in Soviet districts is apparently forging ahead at a big pace. Agricultural products in 1933 have increased 15 per cent on the average as against 1932. The rise in Mien-che-kang is 20 per cent. In the couple of years following the Soviet revolution agricultural production showed a downward trend, but thanks to the certainty in the division of land, the promotion of the Soviets and the growth of enthusiasm among the masses, production has been moving upwards steadily. In some cases production has been re-stored to its original level, but in others it has exceeded the original level. Fallow land has been cultivated again while new land re-claimed. In many places workers and plough cooperatives have been organized. Wide masses of women have joined the shock work in agricultural production. These are the facts never witnessed under the KMT's rule. Satisfied with the land obtained, encouraged by the Soviets, the peasants have shown a great enthusiasm in working up the land alloted to them. Under present conditions agricultural pro-duction shall be the first task in the economic reconstruction of the Soviets. It shall solve the food problem as well as secure raw mate-rials for articles of every-day use. It shall emphasize afforestation and increase in livestock. Taking the small farm economy as a basis, plans must be worked out for certain branches of agriculture as, for example, cotton whose production shall be fixed for each province.

The Soviets must lead the peasants to solve such vital problems as labour, oxen, fertilizers, seeds, irrigation, etc. Here the organized mobilization of the labour force and the participation of women in production are of vital importance. The Soviets must lead the peas-antry in launching the Spring and Summer ploughing campaigns. About 25 per cent of the peasantry is in need of oxen, hence the necessity of organizing the oxen cooperatives. The Soviets must direct the greatest attention to irrigation. At present we are not in need of Soviet farms and collective farms, but for agricultural im-provement an experimental station shall be set up in each district. In addition, agricultural research institutes shall be established, agricultural products show rooms arranged.

As a result of the blockade of the enemey difficulties have arisen in our exportation, and many handicraft industries in the Soviet dis-tricts have declined. Tobacco and paper have suffered most. But these difficulties are by no means invincible. Owing to the large consumption of the people the Soviet goods can find a big market within the Soviet territory. In the first half of 1933 the efforts of the Soviets and the development of the cooperatives resulted in the revival of many industries as, *e.g.*, tobacco, paper, tungston, camphor, fertilizers, agricultural instruments, etc. Attention shall be directed to cloth, drugs, sugar industries. New industries have sprung up in Mien-che-kang province (paper, cloth, etc.). To relieve the shortage in salt nitrate-salt has been manufactured. It is hard to map out a plan for the scattered handicraft industries but it is possible to elaborate a plan for the leading industries, above all, for the undertakings operated by the state and cooperatives. The Soviet and cooperative-controlled enterprises shall make an appraisal of the production of materials (raw) as well as the market both in the white and red districts.

The Soviet shall organize foreign trade and directly control the flow of such goods as the importation of salt and clothes, the exportation of food and tungston. It shall see to it that food be equally distributed within the Soviet districts. This work began in Mienche-kang at an early date, followed by Kiangsi in the Spring of 1933. The inauguration of the foreign trade bureau produced the initial success in this direction.

In the Soviet territory national economy is composed of three parts, namely state, cooperative and private enterprises. The state undertakings are at present very much limited in scope but have a bright prospect in future. Within the pale of law private economy is, far from being restricted, rather encouraged, owing to the Soviets' need for private economy. Not only at the present time, but for a long time to come, private economy is predominant. Now it assumes the form of small capital in the Soviet districts.

The cooperative enterprises are making a rapid advance. According to the statistics of September, 1933, there are 1,423 cooperatives with a capital of $305,531 in 17 hsiens. In certain hsiens like Suikin and Sinkuo the number of cooperatives has doubled owing to the encouragement of the economic conference. At present the consumption and food cooperatives are of major importance. They overshadow the production cooperatives. As to the credit cooperatives, they are just in the initial stage. No doubt the development of the cooperatives constitutes an important lever of Soviet economy. Combined with state enterprises, it will become a mighty force in the economic field, assert its supremacy over private economy in a protracted struggle, create conditions for transition of Soviet economy to socialist economy. State enterprises shall be pushed together with the big-scale development of the cooperatives, at the same time, private economy be encouraged.

As an aid to the development of the state enterprises and the cooperatives $3,000,000 economic reconstruction bonds have been issued thus enlisting the support of the masses to the Soviet economic construction. In face of millions of starving people and with an impoverished country, the Soviets alone boldly embark on economic reconstruction in a planned way which will carry out the task of saving millions now in distress from final collapse.

Soviet Culture

For making sure the victory of the revolution, for consolidating the Soviets, for drawing the gigantic forces of the masses in the revolutionary class struggle, for creating a new revolutionary generation the Soviets must proceed with far-reaching cultural reforms designed to shake off the spiritual yoke of the reactionary ruling class as well as to create a new Soviet culture for the workers and peasants.

As is known to all, cultural institutions of the KMT are without exception in the hands of the landlord and bourgeoisie, employed to spread demagogical propaganda to check the revolutionary thought of the oppressed classes. In support of illiteracy they exclude the workers and peasants from education. Educational appropriations have been used for the attack on the revolution. Legions of colleges and universities have closed down, throwing out thousands of students. Over 80 per cent of the population under the KMT is still illiterate. Left wing thought has been ruthlessly suppressed by the white terror. Left writers arrested by the Fascist thugs. Educational institutions have become a hell for the masses, a fact that characterizes the educational policy of the KMT.

But in the Soviet territory all cultural and educational institutions are under the direct control of the workers and peasants, giving their children a preferred right to enjoy education. The Soviets have done its best in raising the cultural level of the masses. In spite of the Soviets located in a backward region threatened by war from all sides, cultural reconstruction has been going on at an accelerated pace.

For the 2,931 villages in Kiangsi, Fukien and Yeh-kang provinces there are 3,052 Leninist primary schools with 89,710 pupils, 64,612 evening schools with an attendance of 94,517; 32,388 reading groups with a membership of 155,371; 1,656 clubs with 49,668 workers. These are only the statistics compiled up from the data in the central Soviet districts.[2]

A majority of the school children have attended the Leninist primaries. For instance, out of the 20,969 school children in Sinkuo, 12,860 have attended the Leninist primaries. The school children spend most of the time in reading and reserve only a small fraction of the time for family work. They also join the red boy scouts and learn practical communism therein.

Women are very enthusiastic for education, too. In Sinkuo there are 15,740 pupils for the evening schools, out of which 4,988 are men or 31 per cent, and 10,752 are women or 69 per cent. Among the reading groups of Sinkuo we find that 40 per cent of the membership is men, while the female members amount to as high as

[2] These statistics are hardly correct: how is it possible that in 64,612 evening schools there are only 94,517 pupils? (V. Y.)

60 per cent. Not only eager for education, some of the women have occupied high positions in the cultural institutions. They serve as heads of the primaries or evening schools, or as director of the reading groups. The delegate council of woman workers and peasants is almost universal in the Soviets, directing close attention to the interests of the toiling women, including education.

A vigorous campaign against illiteracy is in full swing. Evening schools for reading have been established (in Sinkuo from 22,529 joined the reading groups scattered all over the hsien—3,387—). To help reading, signboards inscribed with characters have been set up close to the highways.

The cultural advance of the Soviets may be illustrated by the increase in the circulation of the papers. In the Central Soviet district we have some 34 papers big and small. The Red China, organ of the Soviet government, has increased from 3,000 to 40,000; the True Word of the Youth up to 28,000; the Struggle (organ of the Central Committee of the Communist Party), 27,000; the Red Star (organ of the red army), 17,300, an increase that testifies to the rapid advance of the masses in the cultural field.

The revolutionary arts of the Soviets have already made a good start with the formation of the worker and peasant dramatics club and the commencement of the blue-shirt movement extending in all directions in the villages. Red sports have been gaining ground everywhere. Gymnasium fields may be seen here and there.

Now the Soviets, though having not much to show in the construction of technical education, have nevertheless succeeded in establishing the red army university. The Soviet University, the Communist University and many higher schools under the direct control of the ministry of education, all calculated to train leaders for the revolutionary leadership. Colleges and high schools must follow closely on the heels of the development of the ordinary schools as is scheduled in the educational plan.

For training the revolutionary intelligentsia, for the development of education and culture the Soviets have utilized the services of the landlord-bourgeoisie intelligentsia—a point that cannot be overlooked in the cultural policy of the Soviets.

The general line of the cultural policy of the Soviets is to educate the broad masses in the spirit of communism, to subordinate education to the revolutionary war and the class struggle, to link labor with education. In the educational field the central tasks confronting the Soviets are the enforcement of compulsory education throughout the whole land. The development of social education on a wide scale, the rapid liquidation of illiteracy, the training of large numbers of cadres for revolution. All these tasks can be performed only under the Soviets because they signalize the sharpened class struggle and an unprecedented victory for spiritual emancipation.

Marriage under the Soviets

To free women from the most barbarous marriage system handed down through thousands of years the Soviets as early as November, 1931, proclaimed the equality of men and women in marriages by a new set of regulations which declared complete liberty of marriage and divorce, abolish the sale of women as wives, interdict child marriage, provisions that have been enforced throughout the Soviet territory. As a rule, a man of twenty may marry a girl of 18 by simple registration with the Soviets provided he is free from dangerous disease. Lineal descendants from the same grandfather, however, cannot marry each other within five generations. Divorce may be granted by the Soviets if one of the parties to the marriage insist on it.

This libration of women from the feudal marriage fetters is made possible only under the democratic dictatorship of the workers and peasants subsequent to the overthrow of the landlord-bourgeoisie and the accomplishment of the land revolution. Men and women, particularly the latter, must have first of all political liberty and also some measure of economic liberty as a guarantee for free marriage. More oppressed by the feudal marriage system than men, women have been given more protection in the matter of marriage, and the burden arising from divorce is imposed for the most part on the shoulders of men.

Of vital importance to the revolution are children who we may say are new revolutionists, to whom protection must be afforded. The Soviets recognize the illegal children and give them protection. The protection of children has been laid down in the Soviet Law.

National Policy of Soviets

The point of departure for the Soviet national policy is the capture of all the oppressed minorities around the Soviets as a means to increase the strength of the revolution against imperialism and KMT. The oppressed minorities such as the Mongols, Thibetans, Koreans, Annamites, Miaos, etc., are all oppressed by Chinese monarchs, militarists, etc., General Geng Yu-hsiang massacred the Mohammedans in Kansu while General Pei Tsung-shi butchered the Miaos in Kwangsi to mention but two recent examples of the Kuomintang in maltreating the minorities. On the other hand, the ruling classes of the minorities such as princes, living Buddas,

Lamas, etc., have allied with the KMT in oppressing and exploiting the mass of people, especially the toilers. In the case of Thibet, Sinkiang and Inner Mongolia the ruling classes have directly surrendered to imperialism and accelerated the colonization of their country.

The Soviets, on the other hand, are decisively against the exploitation of the minorities by imperialism and KMT. The Constitution of the Soviets as paassed by the 1st Soviet Congress in November, 1931, is quite clear on this point (Article 14):

"Soviet China recognizes the complete self-determination of the minorities who may go so far as to secede and form independent free states. Soviet China shall see to it that the minorities be freed from the misrule of imperialism and KMT and secure complete emancipation from the misrule of their own princes and Lamas. In this regard the Soviets will gladly aid the minorities in carrying out this task. The Soviets will permit the development of national culture and languages among these minorities."

Article 15 of the same constitution provides that "Soviet China will give the right of asylum to the revolutionaries either from the nationalities in China or from other countries who should have been persecuted by the reactionary rule; it will help them in securing complete victory for the revolutionary movement sponsored by them."

The fact that many Korean, Annam and Taiwan comrades attended the 1st Soviet Congress and 2nd Soviet Congress is a concrete proof that the Soviets mean what it says. The common revolutionary interests will unite the toilers of China with those of the oppressed minorities in a firm alliance. The free union of nationalities will replace national oppression, an event that is possible only under the Soviets. To achieve complete emancipation the minority nationality shall, on its part, assist the Soviet revolution in securing a victory on a national scale.

Concrete Tasks Confronting the Soviets in Shattering the Fifth Campaign of Imperialism and KMT

In the past two years the Soviets have scored successive victories over the KMT, as a result of which the relation of power between the Soviets and KMT has apparently changed in favor of the former, but at the expense of the latter. The Soviets have consolidated but the KMT has been steadily on the decline. The masses in KMT territory have put up the revolutionary flag. But owing to the fact that the Soviets are situated in a region economically backward with only a comparatively small area, we must extend our territory and fight for the realization of the task of capturing one or more provinces. We must shatter the illusions of those who are satisfied with the present limited area of the Soviets. The revolutionary masses under the Soviets are called on to fight for the carrying out of the following urgent tasks:

Reconstruction of Red Army

First of all the central revolutionary military committee shall be strengthened in its leadership of the whole red army so as to make it possible for the red armies to act more efficiently under a unified, strengthened command. In the second place, the expansion of the red army to 1,000,000 as a slogan must be popularized among the toiling masses, enabling them to understand that 1,000,000 red army is a decisive factor in the struggle against imperialism and KMT. Recruiting shall be made through political agitation instead of compulsion. At the same time, a sharp class struggle together with the Soviet laws shall be directed against the alien elements who blocked the expansion of the red army by desertions. The families of the red armists shall be treated in a better way. Land shall be cultivated and ploughed for them, articles of every-day use supplied to them, in order to comfort them spiritually. The Soviets shall see to it that all those who sabotage the work in this respect shall be punished by law.

To consolidate the red army a political education is of special importance. It will enable the red armists to fight consciously for the victory of the Soviets, to value conscious discipline as a guarantee for the victory of the revolution. The system of the political commissioners shall be observed in all the units of the red army, more workers drawn in to act as military or political directors, more cadres turned out from the red army schools, decisive blows directed against the landlord-bourgeois elements who try to steal into the red army, technique of the red army improved.

The red guards and youth vanguards shall be universally formed in all the Soviet districts, all the grown boys and girls armed as a reserve in defense of the rear. Every youth vanguardist shall be made to understand that conscription plays a big rôle in the future big-scale civil wars against imperialism and the KMT. Conscription in general shall be popularized among the masses, model youth vanguards be incorporated into formal red armies, more red partisans organized in the bordering districts who may penetrate far into the white regions. A closer relation shall be maintained between the red armies and the toiling masses.

The supplies and transport for the red armies shall be assured and taken care of by the financial and economic organs of the Soviets as well as by the transport and sanitary organs of the red army.

Soviet Economic Reconstruction

To crush the economic blockade of the enemy, to counteract the manipulation of the wicked merchants, to assure the revolutionary needs, to improve the lot of the workers and peasants, the Soviets must proceed at once with economic reconstruction in various fields.

In the first place, agricultural production shall be raised, enthusiasm of the masses for such production aroused, propaganda campaigns in ploughing and harvest time launched, all peasantry drawn into the production campaign (including peasant women). Labor mutual assistance and ploughing corps shall be widely organized, the oxen and seed problems solved with the aid of the Soviets. Our fighting slogans are "Liquidate all fallow land." "Increase the crops by 20 per cent." The food bureau of the Soviets shall maintain a more close relation with the food cooperatives to assure ample food for the red army and the masses. The commissar of national economy shall map out a plan for the more important branches of agriculture, as food and cotton.

The tasks of the Soviet economic reconstruction rest on the need of the revival of the handicraft industry and the needs of the war. In elaborating the plans for economic reconstruction, consideration must be taken of the needs of the revolutionary war, the needs of the masses and the possibility of exports to the white regions. Maximum energy shall be devoted to the leading industries as Tungston, coal, iron, lime, agricultural instruments, tobacco, paper, cloth, sugar, drugs, nitrate-salt, lumber, camphor, etc. Production cooperatives shall be organized for these industries, drawing in the unemployed, independent workers and peasants. Private investment being permitted, the Soviets shall not monopolize all the productive enterprises but concentrate on those beneficial to the state. The vital means to raise production are more incentive to labor, competition in production, reward to those who have made achievements on the production front.

The exchange of Soviet surpluses (as food, tungston, lumber, tobacco, paper) with salt, cloth, oils, etc., from the white regions as may be made possible through the development of foreign trade serves as an important lever in breaking through the blockade of the enemy and in promoting the development of our national economy. The commercial institutions of the Soviets shall be consolidated while private merchants be encouraged for exportation and importation of necessaries. Wide masses of the workers and peasants shall be organized in consumption cooperatives to be set up everywhere, and thus enabled to buy cheap but sell at higher prices their products to the white regions, a possibility that plays a vital rôle in the economic reconstruction of the Soviets. The Soviets must strengthen their leadership of the central consumption cooperatives, and see to it that such centrals be established where they do not yet exist.

The solution of the capital problem as involved in economic reconstruction is found in the absorption of capital from the masses through the development credit cooperatives which will smash usury to pieces. The money of the masses will flow into the state enterprises through such channels as economic bonds, subscriptions, to the stock of the state bank, etc. Capital in the Soviet districts will be made mobile through the encouragement of the private capital. The note issue of the Soviet banks shall correspond to the needs of the market and absorb the deposits from the masses, to lend the money so gathered to production enterprises. The Soviet banks shall provide financial relief within the Soviet territory and lead the struggle of the cooperatives against the speculative merchants.

Reconstruction of Soviets

The Central Soviet Government inaugurated as the supreme leader of the Soviet movement in China has a vital significance, and has in the past two years scored glorious success in the fight against imperialism and KMT, but many weaknesses are found in the organization and work of the central government. The organization and work of the presidium of the central executive committee shall be improved and strengthened, the commissariats shall have a sufficient working staff, more commissariats created, if necessary, so that the central government can fulfill its rôle as the supreme leader of the revolution.

As an important link with the central government as well as with local Soviets, the provincial Soviet government has been lax in its work in certain respects, a defect which shall be overcome hereafter.

The village and town Soviets constitute the basis of the Soviet system and for this simple reason merit the utmost attention. Congresses shall be established in places where they do not yet exist, and their work strengthened. Presidea shall be set up, committees moved into the villages, militant workers and peasants drawn into the Soviets, relation between a delegate and a number of inhabitants established, each village shall have a general delegate, permitting him to call a conference of the delegates and inhabitants to discuss the work to be done. The village and town Soviets are the direct organs for the mobilization of the masses and do practical work in the village and street. The latter may compete with each other in order to raise the efficiency of their work. As regards the work done by local Soviets, the system of inspection shall rigorously be enforced. The district Soviets shall give an efficient leadership in regard to the lower Soviets.

The provincial Soviets shall direct maximum attention to the work in new Soviet territory where a revolutionary committee exists in place of the Soviets. In regard to organization and work, the revolutionary committee differs radically from the Soviets and its work (as arming the inhabitants, waging the mass struggle, clearing the counter-revolutionaries, etc.) shall be strengthened.

Soviet democracy has progressed far but not enough. A struggle shall be waged against bureaucratism and dictation still remaining among the Soviet functionaries. Persuasion shall replace dictation vis-à-vis the masses. The worker and peasant inspection commissariat shall draw in large masses for the critical examination of the work of the Soviet functionaries and lead the struggle in criticizing the evil functionaries, even punish them in accordance with Soviet laws, thus maintaining the good relations between the Soviets and the masses. In the Soviet elections more electors shall be drawn in and alien elements, bureaucrats, etc., barred. More workers shall be attracted into the Soviets in order to strengthen the workers' hegemony in the government. In order to get close to the masses the Soviets must establish an intimate connection with the labor unions, the poor peasant unions, cooperatives, etc.

All the work of the Soviets shall be adapted to the needs of the revolutionary war, any relaxation among the Soviet functionaries be stamped out, the functionaries aroused to enthusiasm and consciousness that they work for the worker and peasant democratic dictatorship. Slogans shall be put forward "Subordinate all work to the revolutionary war," "For the greater speed and better quality of the work," all to be brought before the functionaries of the Soviets. In this respect the responsible leaders of the Soviets, especially the worker and peasant inspection commissariat, must win over the Soviet functionaries by persistent persuasion and education.

The Soviets shall enforce the following laws: labor (eight-hours, minimum wages, etc.), land revolution (confiscation of land of the landlord, land inspection, etc.), culture and education, and, finally, all the laws and orders against the counter-revolutionaries (GPU and Soviet courts drawing in large masses in the struggle against the reactionaries).

Anti-Imperialist Work

The Soviets must strengthen its leadership of the anti-imperialist struggle throughout the whole country as well as of the revolutionary struggle of the workers and peasants against the KMT in the white territory. Passivity on the part of the Soviets in this direction means connivance at the aggression of imperialism, prolongation of the KMT misrule and limitation on the development of the Soviets in the territorial aspect. The Soviets must look forward to the vast area of the KMT and lead the workers, peasants and petty bourgeoisie there in the struggle against imperialism and KMT. By utilizing the concrete facts of the KMT's surrender to imperialism the Soviets may arouse the masses in the white regions to a sharp struggle against imperialism and its lackey, the Kuomintang. The Soviets shall call on the masses to organize and arm themselves, to fight for the independence of China, to drive imperialism out of China; in Manchuria and Jehol where Japanese imperialism still marches on with bayonets, the people, revolutionary army and volunteers shall be organized, the existing volunteers be alienated from the influence of the KMT in a determined fight against Japanese imperialism. The Soviets must give aid to every anti-imperialist struggle of the workers, peasants and petty-bourgeoisie.

The Soviets shall aid in every way possible the revolutionary struggle of the workers against capital and of the peasants against the landlord, and lead it to victory. The functionaries of the Soviets must understand that expansion of the Soviet territory and success of the revolution on a national scale depends much on the work of the Soviets in the KMT area, that they have to devote the greatest attention to the white regions where the masses are subject to the military slavery and other exactions are most apt to accept our influence, the more so in the districts bordering on the Soviets.

By making use of every opportunity the Soviets in the borderland shall establish regular contact with the masses, organize their everyday struggle, organize their revolt, develop partisan fighting, bring the new districts under the control of the Soviets. The work in the borderland is of special importance. The partisans must observe the fundamental policy of the Soviets and refrain from making indiscriminate attacks on the Tuhao without any regard to class distinctions. In addition, the opposition of the reds to the whites, the flight of the masses, the salt question, the refugee problem, etc., shall be solved on the class principle and in accordance with the principle of mass work. The causes of the opposition of the reds to the whites and the flight of the masses have to be removed, and in the work in the borderland to be improved, factors that can play a decisive rôle in changing the white into red districts.

(Thunderous and prolonged applause.)

CHRONOLOGY

1851–1864 Taiping Rebellion.

1858   Tientsin Treaty, between China, England, France, Russia and the U. S. A.

1860   Peking Treaty, recognizing the Maritime Province as Russian.

1895   Dr. Sun Yat-sen organizes a revolutionary party, Hsing-Chung-Hui.

1896   Sino-Russian Treaty of mutual support (Li-Lobanov).

1897   Germany occupies Kiao-chow.

1898   Concessions "granted" by China to Russia in Liao-tung, to England in Wei-hai-wei, to France in Kuan-chan-wan.

1899–1900 American notes on the "Open Door" in China.

1900   Boxer Uprising.

1901   International agreement about China, liquidating the Boxer Uprising.

1905   Ke-ming-tang, the Revolutionary Party of China founded.

1905   Treaty of Portsmouth, and the Sino-Japanese agreement of Peking.

1909   The American Secretary of State, Knox, suggests neutralization of the railroads in China.

1911   The Chinese Revolution begins in Wuhan. First "Socialist" newspaper in China, *The Star,* appears.

1911   Mongolia proclaims independence.

1912   China—a Republic.

1912   Russo-Mongolian Treaty and Russo-Japanese Treaty on Mongolia.

1913   Yuan Shih-kai proclaimed President of China.

1913   Sino-Russian Mongolian agreement.

1913   First modern strikes reported in China.

1914–1918 The World War.

1915   The "Twenty-One Demands."

1916   Yuan Shih-kai attempts restoration of the Monarchy.

1917   China enters the War on the side of the Allies.

1917   Revolution in Russia.

1918   About 140,000 Chinese coolies sent to Europe to dig trenches at the front.

1918–1922 Allied intervention in Asiatic possessions of Russia.

1919   China declines to sign the Versailles Treaty. Student movement begins in Peking. Anti-Japanese boycott.

1920   First Communist group organized in Shanghai.
            Four-Power Consortium for China.
            May 1st, Labor Day observed in Peking and Canton.
            Hong Kong strike (9,000 participating).
            Hankow riksha-pullers' Union, the first of the kind, organized.

1921   Provisional Revolutionary Mongol People's Government.
            Urga occupied by the Soviet troops; the "Whites" routed.
            Washington Conference. Japan returns Tsingtao to China. Red International of Labor Unions organized.
            Hunan miners strike. Wave of strikes in the Japanese-owned mills at Shanghai and Tsingtao.

1922   The Four-Power Treaty and the Nine-Power Treaty signed at Washington.
            Soviet Russia-Mongolia Treaty.
            Hong Kong seamen strike (about 60,000 workers involved).
            National Labor Conference held at Canton.
            Hupeh Provincial Federation of Labor representing over 400,000 workers.
            Membership of some 80 Unions at Shanghai estimated at 80,000.

1923   Revolutionary South China starts war against the reactionary North.
            Michael Borodin and other Russian advisers arrive in China.

1924   First National Congress of the Kuo-min-tang. Communists admitted into the Kuo-min-tang. Revival of revolutionary labor activities.
            May 1st—Agreement signed with Soviet Russia at Peking.
            September—Treaty of Mukden signed by the Russians and Chan Tso-lin.
            Failure of Canton coup against Dr. Sun. As the head of the Nationalist Government, Dr. Sun promulgates Trade-Union Regulations legalizing the Labor Unions.

1925   March 12th—Death of Dr. Sun Yat-sen.
        Post-office strike at Shanghai.
        Second National Labor Conference at Canton.
        All-China Federation of Labor formed, and decides to
            affiliate with the Red International of the Labor-
            Unions.
        Lockout in the textile industry at Shanghai; general
            strike; students' demonstration.
        June—Shooting of coolies by British marines at Han-
            kow.
        Incident at Kiu-kiang. Shameen incident.
        Canton—Hong Kong boycott of British goods, and gen-
            eral strike.
        December—Nationalists occupy Tientsin.
        Peasants' Unions spread all over Southern China.
1926   March—Chiang Kai-shek *coup-d'état* at Canton.
        May—Third National Labor Conference at Canton.
        July—Beginning of the Northern Expedition.
        August—Post-office strike in Canton.
        Hong Kong boycott of British goods ends.
        Great Britain announces new Chinese policy.
        White terror begins in Southern China. Labor activities
            restricted.
        Second National Congress of Kuo-min-tang held at
            Canton.
1927   February—First general strike at Shanghai to help the
            Northern Expedition.
        March—Second strike at Shanghai involving over
            100,000.
        March 27th—"Nanking Incident."
        April—Kuo-min-tang is split; and parts with the Com-
            munists. Nanking Government formed.
        June—Fourth Labor Conference and First Pan-Pacific
            Trade-Union Conference held at Hankow.
        Shanghai Labor Federation ordered closed by Chiang.
        July—Borodin departs from China.
        July-August—Nanchang rebellion.
        November—Hailofong Soviet Republic established.
        December—The Canton Commune. Chiang Kai-shek
            intensifies the White terror.
1928   February—Plenary session of the Kuo-min-tang. Soviet
            régime established in Yungtin, Fukien province.
        April—Japan in Shantung. Tsinanfu incident. End of
            the Soviet régime in Liling, Hunan.

May—Japan's Ultimatum to China.
Congress of workers, peasants, and Red soldiers in Eastern Kiangsi.
June—Peking surrenders to the Nationalists.
Chang Tso-lin assassinated.
July—U. S. A. recognizes the Nanking régime.
September—Chiang Kai-shek "President" of the Nationalist Government.
September-October—Soviet régime in Wunan, Kiangsi.
December—Great Britain recognizes Nanking.

1929   January—Tariff autonomy of China.
Soviets in Kwangtung.
March—Third Congress of Kuo-min-tang at Nanking.
April—Soviet Government at Juichin, Kiangsi.
May—Pro-Soviet movement in Hupeh province.
Chinese delegation to the Geneva Labor Conference.
Second Pan-Pacific Trade-Union Conference at Khabarovsk.
Chinese raid on the USSR Consulate at Harbin.
June—Soviets organized in Northwest Hupeh.
July—Chinese arrest the Russian Manager of the Chinese-Eastern Railway and take control over that road.
Soviets organized in Szechwan province.
August—First Congress of Soviets in Taseu county, Kiangsi.
First Soviet Conference at Tingchow, Fukien.
Committee formed for the inauguration of the Provisional Government of the Soviet Republic of China.
September—Soviet Government organized in the Sangchi county of Northwestern Hunan.
October—Soviet Government organized in Yanping, Kwangtung.
New Labor-Union Law issued by Nanking.
November—First Congress of workers, peasants and soldiers' deputies in Sinkan, Kiangsi.
November 26th—Mukden accepts Moscow conditions for starting negotiations on the C.-E. Railway conflict.
December—Soviet movement spreads over Hupeh and Hunan.
Anti-Japanese boycott at Hankow.
Sino-Russian Protocol signed at Khabarovsk, reëstab-

lishing the *status-quo-ante* on the Chinese-Eastern Railway.

1930 January—China unilaterally abolishes extraterritoriality; Italy notifies Nanking that she does not recognize that act as valid.

Soviets organized in a number of counties of Kiangsi and Kiangsu.

Yen and Feng agree to set up a Provisional Government at Peiping.

First Congress of Soviets in Southwestern Kiangsi.

March—Red Armies occupy Anfu, Feni, and Itsun in Kiangsi.

Second Congress of Soviets in Tsiensien, Kiangsi.

Soviet Government organized in Hoyun, Kwangtung.

Red "partisans" occupy Tungshen, Hupeh.

Soviet régime in Lichwang, Kiangsi.

April—Red Army occupies Singfeng, Kiangsi.

May—Soviet movement spreads further in Kwangtung.

First All-China Soviet Conference at Shanghai. Labour and Land Laws adopted.

June—Red Army captures several towns in Hupeh.

July—Soviet régime spreads over several more counties of Hupeh.

First Congress of Soviets in Pinkiang county, Hunan.

Red Army occupies several towns in Kiangsi.

Soviet régime established in Shantangkiang, Kiangsu.

Second Congress of the workers, peasants and soldiers' deputies in Western Fukien.

27th—Changsha occupied by the Reds, and held for ten days.

August—Soviet Government in Kiangsu, 100 miles from Shanghai.

Soviets in Manchuria; in Kirin-Tunhua district.

Red Army occupies Latien and Macheng in Hupeh.

Soviets in the Hainan Island, Kwangtung.

Soviets in Yiyang, near Changsha.

Red Army reoccupies Singfeng and other towns in Kiangsi.

Growth of the Soviet movement in Anhwei province.

Soviets organized in a number of places of Chekiang province.

Red Army occupies Kwangtsi in Hupeh and Yutu in Kwangsi.

October—First Congress of Soviets in Eastern Hupeh.
Soviet Conference in Western Kwangsi.
Red Army occupies Loshan in Honan and Tsiensien
in Kiangsi.
Troops of the Yunnan province rebel and join the
Reds.
November—"Anti-Bolshevik" Party discovered and sup-
pressed in the Red Army in Fukien.
A Brigade rebels in Szechwan and forms a Red unit.
December—Nanking starts his First Anti-Red Cam-
paign.
50th and 18th Nanking Divisions routed.

1931   January—Soldiers in Shansi refuse to fight against the
Reds.
General Conference of the Chinese Communist Party.
First Anti-Red Campaign ended in failure.
February—The 12th and 34th Divisions of Nanking
desert and join the Reds.
Rebellion in the 33rd Nanking Division.
March—Counter-revolutionary plots discovered and
frustrated in Fukien.
Second Campaign against the Reds started by Nan-
king.
May—All-China National Assembly convened at Nan-
king.
Second Anti-Red Campaign ended in failure.
June—Nanking starts a new campaign against the Reds.
July—Tungku captured by Chiang's forces and burned.
August—Climax of Nanking advance.
Red Army reoccupies Yutu in Kiangsi and takes the
offensive against the Government troops.
September—Japan starts her Manchurian campaign.
Chiang Kai-shek orders the anti-Red Campaign dis-
continued.
Representatives of eight Provisional Soviet Govern-
ments published a declaration on the Japanese
activities in Manchuria.
Reds re-occupy Tungku in Kiangsi.
October—Nanking-Canton "Reconciliation Conference."
November—First All-China Congress of Soviets. Pro-
visional Government of Soviet China formed.
December—A counter-revolutionary group of "reorgan-
izationists" discovered and suppressed by the Reds.
Government soldiers rebel in a number of Divisions.

1932   January—Red Army occupies Puchi in Hupeh, near Hunan.

10,000 Nanking troops join the Reds in Fukien.

Tenth Corps of the Red Army occupies Tesin.

February—The Fourth Campaign against the Reds started by Nanking.

Nanking troops force the Reds to retreat from a number of towns.

Red Army occupies Yingshan in Hupeh.

March—Canton militarists also start a campaign against the Reds in Kiangsi.

Reds launch a counter-offensive.

Nanking troops (3rd, 6th, and 10th Brigades) routed by Ho-Lung's troops.

Soldier rebellion in the 34th Division; six regiments of Nanking join the Reds.

The 21st Division of Nanking defeated.

Two regiments of the 48th Division join the Reds.

April—The 40th, 41st, 44th and 48th Divisions of Nanking routed near Peiping-Hankow Railway in Hupeh.

46th and 56th Brigades of Nanking defeated by the Reds in Anhwei.

Several towns occupied by the Reds in Fukien.

May—Nanking Government convenes an anti-Red Conference.

Reds occupy several more towns in Anhwei.

Chaing Kai-shek is appointed Generalissimo to lead the expedition against the Soviets in Hupeh, Hunan and Anhwei.

The Fourth anti-Red Campaign fails at the end of May.

June—Linan occupied by the Reds.

The Fifth "Punitive Campaign" (Fourth in Nanking's terminology) started.

Red Army occupies Sinan on the Peiping-Hankow Railway.

The 30th and 31st Divisions of Nanking join the Reds.

Red Army occupies Singfeng in Kiangsi and Lilin in Kwangtung.

July—The 85th Nanking Division routed by the Reds.

Soldiers of the 19th Kuo-min-tang Army refuse to fight.

August—Red Army advances and is close to Hankow.
Kuo-min-tang Conference at Looshan.
September—Kuo-min-tang issues regulations for the rehabilitation of districts taken from the Communists.
October—Soviet Government of China floats a loan (internal).
Nanking troops occupy large part of the Soviet area in Hupeh-Hunan-Anhwei.
Red Armies take offensive in Central area.
October-November—Reds retreat from Hupeh. Part of their Army concentrates in Szechwan.
December—Growth of Sovietized area in Szechwan.

1933   January—Nanking troops routed in Kiangsi (the 5th, 11th, 14th, 53rd, 56th and 57th Divisions).
February-May—Further reverses suffered by the Nanking troops.
Most of the territories lost late in 1932 reoccupied by the Reds.
September-November—New Anti-Red Campaign of Chiang.
December—The Fukien Revolt.

INDEX

294 INDEX